THEODORE ROOSEVELT
THE
ADVENTUROUS PRESIDENT

By the Editors of TIME FOR KIDS
WITH LISA deMAURO

LIBERTY
STREET

About the Author: Lisa deMauro is the author of several books and magazine articles for young people. She lives in Westchester County, New York, with her husband and two children. The author has been a lifelong fan of Theodore Roosevelt.

Photo locators denoted as follows: Top (T), Center (C), Bottom (B), Left (L), Right (R), Background (Bkgd)

Cover: (C) Underwood And Underwood/Getty Images, (TR) Smithsonian Institution Libraries. **Back Cover:** Library of Congress Prints and Photographs Division [LC-USZ62-49955].

Images:
Title page Sygma/Corbis; **TOC** Stock Montage/Getty Images; **0** Corbis; **2** Library of Congress Prints and Photographs Division [LC-USZ62-8689]; **3** Ewing Galloway/Alamy; **4** Theodore Roosevelt Collection; **5** (T), (B) Theodore Roosevelt Collection; **6** (L), (B) Theodore Roosevelt Collection; **8** (T) Eric Isselee/Shutterstock, (B) Oleg Kozlov/Fotolia; **9** Theodore Roosevelt Collection; **10** G.E. Kidder Smith/Corbis; **11** Theodore Roosevelt Collection; **12** Everett Collection; **13** Theodore Roosevelt Collection; **14** (T) Theodore Roosevelt Collection, (B) Library of Congress Prints and Photographs Division [HABS NY,30-OYSTB,2–22]; **16** Corbis; **17** Eric Isselee/Shutterstock; 18 Theodore Roosevelt Collection; **19** Paul A. Souders/Corbis; **20** Theodore Roosevelt Collection; **21** The Granger Collection, New York; 22, 23 Theodore Roosevelt Collection; **24** (T) Library of Congress Prints and Photographs Division [LC-DIG-det-4a25824], (B) Theodore Roosevelt Collection; **26, 27** Theodore Roosevelt Collection; **28** (T) Library of Congress Prints and Photographs Division [LC-USZ62-137560], (B) The Granger Collection, New York; **30** (T) Dickinson State University/Theodore Roosevelt Digital Library, (B) Urosr/Fotolia; **31** Library of Congress Prints and Photographs Division [LC-USZ62-59646]; **32** Library of Congress Prints and Photographs Division [LC-DIG-ggbain-17283]; **34** Imagno/Getty Images, 35, 36 Bettmann/Corbis; **37** (T) Universal History Archive/UIG/Getty Images, (B) Smithsonian Institution Libraries; **38** Library of Congress Prints and Photographs Division [LC-USZ62-47683]; **40** Bettmann/Corbis; **41** AP Images; **42** Charles Markis; **43** (T) Carl & Ann Purcell/Corbis, (B) Bill Ross/Corbis; **44** (T) Library of Congress Prints and Photographs Division [LC-USZ62-49955], (CL) Library of Congress Prints and Photographs Division [LC-B8171-0440], (CR) Library of Congress Prints and Photographs Division [LC-DIG-ppprs-00699], (B) Library of Congress Prints and Photographs Division [LC-USZC4-7507].

go Find out more at timeforkids.com/photos-video/video/roosevelts-home-289856

ISBN-13: 978-0-328-94959-5
ISBN-10: 0-328-94959-0

7 19

To Sara, Ginny and Jamie
May you leave your children a better world than we have left you.

Contents

The state is the great fictitious entity by which everyone seeks to live at the expense of everyone else.

-Frederic Bastiat

A Different Kind of Retirement Book

THIS IS A DIFFERENT KIND OF RETIREMENT BOOK. I DON'T PEDDLE FANTASIES about how pleasant your retirement will be. I tell the truth. For the vast majority of the 78 million Baby Boomers fast approaching 65 — and very possibly for you — retirement will be a bitter pill.

To recycle a Boomer phrase from the 1960s, I "tell it like it is." When you wake up 20 years from now, shaking your head of thinning white hair (those of you who have hair), groping for your bifocals, and feeling all out of sorts because your "golden" years have become as shop-worn as cheap costume jewelry, you'll know whom to blame. Just look in the mirror and take a long, hard look at the miscreant who failed to save enough money, despite abundant warnings that retirement would be very, very expensive. Then head to East Capitol Street, N.E., Washington, D.C., where you can accost any number of the 535 members of Congress who, through successive decisions more short-sighted than your own rheumy eyeballs, racked up mountains of debt, presided over the disintegration of the United States retirement safety net, and ruined whatever shot you had at living an old age where the words "happy," "carefree" and "solvent" applied.

If you are truly attached to the delusion that your retirement will be a period of freedom and fulfillment spent touring the great cities of Europe or just strolling along the beach hand-in-hand with your honey of 50 years, I would advise you to purchase a different book. You can find one of these actual titles on Amazon.com:

How to Retire Happy, Wild and Free: Retirement Wisdom You Won't Get from Your Financial Advisor
How to Love Your Retirement: Advice from Hundreds of Retirees

The Joy of Retirement: Finding Happiness, Freedom
and the Life You Always Wanted

I wouldn't blame you for picking one of those fantasy titles in pref-
erence to this jeremiad. Reading other retirement books is like reading
romance novels — they fuel the fires of the wishful imagination. By
contrast, contemplating the hellish future in store for the United States,
the world and, in all likelihood, you personally is about as fun as drilling
your own tooth. Unfortunately, the other retirement books depict nothing resembling a reality you are likely to encounter.

The sad fact is, the retirement books being written today are based
on the experience of the Silent Generation, today's seniors who were
born between 1925 and 1945. Having come along at just the right time
and in just the right numbers, the Silent Generation has set high expectations for care-free retirement. The Silent Ones reached adulthood
when the United States economy was the world's strongest and employers could afford to offer generous pension plans. Establishing their
spending and saving habits before credit cards and home-equity loans
created a culture of indebtedness, they were restrained in their borrowing and disciplined in their saving. As a consequence, they built up
hefty retirement nest eggs. Entering the real estate market when houses
were cheap, they rode the decades-long rise in housing prices; many
had retired, downsized to less expensive dwellings and cashed out their
equity before the housing market crashed in the late 2000s. Finally, because the size of the Silent Generation is far smaller than the G.I. generation that preceded it and the Boomers who followed, politicians
could raise Social Security and Medicare benefits without bankrupting
the country — at least not while they were still in office.

The Silent Ones retired, on average, at age 62 with the longest life
expectancies in U.S. history. With two decades of leisure to look for-

ward to, they have both the time and the means to enjoy retirement. Joy, freedom and happiness are things the Silent Generation can realistically aspire to in the final season of their lives.

The fate of the Baby Boomers will be very different. Born in the prosperous post-World War II era when American economic power knew no equal, Boomers never experienced sustained economic hardship, and they earned more money than any previous generation. But that blessing proved to be their undoing. They were young adults in the early 1980s when credit cards morphed from a perk of the elite into plastic for the masses. Around the same time, banks began marketing home equity loans aggressively, and car companies began peddling lease financing for automobiles. Never before had it been so easy to live in a McMansion, own a Beemer and spend a week sipping rum drinks in Mexico. The "democratization of credit" had a dark side: Many Boomers became addicted to debt. Money they could have been saving went to pay off the finance companies. Saving rates plummeted.

The decline in personal savings coincided with the slow disintegration of the fixed pension. Corporations sought to control the cost of their fringe benefits by reducing their exposure to expensive Defined Benefit plans, which guaranteed pension incomes and often required big infusions of cash to keep fully funded. Companies shifted market risks to their employees by offering 401(k) plans, to which companies made defined contributions but bore no further obligation. This new retirement vehicle created great wealth on paper as long as stock market prices rose. But when the market crashed, so did the Boomers' net worth. The Boomers were unfortunate in another way. While they, too, rode the rise in housing prices, very few had retired or downsized their dwellings when the housing market crashed. As a result, they lost much of the equity they had built up over their lifetimes.

Even before the Global Financial Crisis of 2007-2009, retirement experts were warning that Boomers were not saving enough to replace their pre-retirement earnings. The meltdown of the housing and stock markets only made a bad situation worse. In their paper, "The Wealth of the Baby Boom Cohorts after the Collapse of the Housing Bubble," David Rosnick and Dean Baker calculated that Boomers between the ages of 55 and 64 saw their median household net worth drop by half between 2004 and 2009. Younger Boomers, between 45 and 54, experienced a drop of 45 percent.

"This analysis indicates that the loss of wealth due to the collapse of the housing bubble and the plunge in the stock market will make the baby boomers far more dependent on Social Security and Medicare than prior generations," Rosnick and Baker wrote gravely. "The baby boom generation for the most part has insufficient time remaining before retirement to accumulate substantial savings."[1]

In consumer surveys conducted since the crash, Boomers have expressed remorse for all the money they squandered and have evinced an intention to do all the right things: Pay down debt, save more money and invest more. But that will be easier said than done — and not just because many Boomers have been laid off or seen their work hours cut during the recession. As the first true "sandwich" generation, Boomers are usually the chief bread winners in their extended families, and they have taken on responsibility both for aging parents, who increasingly need help living independently, and for adult children who, due to the educational demands of the knowledge economy, delay entering the workforce.

Thirty-one percent of the Boomers responding to a 2009 survey by consulting firm Age Wave and polling firm Harris Interactive said they were worried about supporting aging parents. That support takes two forms: informal care-giving assistance and paying for expenses out of pocket. Unpaid caregivers provided $350 billion worth of care to friends and relatives in 2006, the American Association of Homes and Aging has estimated. That is the market-equivalent value of the care — it does not include the lost wages of the caregivers, mostly women, who either quit work or cut back their hours. Among those who find themselves in a care-giving situation, many supplement their time with money. In a

2007 study, Donna Wagner, director of the Center for Productive Aging at Towson State University, conducted in-depth surveys of 1,000 care-givers. Survey takers reported that they spent $5,500 each year on average for expenses such as food, medical equipment, legal fees and modifications to the home.[2] Typically, that burden falls upon less affluent care-givers. Well-off Boomers tend to have well-off parents who don't need the assistance.

At the other end of the generational spectrum, younger Americans are attending college in greater numbers than ever before. Three out of four respondents to a 2009 Pew Research Center survey agreed that college is necessary to "get ahead" in life—that compared to only two out of four a single generation previously, in 1978.[3]

Over those same three decades, college has become increasingly expensive. Tuitions have consistently outpaced incomes. As a result, students and their families have been forced to seek financial assistance. In the 2008-2009 academic year, student borrowing surged an incredible 23 percent in a single year. Two-thirds of all students today end up borrowing money, and they graduate with an average debt load exceeding $23,000. Those numbers are up from 58 percent of students borrowing to pay for college a dozen years earlier and an average amount borrowed per student of less than $13,200.[4]

Many debt-laden graduates, the so-called "boomerang children," go home to live with their Boomer moms and dads. Even when they don't, parents lend a helping hand. A survey last year by VibrantNation.com, a website forum for 50+ women, found that 29 percent of its readers were helping pay for their children's rent, 26 percent for everyday expenses and 17 percent for health care and educational costs. And where does that money come from? For the most part, parents cut back on their own consumption. But one-third of them tapped funds they'd set aside for future needs such as retirement.

"This is a generation of helicopter moms and dads who value their friendships with their children and who [have] had a hard time letting go," observed Carol Osborne, senior strategist for VibrantNation.com. "The jury is still out whether this is a temporary adjustment to tough economic times, or a re-jiggering of multigenerational family models that will have staying power over the long run."[5]

In all likelihood, Boomer subsidies for grown children will continue at high levels, as there is no sign that the escalation in college tuitions is abating. With only a few years left to prepare, Boomers are awakening to the fact that they have saved insufficiently to fund the fantasy retirements they dreamed of, and they have too many family obligations to save much money even if they did have more time.

Aside from buying lottery tickets and praying for a miracle, most Boomers see only one practicable solution. Reversing a century-long trend in which each generation retired earlier than the preceding one, most Boomers have concluded they will have to work several years longer than their parents did. A survey by Age Wave and Harris Interactive found that Boomers expect to work 3.9 more years on average than they had planned.[6] The findings have been replicated by other consumer research firms.

Alas, even working longer may not ameliorate the predicament in which Boomers find themselves. Alicia Munnell and her colleagues at the Center for Retirement Research at Boston College painstakingly compile and update something they call the National Retirement Risk Index, which measures the risk that Americans will be financially "unprepared" for retirement. By "unprepared," the researchers mean the inability to maintain 70 percent of their pre-retirement income after adjusting for the expected increase in health care expenses and the cost of insuring for long-term care. Even if they all work until 65 — about three years past the average retirement age today — and tap the equity in their houses, 52 percent of older Boomers, 64 percent of younger Boomers and 71 percent of Generation Xers are at risk of falling short.[7]

Boomers are concerned about the cost of health care and long-term care, and rightfully so. One in three Americans requires long-term care at some point in their lives. Quality nursing homes can cost up to $77,000 a year. Less than 15 percent of the elderly population could withstand such a drain and still maintain their living standards. For households in the bottom third of wealth distribution, Munnell concludes, the "most reasonable strategy" would be to rely upon Medicaid to cover expenses should long-term care be required. Although households in the middle third might benefit from long-term care insurance, many may find the price tag too steep — $7,300 a year at age 75 — suggesting that an optimal strategy would be to take their chances and fall back on Medicaid if they exhaust their resources.

Munnell is assuming, of course, that Social Security, Medicare and Medicaid will remain intact, that in spite of spiraling costs for health care, the U.S. government will continue to pay out benefits more or less on the same terms as today. What happens if it can't? What happens if chronic deficits, rising interest rates, compounding payments on the fast-rising national debt and dependence upon foreign lenders force the U.S. into default? What happens if no one will lend to Uncle Sam anymore?

What would Baby Boomers' retirement prospects look like if their Social Security, Medicare and Medicaid benefits were arbitrarily slashed by 25 percent or more as the U.S. government desperately sought to preserve its solvency? How "happy, wild and free" would anybody's retirement look then?

Those are the questions that I will address in this book. In the first five chapters, I will try to persuade you that the nightmare scenario of government insolvency isn't just a paranoid delusion of fiscal conservatives, but a near inevitability given the myopic, corrupt and gridlocked political culture of Washington, D.C. I also will try to convince you that the default of the federal government and the inability to support spending through borrowing — an event that I refer to as "Boomergeddon" — is not merely a legacy that we Boomers bequeath our children and grandchildren, it is an affliction we foist upon ourselves in our lifetimes, most likely when we are retired, exhausting our savings, feeling weak and frail, and reliant upon the government social safety net for our financial security.

In chapters six and seven, I will explore what Boomergeddon means for Americans: first the collapse of the American sphere of influence around the world, retrenchment of world trade and the spread of war and anarchy; and second, the radical truncation of the American welfare state, including the Social Security, Medicare and Medicaid that you'll be depending upon to help finance your old age.

In the final two chapters, I will explore survival strategies. I will outline what you can do personally to brace for Boomergeddon and to adapt to the fiscal shock of a federal government in default. And, finally, so as not to leave you in utter despair, I will lay out five strategies for salvaging the nation's fiscal health (and, thereby, your retirement) should the American people in their righteous wrath and indignation wrest power back from the big corporations, the big unions, the special interests and the political class of lobbyists and fixers in Washington, D.C.

If you're looking for smiley-face advice on a blissful retirement, this isn't it. If, in the immortal words of Col. Nathan R. Jessep in the movie, "A Few Good Men," "You can't handle the truth," then stick your ostrich head back into your hole. But if you are of a combative frame of mind and want to know where the country is heading and how to survive the greatest crisis in the American system of government since the Great Depression — possibly since the Civil War — then read on.

Chapter 1
The Imperial City

He Did It, Mom. No, He Did It!

ON JAN. 18, 2001, PRESIDENT BILL CLINTON SAT IN THE OVAL OFFICE and gave his farewell address to the American people. The nation had enjoyed eight years of peace and prosperity, he said proudly. The economy had created 22 million new jobs. And the fiscal health of the nation had never been stronger. As the nation looked ahead, he said, it needed to maintain its record of fiscal responsibility.

Through our last four budgets we've turned record deficits to record surpluses, and we've been able to pay down $600 billion of our national debt, on track to be debt-free by the end of the decade for the first time since 1835. Staying on that course will bring lower interest rates, greater prosperity, and the opportunity to meet our big challenges. If we choose wisely, we can pay down the debt, deal with the retirement of the baby boomers, invest more in our future, and provide tax relief.[8]

Americans faced a very different kind of budget quandary back then than they do today. Budget projections indicated that surpluses would grow to $625 billion a year by the end of the decade.[9] The big question was what to do with all the money. Cut taxes? Invest in education and the environment? Put Social Security in a "lock box"? Pay off the $5.7 trillion national debt?

It was a wonderful dilemma to ponder. But it didn't last long. Consider where we stand today.

The total national debt has surged past the $13 trillion mark — more than double the level when Clinton gave his speech — and the

Obama administration has forecast that the nation will surpass $20 trillion by 2020.[10] The Congressional Budget Office is even more pessimistic, projecting an extra $1 trillion in deficits by the end of the decade.[11] If the feds conducted 20-year forecasts, the picture would look far worse. The really big expenditures on Medicare, Medicaid and Social Security don't start until a decade from now, when most Boomers have reached retirement. That's when the deficits get really ugly. Today the question isn't whether we should pay off the national debt, it's how long we can continue adding to it before the whole system collapses.

How did we reach such a state of affairs in nine short years?

The two dominant political clans — the Hatfields and McCoys of American politics otherwise known as the Democratic and Republican Parties — would have you believe that it's all the other's fault. The sad truth is, there is plenty of blame for both. Since 2001, neither party has been serious about controlling the deficit.

The point may seem obvious to some, but it apparently eludes bloggers and TV's talking heads who parrot official party talking points, admitting no flaw and conceding no weakness. I dwell upon the issue because in my experience in personal conversations and as moderator of the *Bacon's Rebellion* blog, an Internet forum where people of diverse perspectives manage to debate civilly, many people are more interested in exonerating their partisan champions than fixing the problem. The sad reality is that, while balancing the budget is something that everyone says the U.S. ought to do, it isn't at the top of anybody's list of priorities. Given a choice, Democrats would rather jack up domestic spending and entitlements every time. Republicans would rather cut taxes and project national might overseas. As long as the elephants can pin the blame on the donkey and vice versa, no one has to take ownership of their own actions.

With the benefit of hindsight, we now know that the nation's fiscal health was not as sound in January 2001 as President Clinton thought it was. Indeed, following the collapse of the dot.com bubble, the economy slipped into recession in March — only two months after Clinton's speech. Then on September 11 the unthinkable happened: Islamic terrorists hijacked four jets and slammed two of them into the twin towers of the World Trade Center, striking the heart of the financial system. Markets panicked and the slump deepened. Federal revenues took a dive and the surplus evaporated.

The terrorist attack also highlighted the nation's lack of preparedness. Responding to the challenge of fundamentalist Islamic terrorism, the Bush administration ramped up spending across the board on the military, homeland security and intelligence — with broad support from Democrats in Congress. While the invasion of Iraq was discretionary and arguably unnecessary, few disputed the necessity of spending more money to ensure that 9/11 was never repeated.

Finally, against the backdrop of the wobbly economy and war on terror, the Congress let expire in 2002 a piece of legislation that had been crucial to holding deficit spending in check over the previous decade. Back in 1990, President George H.W. Bush had reneged on his famous vow, "Read my lips: no new taxes." By acceding to modest tax increases, he had won important spending caps that helped his successor, Clinton, restrain spending through his eight years in office. Unfortunately, Bush's son, George W., had to work with a Congress that had no such institutional brake on its appetites.

Democrat spin-meisters tend to forget that Clinton had a partner in restraining spending: a Republican Congress. By putting Republicans in charge of both houses of Congress in 1994 for the first time in 40 years, voters sent a clear message that they wanted an end to fiscal business as usual. A champion of smaller government, House Speaker Newt Gingrich was instrumental in pushing through welfare reform and other budget-tightening measures. By 1996, small-government Republicans were so firmly in control of Congress that Clinton acknowledged what seemed obvious at the time, declaring, "The era of big government is over."[12]

While Republicans and Democrats alike share credit for balancing the budget in the 1990s, President George W. Bush bears much of the responsibility for letting deficits run amuck in the 2000s. Bush's defenders could argue, like President Obama does today, that he inherited his fiscal problems. After all, the economy went into the tank two months after he stepped into office, and 9/11 took place eight months later, dealing a blow to the economy and prodding the nation into ramping up defense, intelligence and homeland security spending. But other big fiscal decisions were his. Bush fought for tax cuts as an economic stimulus. He led the nation into the budget-busting war in Iraq. He launched the two biggest entitlement expansions in years, the State Childrens' Health Insurance Program (SCHIP) and Medicare Part D, the prescription drug benefit. He signed onto a ramp-up of massive agricultural subsidies. And he tolerated Congress' growing predilection for pork, allowing earmarks to multiply like feral swine.

The administration's insouciance toward deficits was captured in a famous story told by Bush's first Treasury Secretary, Paul O'Neill. During a meeting of the Economic Policy Group, O'Neill argued against the proposed tax cut. Government, he argued, needed the money to fix Social Security and Medicare, redesign the tax system and fund the ongoing war on terror. Vice President Dick Cheney disagreed. As O'Neill remembered Cheney's retort: "When Ronald Reagan was here, he proved that deficits don't really matter."[13]

Animated by Cheney's advice, the Bush administration followed the easy fiscal path, borrowing record sums to pay for guns and butter. On the day Bush took office, the national debt stood at $5.73 trillion. On the day he left office, it had risen to $10.63 trillion — an increase of $4.9 trillion, and the most spectacular run-up since the United States had mobilized for total war in 1942.

President Barack Obama rightfully criticized Bush's fiscal recklessness during his presidential campaign, but he conveniently overlooked the fact that the Democrats, who had recaptured control of Congress for Bush's final two years, passed the budget bills that he was now denouncing. Posturing as a fiscal hawk, Obama continued to blame his predecessor for the worsening fiscal straits when he took office. As he said during a high-level summit one month into the job:

> *This administration has inherited a $1.3 trillion deficit — the largest in our nation's history, and our investments to rescue the nation's economy will add to that deficit. We cannot and will not sustain deficits like these without end. Contrary to the prevailing wisdom in Washington these past few years, we cannot simply spend as we please and defer the consequences to the next budget, the next administration or the next generation.*[14]

After saying all the right things, Obama proceeded to ignore his own advice. He signed a $797 billion stimulus package, to be paid for all with borrowed money, employed TARP money to bail out Chrysler and General Motors, a use which Congress had never contemplated, and made his top legislative priority the overhaul of the U.S. health care system, the biggest expansion in entitlement spending since the days of the Great Society.

Democrats may believe Obama's rhetoric about fiscal responsibility, but the American people do not. Toward the end of 2009, public opinion polls showed flagging approval ratings for Obama's policies, opposition to "ObamaCare" specifically, and a throw-the-bums-out mindset universally. Despite Obama's personal popularity, Americans disapproved in September of his handling of the federal deficit by 58 percent to 38 percent.[15] As the year came to a close, the public mood soured even more. A November 30 Rasmussen poll showed that 71 percent of voters said they were angry at the policies of the federal government — up five points from September — and 46 percent were very angry.[16] In January the election of Scott Brown, a moderate Republican, in the Massachusetts Senate seat long occupied by liberal lion Teddy Kennedy made it manifestly clear that the American people had had enough.

Voters focused on something that the political class in Washington, D.C., growing fat on unprecedented spending, mainly gave lip service to: runaway federal government spending and the massive unfunded liabilities in Social Security and health care. With no credible plan for making good on the old entitlements, many Americans felt, the nation could not afford to make new entitlements. The bail-out and stimulus money may have helped Wall Street tycoons, the United Auto Workers and incumbent Democratic Congressmen, but it wasn't helping ordinary Americans. All the tax-paying public got from a year of big-government activism was a mountain of debt that propelled the nation ever faster toward the final day of fiscal reckoning.

If it were only a matter of "throwing the bums out," voters could impose their wishes upon Washington, D.C. But they've tried that, and it didn't work. The Gingrich insurrection made a difference for a few years in the 1990s, but the Republicans' zeal for reform burned itself out and deficit spending resumed like it had never gone out of style. In 2006, the country put the Democrats back in charge of Congress and voted in 2008 for "hope and change." But nothing changed except the number of digits measuring the size of the budget deficit. In their desperation, voters now show every sign of shifting back to the Republicans.

The problem with America today is much bigger than which political party controls Congress and the White House. Voting out one bunch of bums and replacing it with another bunch fails to bring about lasting change because the bums aren't fully in charge. Washington, D.C., is, for all practical purposes, ruled by a permanently entrenched political class that occupies the high ground, the low ground and every vantage point of tactical political value in the nations' capital.

Only when you comprehend how laws are made, regulations written, money spent, and capital allocated in this country, will you understand why the United States has racked up a $13 trillion national debt and why that debt is spiraling out of control. Only when you grasp how an avaricious political elite has tightened its chokehold on the nation will you understand why the U.S. chronically shows so little fiscal discipline, why the U.S. government will be driven to default, and why, when push comes to shove, the retirement benefits you have contributed to all your life are now in jeopardy.

America's Ruling Class

There are two levels of political power in Washington, D.C. The visible layer revolves around the endless struggle between Democrats and Republicans. The invisible layer consists of permanent special interests and the mercenary lobbyists that support them: the political class. This governing elite goes about its business regardless of whether the Ds or Rs are in nominally charge. Its practitioners are inherently biased toward bigger, more powerful government because the very reason for their existence is to seek favors from government. By definition, bigger government means more power to dispense favors and privileges, and more petitioners seeking those favors.

The American people are only dimly aware that a distinct political class even exists. That's because the mainstream media narrative frames national politics as a battle between the two dominant political parties. Differences between Democrats and Republicans, especially in the realm of cultural issues such as "God, guns and gays," are hyped while common attitudes toward fiscal philosophy — such as the notion that budget deficits are reckless and irresponsible when the other party is in power but an unfortunate necessity when the good guys are in charge — are played down. The illusion of a significant divide between the two is maintained by the close attention given to minor differences within a narrow band of public policy options.

Think of the two political parties as tribes divided by their distinctive totems, traditions and personal loyalties. Partisans of the Donkey Clan are pitted in undying enmity against partisans of the Elephant Clan. Oblivious to their common support for a large, interventionist federal government, they dwell upon what separates them. The top tax bracket for the rich should be 28 percent — no it should be 35 percent — or the economy will go straight to hell! In doing so, the Donkeys and Elephants resemble nothing so much as tribesmen of the Papua New Guinea highlands. As a Papua village chief might say, "Our two clans have nothing in common. My clan is descended from the noble crocodile, their clan from the contemptible tree kangaroo. We color our scars with beautiful red ash, they do it with ugly black ash."

"But, dude," responds the outside observer, "you both practice scarification and you both think you're descended from animals!"

In the New Guinea highlands, the tribes engage in endemic but ritualized warfare that results in the occasional fatality. In Washington, the clans do the same, although the ritual battles usually take the form of press conferences and Congressional votes, and political death usually means losing an election, not having one's brains ritually consumed by the victor (although, as political rhetoric becomes increasingly overwrought, it won't be long before the two sides start accusing each other of cannibalism). The clash of the clans generates considerable heat and dominates the media's coverage of politics because of the all-too-human tendency to view complex and abstract issues through the prism of people and personalities. Thus, Rush Limbaugh depicts Sen. "Dingy" Harry Reid, the Senate Majority Leader, as lugubrious, sour-faced and nefarious. In turn, the Obama White House paints Limbaugh as a polarizing, drug-addled racist who, by the way, is the real leader of the Republican Party. All the while, bloggers and cable-news talking heads engage in personal attacks, characterizing their foes as incompetent, dishonest, stupid or corrupt. The American people get so caught up in the petty hypocrisies, sexual dalliances and other human failings of Donkey Clan and Elephant Clan leaders that they miss the substance of what goes on in Washington.

The business of Washington, D.C. is the federal government. Regardless of the political power in power, the central activity that takes place is the redistribution of wealth — using the coercive power of the state to take from some and dispense it to others. Regardless of the political party in power, a permanent political class consisting of bureaucrats, policy junkies, party hacks, lawyers, lobbyists, contractors, special pleaders and fixers fight like lions and jackals over the economic spoils.

The size and scope of those spoils is extraordinary. Budget outlays in 2010 amount to $3.7 trillion, or more than a quarter of the national economy. Admittedly, much of that money is simply sucked in and spewed back out in the form of Social Security and Medicare checks, but Congress and the federal bureaucrats still set the formulas that determine who gets the checks, how big the checks are and when people get them. What's more, those trillions of dollars represent only a fraction of the resources controlled by the federal government.

Congress also dispenses multibillion-dollar favors by means of tax breaks for particular classes of individuals and businesses. In a 2008 paper, Leonard Burman, Eric Toder and Christopher Geissler estimated that "tax expenditures" for individuals reduced 2007 federal income tax receipts by as much as $761 billion, a sum that exceeded total spending for all non-defense discretionary programs.[17] Many of these tax breaks are highly popular, such as exclusion of interest on life insurance savings, deductibility of student loans, deductibility of mortgage interest, child care credit and others. But the end result is the loss of three-quarters of a trillion dollars that could be used to lower tax rates generally – – or balance the budget. Needless to say, under the guise of protecting the general welfare, the tax breaks are defended tenaciously by a coterie of special business interests that benefit from them indirectly: insurance companies that can sell more insurance, for instance, or real estate companies that can sell more, higher-priced houses. Over and above the breaks granted to individuals, tax breaks for businesses amounted to more than $105 billion, estimated a 2008 report prepared for the House Committee on Ways and Means in an analysis that included only expenditures exceeding $500 million.[18] Tax expenditures receive very little public scrutiny, and they tend to accumulate as lobbyists succeed in getting more exemptions added to the tax code every year.

By a variety of means, Congress, the executive branch and the theoretically independent Federal Reserve Bank play a major role in allocating the nation's financial capital. Currently, the system favors banks, the housing sector, state/local government and narrow-bore causes like foreign exports and green power. The latest ploy for steering capital to favored sectors is the Build America Bonds, authorized by the 2009 fiscal stimulus as a temporary measure to open up credit markets to state and municipal governments. These bonds aren't tax-free, but the federal government pays 35 percent of the interest, resulting in lower interest charges to local government authorities. By the end of 2010, bankers estimate, $150 billion of the bonds will have been sold. As of March, Wall Street had generated some $1 billion in fees.[19]

Meanwhile, capital for politically powerless small businesses has been severely constricted in two ways: Banks have taken large write-offs for bad real estate loans and government has steered capital to favored constituencies. As economist David Malpass described the nation's politically driven capital markets:

> *Capital is being rationed not on price but on availability and connections. The government gets the most, foreigners second, Wall Street and big companies third, with not much left over. . . . For small businesses and new workers capital rationing is devastating, spelling business failures and painful layoffs. Thousands of start-ups won't launch due to credit shortages, in part because the government and corporations took more credit than they needed (because it was so cheap).*[20]

Through direct grants and subsidies, tax breaks, the allocation of capital and, of course, the writing of regulations, the political class enhances or diminishes the competitive advantage of business after business, industry after industry. Even the world-beating technology titans of Silicon Valley and Redmond, Wash., have discovered that Washington can make or break their enterprises. Thus, the likes of Google and Microsoft compete on a regulatory and legislative playing field, not just in the marketplace.

Presidents and their acolytes come and go. So do Congressmen and their minions. But the interests of the business world endure. Virtually every segment of the American economy is organized in a trade association, every occupation organized in a trade union or a professional association, and every conceivable special interest group organized in an advocacy organization. Once upon a time, these councils and associations were scattered around the country, springing up amidst the industries and communities they served. Today, they congregate in the Washington area, some of them in the famous K Street corridor in the District of Columbia itself, but frequently just across the Potomac River in Arlington or Alexandria. While trade associations still do the things traditionally associated with such groups, such as organize conferences, publish statistics and provide services to members, their role increasingly is to influence the federal government.

These associations number in the hundreds, running the gamut from A to Z — well, A to Y. Apparently, no one has gotten around to forming a Zebra Breeders Association yet. Their concerns include influencing the regulatory process, lobbying for trade protection, petitioning for grants and subsidies, and seeking special treatment in the tax code. Most of the work occurs outside the public eye, unseen by the national media. The Adhesive and Sealants Council, to pick an association at random near the beginning of the alphabet, notes on its website that its recent accomplishments include working with the Environmental Protection Agency to address the emission of Volatile Organic Compounds in adhesive applications — not exactly headline news to most of us, but vitally important to manufacturers of sealants. Similarly, the Writing Instrument Manufacturers Association (WIMA), representing the $4 billion industry that manufactures pens, scrutinizes something called the "Generalized System of Preferences," which dictate which nations receive special trade consideration. Consumers don't give much thought to whether their ball-point pens are manufactured in China or the U.S., but the WIMA surely does.

There are trade associations for home builders and for Realtors, associations for toy companies and for greeting card manufacturers, associations for trains, for airplanes and for automobiles. There are associations for egg producers and soy farmers, for banks and for newspapers, for the construction trades, for the health care professions and for every sector of the energy economy. There is even a National Pork Producers Council, although its membership apparently does not extend to the world's largest generator of pork, Congress.

These groups exercise their influence both directly and indirectly. Through their Political Action Committees (PACs), the major industries and professions pour vast sums into the campaign coffers of incumbent congressmen. The giving of money doesn't guarantee that a congressman will vote the way a contributor wants, but it usually does guarantee access — an assurance that the donor's argument will be respectfully listened to. Although donors cover their bets by contributing to both parties, they typically favor the faction in power, which in the current Congress happens to be the Donkey Clan.

The special interest groups also influence the legislative and regulatory process through lobbying. In 2009, there were 13,426 lobbyists listed in the federal lobbyist registration database, according to OpenSecrets.org. That was up 26 percent since 1998, making lobbying one of the strongest growth industries in the U.S. economy. The number of lobbyists actually peaked in 2007 at a number exceeding 15,000, but the number has fallen as many lobbyists de-registered in response to President Obama's executive order restricting the movement of lobbyists directly into the federal government. However, the decline in the number of lobbyists may be more apparent than real. Reports OpenSecrets.org:

Thousands of lobbyists who appear to have left their line of work may not have actually done so. At the federal level, many people working in the lobbying industry are not registered lobbyists, instead adopting titles such as "senior advisor" or other executive monikers, thereby avoiding federal disclosure requirements under the Lobbying Disclosure Act.[21]

Given Obama's ambitious legislative agenda, which would expand the federal government's role in the financial, health care and energy sectors, it would be no surprise to find that the number of actual lobbyists, whether registered or not, has increased dramatically since he came to office.

The small business members of the Indoor Tanning Association are only one of the trade groups that have learned the hard way that in Washington, if you snooze, you lose. During the frenzied negotiations leading up to the final version of the Senate's health care overhaul in late 2009, the American Academy of Dermatology lobbied furiously to remove the so-called Botax (the 5 percent levy on plastic surgery procedures, including Botox) by persuading Senate solons that a better alternative would be to slap a 10 percent tax on tanning services, which, they argued, would reduce the incidence of skin cancer down the road. The switcheroo caught the tanning lobby by surprise. (Yes, the 20,000 tanning salons across the country also see the need to hire lobbyists.) But Big Tanning was no match for Big Medicine, and the tanning tax stuck.[22]

What makes the legislative process so insidious is the "revolving door" between government positions on the one hand and lobbying firms on the other. When Congressmen resign or lose an election, they and their staffs frequently find employment with an outfit whose job is to influence the legislative process. Likewise, presidents and congressmen draw heavily from the ranks of Washington's permanent political class to fill important appointments.

The Center for Responsive Politics, a non-partisan research group that tracks the money in U.S. politics and publishes the OpenSecrets.org website, has done a magnificent job of tracking this migration between the public and private sectors. As of Nov. 30, 2009, for instance, the Center had identified 482 individuals who had moved from the White House staff over successive administrations to a private-sector lobbying position, 456 people who had done so from the Department of Defense, 340 from the Department of Commerce, and thousands more from other branches of government. Writes OpenSecrets.org:

> *Former employees of federal agencies can often find good (and lucrative) jobs as lobbyists, capitalizing on the connections that they forged while in public service. An Environmental Protection Agency administrator may go on to lobby his former colleagues on environmental issues, and a White House staffer can tap her West Wing connections when she starts a new job on K Street.*[23]

Congressional staffers also fare well in the private sector. OpenSecrets.org has identified 141 individuals who have shifted from the House Energy & Finance Committee to a lobbying position, 101 who have done the same from the Senate Judiciary Committee, and many hundreds more from other committees.

President Obama understands all of this, and his lobbying reforms were designed to slow the movement of lobbyists and government employees through that revolving door. What the president evidently fails to appreciate is a fundamental tenet of human nature: Given sufficient motivation — and $3.8 trillion in spending, nearly $1 trillion in tax breaks, and the ability to influence regulations and the allocation of capital is considerable motivation — people will find to a way to skirt the intent of the rules.

Perhaps no one epitomizes the system better than Rahm Emanuel, President Obama's chief of staff. The former Chicago politician and Wall Street investment banker has moved amphibian-like between the realms of business and politics.

Top Contributors to Congress

			Dem %	GOP % Top Recipient
1	Lawyers/Law Firms	$21,873,666	83%	17% Harry Reid (D-Nev)
2	Health Professionals	$13,611,257	63%	37% Harry Reid (D-Nev)
3	Retired	$11,433,765	56%	44% Mark Kirk (R-Ill)
4	Securities/Invest	$10,299,538	74%	26% Charles E Schumer (D-NY)
5	Real Estate	$10,061,748	65%	35% Charles E Schumer (D-NY)
6	Insurance	$8,405,172	58%	42% Charles E Schumer (D-NY)
7	Lobbyists	$7,631,276	68%	31% Harry Reid (D-Nev)
8	Leadership PACs	$6,354,659	63%	37% Roy Blunt (R-Mo)
9	Bldg Trade Unions	$5,693,745	92%	8% Judy Chu (D-Calif)
10	Pharm/Health Prod	$5,434,796	61%	39% Richard Burr (R-NC)
11	Electric Utilities	$5,339,404	60%	40% Byron L Dorgan (D-ND)
12	Misc Finance	$5,248,219	62%	38% Charles E Schumer (D-NY)
13	Democratic/Liberal	$5,114,851	100%	0% Michael F Bennet (D-Colo)
14	Oil & Gas	$4,443,128	40%	60% Blanche Lincoln (D-Ark)
15	TV/Movies/Music	$4,376,500	70%	30% Patrick Leahy (D-Vt)
16	Business Services	$4,184,329	73%	27% Harry Reid (D-Nev)
17	Transport Unions	$3,954,388	87%	13% Michael E McMahon (D-NY)
18	Commercial Banks	$3,898,696	51%	49% Kirsten Gillibrand (D-NY)
19	Hospitals/Nurs Homes	$3,872,639	74%	26% Charles E Schumer (D-NY)
20	Public Sector Unions	$3,711,520	93%	7% Scott Murphy (D-NY)
21	Industrial Unions	$3,641,976	98%	2% Mark Schauer (D-Mich)
22	Crop Production	$3,463,666	62%	38% Blanche Lincoln (D-Ark)
23	Air Transport	$3,327,586	56%	44% Byron L Dorgan (D-ND)
24	Misc Mfg/Distrib	$3,038,709	57%	43% Charles E Schumer (D-NY)
25	Defense Aerospace	$3,008,925	61%	39% Patty Murray (D-Wash)
26	Computers/Internet	$3,001,771	71%	29% Charles E Schumer (D-NY)
27	General Contractors	$2,792,843	51%	49% Charles E Schumer (D-NY)
28	Beer, Wine & Liquor	$2,733,174	61%	39% Mike Thompson (D-Calif)
29	Retail Sales	$2,727,937	55%	45% Blanche Lincoln (D-Ark)
30	Accountants	$2,722,040	51%	49% Charles E Schumer (D-NY)
31	Candidate Cmtes	$2,612,618	81%	19% Scott Murphy (D-NY)
32	Railroads	$2,605,795	60%	40% Corrine Brown (D-Fla)
33	Construction Svcs	$2,493,180	66%	34% Harry Reid (D-Nev)
34	Misc Business	$2,415,903	70%	29% Al Franken (D-Minn)
35	Telephone Utilities	$2,379,157	56%	44% Rick Boucher (D-Va)
36	Education	$2,279,328	82%	18% Harry Reid (D-Nev)
37	Health Services	$2,249,688	69%	31% Charles E Schumer (D-NY)
38	Defense Electronics	$2,072,065	63%	37% John P Murtha (D-Pa)
39	Agricultural Svcs	$1,854,989	55%	45% Blanche Lincoln (D-Ark)
40	Casinos/Gambling	$1,806,938	76%	24% Shelley Berkley (D-Nev)
41	Food & Beverage	$1,756,772	55%	45% Blanche Lincoln (D-Ark)
42	Pro-Israel	$1,562,496	70%	30% Harry Reid (D-Nev)
43	Misc Defense	$1,534,459	63%	37% Daniel K Inouye (D-Hawaii)
44	Finance/Credit	$1,500,228	57%	43% Harry Reid (D-Nev)
45	Telecom Svcs/Equip	$1,456,889	69%	31% Rick Boucher (D-Va)
46	Food Process/Sales	$1,394,558	54%	46% Blanche Lincoln (D-Ark)
47	Automotive	$1,383,219	46%	54% Roy Blunt (R-Mo)
48	Chemicals	$1,358,649	56%	44% Vernon Buchanan (R-Fla)
49	Publishing	$1,290,133	77%	23% Kirsten Gillibrand (D-NY)
50	Misc Unions	$1,249,270	100%	0% Scott Murphy (D-NY)

Source: Open Secrets.org "Top Industries Giving to Members of Congress, 2010 Cycle."
Note: Sums include only donations made to current incumbents in Congress.

Starting out in Illinois politics, Emanuel joined the presidential campaign of Bill Clinton as a fund raiser, then served the president as a senior advisor. Tapping the contacts he made during his fund-raising activities, he left in 1998 to become an investment banker at Wasserstein Perella; a year later, he was managing the firm's Chicago office. In a two-and-a-half-year stint, he worked on eight deals that netted him $16.2 million — not bad money for a young man with no formal deal-making experience in investment banking. After making his millions, he ran for Congress, served five terms, and then joined the Obama campaign. Now, at 50 years old, he is one of the most powerful men in Washington.

Another paragon of the political class is Tom Daschle, a former U.S. Senate Majority Leader who was defeated for re-election in 2004. Shortly after his loss, he took a job as "senior counsel" with the K Street law firm, Alston & Bird. The firm's lobbying clients included some of the biggest names in the health care industry, including Abbott Laboratories, HealthSouth, Anthem and the American Hospital Association. The firm has generated roughly $8 million a year in lobbying fees over each of the past three years — and that doesn't include non-lobbying legal work done for those groups. Daschle reportedly earned $2 million a year from Alston & Bird as well as $2 million in salary from InterMedia Advisors, the firm made famous for squiring him around with a private car and driver.[24]

When Obama selected Daschle as Secretary of Health and Human Services, unpaid taxes on that limousine derailed his appointment. But the mini-scandal did not stop Daschle from playing a key role behind the scenes in crafting Obama's health care initiative. In August 2009, he talked continually with top White House advisers, some of whom had previously worked for him. He even spoke frequently to the president, meeting with him in the Oval Office. As journalist Timothy P. Carney sums up Daschle's ability to shift between the business and political worlds:

Daschle is not technically a lobbyist — he hasn't registered under the Lobbying Disclosure Act. That means by law he cannot make "lobbying contact" — speaking on behalf of clients to public officials about policy. But he can advise clients on strategies for lobbying. He can also advise his Alston & Bird colleagues — lobbyists — on how to lobby. Finally, he can still talk to government officials about policy — just not on behalf of his clients. So, Tom Daschle works at a lobbying firm, gets paid by health industry clients for his work on health policy, and advises Obama on health care reform — but he's still not a lobbyist. [25]

Emanuel and Daschle stand at the apex of influence in the political class. But there are literally thousands of other lobbyists, lawyers, public relations professionals and other "government affairs" experts from both political parties who have made the same journey between the public and private sectors, and, often, back again.

True Blue

Anyone who understood how Washington works was not beguiled by candidate Obama's message of hope and change, nor his promises to reform the way business conducted in the nation's capital. For businesses, there's too much money at stake. For the political class, there's too much money to be made.

Robert Reich, a Labor Secretary during the Clinton administration and now a professor at Berkeley, described the underlying forces at work in his book, "Supercapitalism." American corporations are driven by the need to maximize shareholder value. Once upon a time, that meant competing in the marketplace. Increasingly, Reich observes, competition has moved into the political arena. "Companies have entered politics to gain or keep advantage over their business rivals. ... Everyday politics within legislatures, committees, and departments and agencies of government has come to be dominated by corporations seeking competitive advantage."[26]

Carney makes much the same point in his 2009 book, "Obama-nomics." It's a myth, he says, to characterize Republicans as the party of the middle class and the Democrats the champions of the powerless. Both parties are in hoc to their necks to the moneyed special interests. Obama lambasted lobbyists and the special interests during his presidential campaign, promising a new kind of politics. But Carney, a *Washington Examiner* columnist, meticulously documents the role of big business in crafting health care legislation, the cap-and-trade bill, tobacco regulation, the economic stimulus package and the financial bail-outs (as well as the role of the auto workers union in the Chrysler and General Motors bail-outs) in the first year of the Obama administration. In issue after issue, Obama's vision for an expansive government won support from corporate interests that stood to benefit from that expansion, whether through government mandates, restricted competition or outright subsidies.

The bias of Washington, D.C., toward bigger-spending government runs even deeper than the lobbyists and corporate interests. The nation may stand at the epicenter of the most powerful nation on the globe, but its inhabitants are just as subject to the laws of human nature as small-town rubes. Washington's political class lives in a privileged bubble. Washingtonians interact with others like themselves, people who share similar mindsets about how the world works, people who rarely contradict deep-seated assumptions regarding the proper role and scope of the federal government.

Not surprisingly for a city that revolves around the passing of laws and writing of regulations, Washington, D.C., is stacked to the gills with lawyers. The District of Columbia Bar Association has 80,000 members. They don't all reside in Washington, but a good many of them do. Lawyers, steeped in the rigors of legal training, are not accustomed to thinking, like businessmen and entrepreneurs do, in terms of creating wealth and adding value through voluntary transactions. The legal thought process gravitates naturally towards legislating solutions that mobilize the coercive power of the state.

The Washington region also is distinctive in having 320,000 federal government employees working there.[27] Most of these are "lifers," making government their career. Their world view centers on the federal government as the single-most indispensable institution of the United States. For the most part, federal government employees also think in terms of government as the natural "solution" to any of society's problems.

Greater Washington, a metropolitan region of 5.6 million people, has a significant private sector but, for the most part it is oriented toward the U.S. federal government, either as a customer or a dispenser of largesse. As the world's largest buyer of goods and services, the federal government hews to rigid, rules-oriented procurement policies designed to thwart graft and corruption. To sell to the feds, a company must master these arcane rules and procedures, and that means maintaining a presence in the Washington region where they can hire people who know the rules and can interact with federal procurement officials as needed. The ranks of public companies headquartered in the region are dominated by the IT, telecommunications, defense and aerospace, and professional services industries, which make their living by selling weaponry to the military or services to federal agencies.

Not all Washington-area companies sell to Uncle Sam. Some were formed to advance public policy goals. Two of the more notorious corporations are Fannie Mae ($22.7 billion in 2008 revenues) and Freddie Mac ($12.3 billion), created with the aim of increasing U.S. home ownership. And that they did. By buying hundreds of billions of dollars of mortgages from millions of Americans regardless of credit worthiness, they helped push home ownership to all-time highs. They also enriched their senior executives and contributed to the excessive lending to subprime borrowers, the over-heating and subsequent collapse of the housing market, and the Global Financial Crisis. After their financial collapse, the federal government has taken over control in every way but name only, subsidizing them with hundreds of billions of dollars and using them to execute the Obama administration's rescue of the housing industry.

The federal government may dominate the Washington business scene, but that's not to say that there isn't a smattering of businesses that lack a strong connection to government — Capital One Financial (credit cards), Marriott International (hotels) and Gannett (newspapers) are examples. There are prominent home building firms and real estate developers to serve the region's growing population, and of course there are health care companies, retailers and personal service providers. But the primary industry that drives the economy and without which all the rest would shrivel and die is the federal government. For all practical purposes, Washington is a one-company town.

The business of redistributing the nation's wealth is a lucrative one. With a per capita income of $49,606, the Washington metropolitan area was the fourth wealthiest MSA in the country in 2007. The region trailed only the San Jose MSA, home to Silicon Valley, the Bridgeport, Conn., MSA, abode of many of Wall Street's richest, and the San Francisco MSA. In contrast to those regions, however, average incomes in the Washington region aren't buoyed by the mega-rich. The main path to super riches in the United States still is building enterprises and managing money. *Forbes Magazine* lists only a handful of its 400 wealthiest Americans as living in the Washington area, and none of them owe their wealth to government work. But making friends and influencing people isn't a bad way to make a living. In a survey of 514 trade and professional associations, labor unions, think tanks and nonprofit organizations active in Washington, the *National Journal* and CEO Update identified 89 top executives who knocked down more than $1 million — a 30 percent increase from a survey two years previously. John Castellani, president of the Business Roundtable, led the list with total compensation of $5.57 million in 2008. Senior lobbyists fared well too. Richard Pollack, head honcho for advocacy and public policy at the American Hospital Association, raked in $1.15 million.[29] Hired-gun lobbyists working for independent firms rarely make those sums, but billing $500 an hour can lead to a pretty comfortable lifestyle. And when thousands of people are doing it, it creates a broad-based affluence.

Moreover, the Imperial City is well insulated from the travails of the general economy. The Washington area has received 10 times as much stimulus money per capita from the American Recovery and Reinvestment Act as the national average. Regional unemployment in January 2009 was far below the national norm: 6.9 percent compared to a national average of 9.7 percent — the second lowest of any metropolitan area with a population of one million or more. The unemployment there resulted from the contraction of the private sector, the construction trades most dramatically, not the public sector. Wages and salaries have held up well, too.

While Americans in the private sector coped with layoffs, reduced working hours and pay freezes during the recession, the number of federal workers earning six-figure salaries exploded. The number of Defense Department employees earning $150,000 or more increased from 1,868 in December 2007 to 10,100 in June 2009, *USA Today* found in an analysis late last year. Eighteen months ago, the Transportation Department had only one person earning a salary of $170,000 or more. Today, 1,690 employees have salaries above $170,000.[30]

The average pay of federal employees is $71,206 compared to $40,331 in the private sector. A spokesperson for the Federal Managers Association justified the discrepancy on the grounds that the federal government employs educated workers such as scientists, physicians and lawyers. Federal employees earn 26 percent less than private workers on comparable jobs. Of course, federal employees also enjoy job security and pension benefits that are far more lucrative than private-sector plans. Additionally, federal employees can count on consistent pay raises. Congress approved across-the-board pay hikes of 3 percent in 2008 and 3.9 percent in 2009. When *USA Today* published its article, Obama was recommending 2 percent more in 2010. In addition to the across-the-board raises, most employees get longevity pay bumps, called steps, that average 1.5 percent per year.

Thus, not only is the political class comprised of hundreds of thousands of people who are "very well off" economically and heavily invested in the idea that a powerful federal government is a good thing, Washingtonians are insulated from the consequences of the policies they inflict upon the nation.

Residents of the Imperial City know to whom they owe their government largesse. Voters skew heavily in favor of the Democrats, the party that openly favors big government, over Republicans, whose rhetoric is hostile to big government even if their voting records aren't. Indeed, the Washington metro area is one of the bluest patches on the national electoral map. If the core Washington metropolitan area were a state, its residents would have voted for Barack Obama by a higher percentage than any other state in the union — 72 percent by my calculation, a hair more than Hawaii, where Obama was born, more than the Peoples' Republic of Vermont, more than Obama's home state of Illinois, and more than the Democrat bastion of Massachusetts.

Washington Metro Election Results - 2008				
	Obama	McCain	% Obama	% McCain
Washington, D.C.	245,800	17,367	92.5	6.5
Prince George's County, Md.	323,396	38,833	88.9	10.4
Arlington County, Va.	78,994	29,876	71.7	27.1
Alexandria, Va.	50,473	19,181	71.7	27.3
Montgomery County, Md.	314,444	118,608	71.6	27
Charles County, Md.	43,635	25,732	62.2	36.7
Fairfax County, Va.	310,359	200,994	60.1	39.0
Prince William County, Va.	93,435	67,621	57.5	41.6
Loudoun County, Va.	74,845	63,336	53.7	45.4
	1,535,381	**581,548**	**72.5**	**27.5**

Source: "2008 Presidential General Election Results"; "Atlas of U. S. Presidential Elections."

In summary, not only does the political class of Washington, D.C., make a very comfortable living from petitioning government on behalf of the nation's vested interests, it comprises an affluent, liberal Democrat mono-culture with few parallels anywhere in the country. You'd have to visit places like Manhattan, San Francisco or Boston-Cambridge to find anything comparable.

While the American people occasionally elect insurgents to overturn the status quo, the reality in such an environment is that small-government rebels don't stay small-government rebels for long. Washington, D.C., the imperial city, is like Beijing at the height of Chinese civilization. Peasants and barbarians periodically conquered the capital and overthrew old, decaying dynasties, but within a generation the new rulers cast off their old culture to ape the ways of the mandarins.

Political convulsions originating in the heartland have left no lasting trace on government spending. Eight years of the Reagan Revolution did not roll back the size and scope of the federal government. Neither did the Gingrich insurrection. The latter small-government incursion, which marched into town in 1994 under the banner of term limits and the Contract with America, took only a few years to lose its way. By 2002, Republicans in Washington were proclaiming that "deficits don't matter," larding their legislation with earmarks and pork, hitting up lobbyists for money in the "K Street project," running up deficits and the national debt, and deciding that term limits weren't such great idea after all.

As long as the U.S. Treasury can continue to heap on the debt, the political class will continue to see its interests as synonymous with an expanding government, will avoid making hard budgetary choices and will continue to spend other peoples' money without restraint. Government will continue growing until the day the political class can borrow no more. That day, Boomergeddon, is coming — probably a lot sooner than you think.

Chapter 2
The Ten-Year Outlook

The Obama Path to Prosperity

STANDING BEFORE BOTH HOUSES OF CONGRESS ON JANUARY 27, 2010, President Barack Obama opened his nationally televised state-of-the-union address by enumerating the challenges besetting the nation when he had taken office a year before: two wars, a severe recession, a financial system on the brink of collapse and a country deeply in debt. As he spoke, the worst appeared to be over: The country had survived the financial meltdown and dodged a major depression. But much work remained to be done. One in ten Americans were out of work, home values had declined, and families were hard-pressed to pay for college tuitions.

Obama then laid out his plan for reviving the economy. He proposed taking $30 billion of repaid bank bailout money and giving it to community banks to lend to small business. He advocated creating jobs by "building the infrastructure of tomorrow" and by establishing incentives to promote "clean energy" like nuclear power, clean coal and bio-fuels. He set the goal of doubling exports by launching a National Export Initiative to help farmers and small businesses. He talked of investing in "the skills and education of our people" by means of charter schools and college-tuition tax credits. And, of course, he made the case for his dramatic overhaul of the United States health care system. The plan, he claimed, would reduce costs for millions of families and businesses and bring down the deficit by as much as $1 trillion over the next two decades.

His predecessor, Obama reminded the American people, had taken a $200 billion surplus and turned it into a $1 trillion deficit by the time he left office. To pay for the initiatives that pulled the economy out of the ditch, Obama conceded, he had added an extra $1 trillion to the national debt. But families across the country were tightening their belts, and the federal government should do the same. To offset that $1 trillion, Obama proposed freezing discretionary, non-defense spending for three years. "Like any cash-strapped family we will work within a budget to invest in what we need and sacrifice what we don't. And if I have to enforce this discipline by veto, I will."

But not right away. The spending freeze, Obama said, would go into effect in the following fiscal year, 2011, "when the economy is stronger." To tackle the nation's long-term structural deficit, he proposed a bipartisan fiscal commission to come up with answers, and he urged Congress to enact earmark reform. "We have finished a difficult year. We have come through a difficult decade," he said. "But a new year has come. A new decade stretches before us. .... Let's seize this moment –– to start anew, to carry the dream forward, and to strengthen our union once more."[32]

Underpinning the president's lofty rhetoric were elaborate spreadsheets projecting the cost of the federal government's spending programs, anticipated revenues, and critical economic variables such as inflation, interest rates and economic growth that could push spending and revenues higher or lower than anticipated. Compiling the budget of the world's largest organization had been a formidable task. Working under the direction of budget boss Peter Orszag, the anonymous gnomes of the Office of Management and Budget (OMB) had delineated the disposition of dollars for 15 federal departments and seven major independent agencies, any one of which were the size of a Fortune 500 company. Not only did the budget detail spending for fiscal year 2011, but it forecast revenue, spending and deficits for the next 10 years.

Obama used his bully pulpit to project an image as a president deeply concerned about escalating deficits and the mounting national debt. Sounding defensive at times, he repeatedly blamed the nation's problems on the failed policies of a certain unnamed president who served between 2001 and 2009 More optimistically, he expressed confidence that his administration had stabilized the worst recession since the Great Depression and asserted that the economy was moving toward recovery. But some numbers in his proposed budget belied the theme of fiscal rectitude. For instance, Obama never once mentioned the extraordinary size of the fiscal 2010 budget: an unimaginable sum, $3.7 trillion. He never noted the projected size of the budget deficit — nearly $1.6 trillion, more than one-tenth of the entire economy — much less of the projected deficit in the year ahead when the economy was projected to be growing vigorously, nearly $1.3 trillion. While Obama saw fit to put numbers on the sorry, eight-year budgetary performance of his predecessor, he omitted the deficits in his own 10-year forecast. Only by poring through the budget documents posted online would anyone know that the annual shortfall in the years to come would never be less than $700 billion and that, even after 10 years of uninterrupted growth, it still would be $1 trillion and growing. Most importantly, never did the president deem it necessary to inform the American people that if the nation pursued the fiscal path he was outlining, the nation would accumulate another $8.5 trillion in national debt by the end of the decade.[31]

Thanks to the transparency of 21st century government, however, all this information is readily accessible to the public. Not only does OMB put the broad-sweep numbers on the World Wide Web, it details the numbers for each department and independent agency, provides the key economic assumptions undergirding revenue and spending forecasts, and explains its thinking in mind-numbing narratives. It's all there for anyone who wants to plow through it.

OMB divides the federal budget into four broad categories. In order of magnitude they are: (1) mandatory programs such as Social Security, Medicare, Medicaid and means-tested entitlements like food stamps and school lunches; (2) spending on security such as defense, homeland security and intelligence; (3) discretionary domestic spending on everything from agriculture, commerce, education and energy to justice, labor, transportation and the interior; and (4) interest on the national debt. Here are the trend lines based on Obama's own numbers:

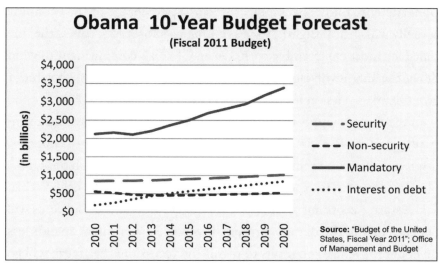

Obama 10-Year Budget Forecast
(Fiscal 2011 Budget)

Source: "Budget of the United States, Fiscal Year 2011"; Office of Management and Budget

The budget buster, the grab-bag of entitlement programs termed "mandatory programs," shoots off the chart like an errant SCUD missile. Obama proposes to address two of the biggest of the entitlements, Medicare and Medicaid, with his plan for health care reform. The issues are so important that they require an extended dissertation, so I shall defer discussion of Obama's approach to health care in the next chapter.

A second area of concern is interest on the national debt. Interest rates are unusually low due to a confluence of factors, including the recent recession, but they will rise as the recovery takes hold. The Obama budget forecast recognizes this reality. As deficits pile up and interest rates climb, according to the Obama budget, payments on the national debt will ratchet steadily higher, reaching nearly $1 trillion a year by the end of the decade. As alarming as that number may sound, it can be argued that OMB has significantly under-estimated interest rates and, therefore, under-estimated payments on the national debt. I shall explain my reasoning in Chapter Four.

There is one piece of comforting news in the budget forecast: The cost of defense and other security programs is projected to increase modestly, at an average rate of less than 2 percent annually. That's slower than the projected rate of economic growth, which means that the national defense burden when measured as a percentage of the economy actually will shrink slightly. Of all of Obama's forecasts, this is the one that I am most comfortable with. Given Obama's commitment to wind down the U.S. involvement in Iraq, the forecast appears defensible. I give Obama a pass on his defense-spending projections.

Finally, there appears to be a piece of good news — nay, extraordinarily good news — in the 2011 budget forecast. Miracle of miracles, discretionary "non-security" spending, the source of so much pork, payola and earmarks, is expected to be lower by the end of the decade than at the start. According to the Obama budget forecast, expenditures will decline early in the decade, presumably as the government spends less on counter-cyclical programs to offset the recession; the freeze will go into effect in 2011, holding down spending for three years; and then discretionary spending inches ever-so-delicately higher, but at nowhere the pace of the other three spending categories. If Obama and budget chief Orszag (the O Team) can keep discretionary, non-defense spending under tight control, that would be a remarkable accomplishment, as such a feat has eluded nearly every president since World War II.

Alas, there is ample reason to think that the O Team has low-balled the deficit forecasts. In an analysis published March 24, 2010, the Congressional Budget Office estimated that the decadal deficit will reach $9.8 trillion. Most ominously the structural deficit will have grown to the point that the shortfall will be nearly $1.3 trillion in a single year, 2020 — even in the absence of recession. As Director Douglas W. Elmendorf summarized the situation, debt held by the public will grow from $7.5 trillion (53 percent of GDP) at the end of 2009 to $20.3 trillion (90 percent of GDP) at the end of 2020 — and that doesn't include debt owned by governmental entities. Net interest on the debt will more than quadruple between 2010 and 2020 in nominal dollars, swelling from 1.4 percent of GDP in 2010 to 4.1 percent in 2020.[33]

Elmendorf's analysis assumes that Congress doesn't get into any more mischief. The OMB bases its analysis upon the laws on the books — not madcap ideas that Congress or the Obama administration might dream up next year or the year after. Like health care reform. As director of Congress' non-partisan, in-house budgetary think tank, Elmendorf cannot say, "Congress has repeatedly broken its vows of fiscal responsibility in the past, and there is no indication, given the people in charge, that it will adhere to its vows in the future."

But we are bound by no such protocols. The chart below tracks discretionary, non-security spending in inflation-adjusted dollars since 1962. The category has headed relentlessly higher for a half century, with one exception — the early years of the Reagan presidency when Obama's political party accused the administration of gutting domestic spending on the backs of the poor, the homeless and the malnourished children. The Reagan years were not known for massive investment in infrastructure, schools, clean energy, health care reform and other items atop Obama's agenda. Presumably, those years are not a period that the president wants to emulate. Even so, despite all of his new spending priorities, Obama thinks he can do a better job of reining in spending than any administration since Harry Truman demobilized the nation after World War II.

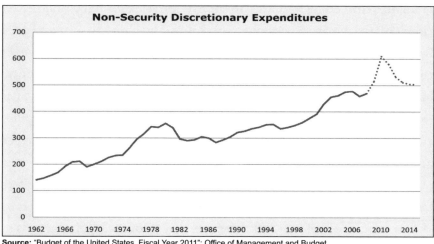

Non-Security Discretionary Expenditures

Source: "Budget of the United States, Fiscal Year 2011"; Office of Management and Budget

Given the expensive goals he has articulated, there are ample grounds for questioning whether Obama will follow through with his promise to freeze discretionary spending. One of the oldest tricks in politics is to announce budget cuts two or three years in the future, by which time the news media's gnat-like attention has moved on to other issues and the promise of austerity can be safely ignored. Even if Obama were sincere about carrying through with his freeze, he would have to prevail against the spending proclivities of Congress in a political economy that favors spending over cutting. Not only are Obama's appetites endless, so are those of the political class.

As I argued in the previous chapter, as long as Congressmen can continue borrowing money instead of making political unpopular cuts, they will continue to borrow the money. But that's just my jaundiced perspective. Obama's admirers will insist that I'm wrong. Ultimately, there's no way to prove or disprove the president's willingness to hang tough. We simply must wait until 2013 and see what he does.

As it happens, discretionary spending is a sideshow in the big budgetary picture. Entitlements alone are enough to send the country into default. Here is the argument that I shall lay out in the rest of this chapter. Social Security is a serious problem but it is not beyond redemption. Tweaks to the system made within the next few years could put the program on a firm enough footing to survive the stress of Baby Boomer retirement and old age — although there is no "lockbox" to protect Social Security in the event of a total fiscal meltdown. Medicare and Medicaid, however, are disasters unfolding before our very eyes. If left on auto-pilot, they will precipitate Boomergeddon. Of course, Obama has not left entitlement spending on auto-pilot. He has risked the reputation of his presidency to enact a new health care entitlement that, he argues, will more than pay for itself.

Finally, there is the interest payment on the national debt. Of all the fiscal challenges facing the nation, this is the least appreciated by the American people — and the most threatening. While there is at least the theoretical possibility that runaway health care costs can be contained, by rationing if nothing else, there is no way to finesse the snow-balling size of the national debt. A debt burden that grows at an accelerating rate is a near mathematical certainty.

As long as we depend upon foreigners to lend us ever-larger sums of money, we have limited options for dealing with that debt. If American citizens were the only significant creditors, as Japanese citizens are the primary creditors to their own government, we could play the usual re-distribution-of-wealth politics that allow us to rob Peter to pay Paul. But the Chinese, Japanese and Persian Gulf oil states are not subject to Congressional jurisdiction. We cannot tax them, fine them or regulate them, nor do we as a practical matter possess the power to sneakily de-value our debt through inflation: At the first whiff of rising prices, lenders will react forcefully. The scary thing is that they don't have to yank their trillions of dollars in loans to bring us to our knees. As long as we're running trillion-dollar deficits, all they have to do is stop lend-ing us new trillions, and it's Boomergeddon time.

What Congress Giveth, Congress Can Taketh Away

Steve, a friend of mine, decided last year to retire. At 63 years old, he was in no hurry to call it quits, but the economic downturn had slammed his consulting business, and he saw Social Security income as a lifeline. The rules allow him to supplement his Social Security with earned in-come, so he plans to make an extra $14,000 a year on the side. By sell-ing his house in a big-city suburb, he and his wife plan to downsize to a smaller place on the South Atlantic coast and pay off the mortgage.

Steve knows that he's taking a financial penalty by signing up for So-cial Security now instead of waiting until the standard retirement age of 65 – his check will be about 25 percent smaller — but he figures he might as well get a piece of the action while he can. He's paid into the system all his life, and his Social Security check will represent a paltry return on his investment, a fact that he resents deeply. However, he's not confident he can even count on the money that Social Security says it will pay him. "People think the U.S. government is too big to fail," he says. "I'm not so sure."

Steve has plenty of company. In its 2010 Retirement Confidence Survey, the Employee Benefit Research Institute (EBRI) detected widespread worries about the viability of Social Security. Current retirees generally expressed confidence in the program — perhaps, speculated the EBRI report, because the widely publicized 2039 depletion date of the trust fund is beyond their life expectancy. However, 70 percent of all workers surveyed said they were either "not too confident" or "not at all confident" that Social Security could continue to provide benefits equal to the value of benefits that retirees receive today.[34]

Sun Life Financial, a financial services firm, found similar skepticism in the American public, the younger generations especially, in a March 2009 "Unretirement Index" poll. Nearly half of all American workers would opt out of Social Security if given the option. Following a consistent pattern, younger workers were the most skeptical of the value provided by the system, and older workers had the most faith in it.[35]

Those in favor of opting out of Social Security
Workers in their . . .

30s	59%
40s	51%
50s	44%
Over 60	33%

Apparently, the public understands that the retirement of the Boomer generation will subject the system to tremendous strain. Perhaps some Americans have paid attention to the annual reports of the Social Security and Medicare boards of trustees, which are easily accessed online. As the trustees stated in their 2009 message to the public, the financial condition of Social Security and Medicare "remains challenging." The programs are "not sustainable" under the current funding streams and benefit payouts.[36]

The good news for Social Security is that, at the moment, the program is taking in more revenues from payroll taxes and interest on its $2.6 trillion trust fund than it is paying out in retirement, survivor and disability benefits. The bad news is that the surplus will end soon, and obligations will be met only by drawing down the trust fund until it runs out. There are three key milestones in the process:

- In 2017, according to the latest estimate for the Old Age and Survivors (OASI) Trust Fund, obligations will exceed income from payroll taxes. That's not as bad as it sounds. Thanks to the interest on the assets in the trust fund, the program still will run a surplus.
- In 2025, benefits paid will exceed payroll taxes and interest combined. The OASI trust fund will start shrinking. That is as bad as it sounds.
- In 2039, the OASI trust fund will be exhausted. That's really bad. Tax income will be sufficient to cover only 76% of scheduled benefits.

(Social Security also maintains a separate trust fund for disability insurance. That smaller fund is a mess — trust funds are expected to be exhausted by 2020.)

None of these projections are certain. Cranking in the latest data and revising the assumptions that go into their model, the trustees revise their estimates each year. The projections could improve as the economy pulls out of the recession and the revenues exceed projections. Or, if the economic recovery stalls, the forecast could get more pessimistic.

Unfortunately, the latest news is grim. Due to early retirements and high unemployment, expenses exceed payroll taxes. In March, the Congressional Budget Office projected that benefit payments will be $37 billion higher while revenues from payroll taxes will fall $12 billion short in 2010. For the first time since the early-1980s reforms, benefit payments will exceed payroll receipts — a development that was not expected to occur until 2017. As the economy rebounds and unemployment declines, Social Security should start running surpluses again. But even a temporary deficit is an ill omen.[37]

Defenders of Spending As Usual say the situation really isn't so bad. Look at the long-term picture: As a percentage of Gross Domestic Product (GDP), Social Security was 4.4 percent in 2008. As the Boomers retire, it will hit a peak around 6.2 percent around 2034, then settle back around 5.8 percent for another 35 years. One or two bad years have a minimal impact on the long-range trends. Unlike Medicare, where runaway health care costs are accelerating like a speed racer on the Bonneville Salt Flats, Social Security expenditures never get out of control. What's more, we have 10 years to patch up Social Security's Disability trust fund and more than 20 years to repair the Old Age trust fund. If we make prudent adjustments now instead of waiting until the last minute, the argument goes, we can put Social Security on a sustainable path with relatively little pain.

Along those lines, the National Academy of Social Insurance produced a report in October 2009 laying out a wide range of options for improving benefits and making up the long-term revenue shortfall.[38] Raising the payroll tax in 2010 from the current 6.2 percent to 7.3 percent — equivalent to tacking on an extra 1.1 percent tax onto payroll — would make the program solvent for the next 75 years.

But no one expects to load the full burden on wage earners all at once. One approach to generating more revenue would be to nudge the tax higher very gradually, one-twentieth of a percentage point per year — too slowly to notice. Other techniques would be to raise the earnings cap on a worker's Social Security payments, thus collecting payroll taxes on salaries over $106,800, or to broaden the payroll tax to apply to nontaxable compensation such as 401(k) contributions.

The Academy also explored many ways to reduce benefits. One idea would be to slowly increase the age at which retirees can collect full Social Security benefits, on the grounds that, hey, if people are living longer, they should work longer. Another idea is to use a less generous index for adjusting Social Security benefits to reflect inflation and wage gains.

Any one of these ideas can be construed as "unfair" to someone. Inevitably, one category of people would wind up paying more or receiving less than if the system were left to drift. (Until the system crashed, of course, and then everyone would end up with a lot less.) However, it should be possible to cobble together a mish-mash of ideas — raise taxes a little, raise the retirement age a little, trim the annual price indexes a little — and smear the pain so thin that no one really feels it. Congress made bigger changes in 1983 when the National Commission on Social Security Reform put the program back on a sustainable path after years of expanded benefits, and there is no reason — aside from the obstinacy of the two political clans — that the problem can't be solved.

The heartening conclusion is that Social Security need not be a major contributor to the nation's deficit death spiral. But don't start plugging those Social Security payments into your retirement calculator just yet.

If Social Security were a fully funded, stand-alone program with walls of protection between its trust funds and the grabby hands in Congress — in other words, if the trust funds were in a "lockbox," as presidential candidate Al Gore called it back in 2000 — Boomers and younger Americans would have no reason to fear. But Congress never got around to creating that lockbox. Americans are not contractually entitled to receive a particular level of Social Security benefits as they are, say, entitled to receive their pension benefits. Americans will receive Social Security at scheduled levels only if future Congresses see fit to make good on the promises of previous Congresses.

Enter, stage left, Ephram Nestor. In 1955 the Bulgarian-born immigrant turned 65, became eligible for Social Security benefits, enrolled in the program and began receiving checks. In 1956, however, he was deported. As it happened, an amendment to the Social Security Act enacted two years previously had provided that anyone deported for various offenses, including subversive activity, did not qualify for old-age benefits — and Nestor had been a member of the Communist Party back in the 1930s. When informed of the circumstances, the Social Security Administration stopped sending him his $55.60-per-month checks. (Those were the days when $55.60 meant more than a teenager's allowance!) In 1958, Nestor filed suit, alleging that the suspension was illegal and unconstitutional. Old-age benefits, he argued, were an "earned right" of the recipient.

The legal precedents were not favorable to Nestor's case, however. In 1937, the U.S. Supreme Court had ruled in Helvering v. Davis that Social Security was not a contributory insurance program: "The proceeds of both the employee and employer taxes are to be paid into the Treasury like any other internal revenue generally, and are not earmarked in any way." When ruling against Nestor in 1958, the high court made it even more explicit that Americans have no "right" to receive Social Security. Wrote the Court: "To engraft upon the Social Security system a concept of 'accrued property rights' would deprive it of the flexibility and boldness in adjustment to ever changing conditions which it demands."[39]

Adjustment to ever changing conditions? Translation: What Congress bestows, Congress can take away. Even Social Security.

It goes without saying that Congress would not lightly deprive Americans of Social Security benefits accrued after decades of paying into the system. Indeed, the first half-century of the program saw a steady expansion of entitlements in order to win votes. But all history and precedent will fly out the window when Boomergeddon strikes.

Just imagine a world in which Social Security is fully funded but all other government programs can spend no more than the U.S. collects in taxes, or about 70 percent of the budget. Imagine military aircraft grounded and soldiers running short on munitions. Imagine aid to states put on hold. Imagine food stamps and assistance to the poor running out. Worst of all, imagine all federal employees, including members of Congress, getting paid in I.O.U.s.! When the day comes that the U.S. Treasury can no longer meet its interest obligations and lenders stop lending, Congress will be desperate to keep the machinery of government running. Social Security might be solvent on paper, but its only assets will consist of I.O.Us (U.S. Treasury bonds) backed by nothing more than the full faith and credit of the government. If the government is broke, the "full faith and credit" of the government will be worthless, and Congress will have nothing with which to pay its Social Security pensioners.

Boomers cannot count on getting all the money promised them, even if Congress patches up the program to make it actuarially sound. Only a fool, or a gambler, would stake his retirement on it.

The Demographics of the Health Care Crisis

There is a keen irony in our budgetary dilemma. One of the great blessings of the modern era is that Americans are living longer than ever. Longevity is not a phenomenon that anyone would want to reverse. But that same longevity is our collective curse, imposing a mounting fiscal burden upon the United States government.

Personally, I'm a huge fan of extended longevity and the medical advances that make it possible. Without the marvels of modern surgery I most likely would have died from a burst appendix some 18 years ago. I'm glad I'm still alive. So, too, is my 12-year-old son. (Or he would be, if he had any sense. It might not occur to him that if I died 18 years ago, he might not be alive today.) I am also taking a prescription drug to treat hypertension, substantially reducing the risk of a stroke, heart disease, kidney failure and a host of other medical problems I'd rather not have. Insofar as I do my share to keep the economy humming and pay enough taxes to keep the U.S. government running for a few nanoseconds every year, I remain a net positive to society thanks to modern medicine.

I am especially grateful to still have the company of my mother, father and step mother, who have outlived their parents by many years. But they are getting old and frail. As Matt Thornhill, president of The Boomer Project, likes to put it, the warranty on our bodies eventually runs out.[39] My parents have passed the 80-year mark and, despite having lived active, healthy lives, each of them requires extensive maintenance and repair. The past few years have seen visits to the doctor and hospital for a succession of ailments ranging from heart disease to cataracts, rheumatism to gout. As they lose their sense of balance, my parents are increasingly vulnerable to falls and broken bones. So far, knock on wood, none of them have required anything hideously expensive like open-heart surgery or cancer treatment. Still, the expense of chronic maladies does add up.

With tens of millions of middle-aged Americans like me requiring prescription drugs and millions more Americans in a condition akin to that of my parents, the aging of the population is inexorably driving up health care costs. Short of saying, "You're too old, too crippled, or too fragile, your life has little value anymore, and we're going to let you die," there is only so much that we can do to prevent the cost curve from arcing higher. Immutable facts of demography and the human condition dictate that health care costs will continue to consume an increasing share of national production and federal budget.

Let's take a closer look at the demographic trends behind the health care funding crisis and see why roughly half of the projected long-term cost increases over the next 20 to 30 years is baked into the system — no matter what Obama or anyone else can do to contain them.

Longer life expectancies. People are living longer. An American born in 1900 could expect on average to reach 47.3 years. At the mid-century mark, thanks largely to improvements in sanitation and the ability to treat communicable diseases, an American could expect to make it to 68.2 years on average — a gain of two decades. By 2000, the average life expectancy of an American born in 2000 advanced to 77.0 years — a pick-up of another decade.[41] Since then, lives have gotten even longer. A child born in the U.S. today can expect to live one year longer on average than a child born at the turn of the millennium.

It doesn't take a Ph.D. in demography to grasp that the longer people live, the more "old" people there will be. The trend can be seen clearly in the chart below,[42] which shows how steadily the percentage of the 65-and-older population has increased since 1950. The 65-year-old threshold is doubly significant because it is the age at which Americans qualify for Medicare and much of the burden of financing their health care shifts from workers and their employers to society as a whole.

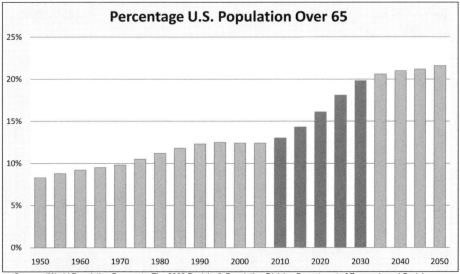

Source: "World Population Prospects: The 2008 Revision"; Population Division Department of Economic and Social Affairs, United Nations.

The Boomer wave. The United States is in the early stages of a spike in the 65-and-older population. As you can see in the darker columns of the graph on above, the percentage over-65 population surges as a percentage of the U.S. population between the years 2005 and 2030.

That reflects the passage of 78 million Baby Boomers into their 60s in vast numbers. Short of a mutant virus that selectively kills people who watch "M*A*S*H" reruns or attend Jimmy Buffett concerts, we are destined to see a spectacular increase in the number of over 65s — and an increasing burden on the Medicare and Medicaid programs.

The "old old" wave. Once upon a time, anyone over the age of 65 was considered "old." But now so many people have hit the 65-year-old milestone that we have to distinguish between the "young old," those who still have the physical and mental vitality to lead active lives, and the "old old," whose disabilities render them increasingly homebound, unable to care for themselves and in a condition that requires chronic medical care. Because the latter group tends to suffer from multiple chronic illnesses, from diabetes to dementia, their medical issues are more persistent and more complex. The "old old" deliver a double whammy to public finances. Their need for medical care drains the coffers of Medicare, while their need for institutional care-giving strains the Medicaid program.

The number of 80-and-olders has increased steadily as a percentage of the U.S. population, from about 1.1 percent in 1950 to 3.8 percent in 2010. The number of "old old" will level off for some 15 years as the

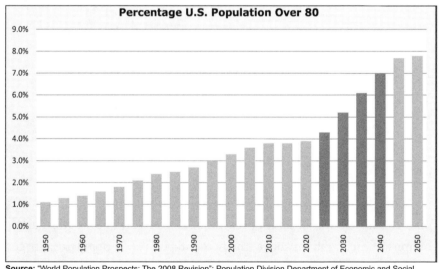

Source: "World Population Prospects: The 2008 Revision"; Population Division Department of Economic and Social Affairs, United Nations.

smaller Silent Generation works its way through the demographic pipeline, and then will start climbing dramatically in the 2020s when the Boomers hit their 80s. In that one decade, the "old old" will increase as a percentage of the U.S. population from 3.9 percent to 5.2 percent.

The fragility of the "old old" population bears closer examination because it is such a key driver of health care costs. As their bodies deteriorate with advancing age, Americans suffer from an increasing number of chronic diseases that require continual monitoring and treatment: maladies such as high blood pressure, high cholesterol, diabetes, dementia, cancer and back problems. The existence of multiple diseases — the percentage of Medicare patients with five or more chronic diseases stands at more than 50 percent — adds complexity to medical treatment, making it all the more expensive.

One chronic disease, diabetes, is pandemic in America, and especially in the over-65 crowd. A recent study by Elbert S. Huang, a University of Chicago researcher, projects that the number of Americans treated for diabetes under Medicare will leap from 8.2 million to 14.6 billion over the next 25 years, while Medicare spending on the disease will surge from $45 billion to $171 billion.[43] Those numbers assume no increase in obesity. But obesity is on the increase! In just one decade, between 1991 and 2000, obesity rates in the U.S. increased by more than 60 percent, and the problem showed no indication of letting up in the 2000s. Researchers estimate that severely overweight people have two-thirds more chronic conditions than normal-weight individuals.

"The health and financial consequences of chronic illness are profound," warns the AARP Public Policy Institute. "People with chronic diseases ... have significantly higher rates of hospitalization and make more emergency room visits. Their health spending (shared among patients and payers) is higher than that for people without chronic disease."[44]

The "old old" population also experiences more disabilities and encounters greater difficulty performing the routines of daily existence. Disabilities range from impaired hearing and sight to difficulty walking, climbing steps, bending over and performing other Activities of Daily Living (ADL). The inability to drive, walk, shop and run errands severely restricts old peoples' ability to live independently.

Incidence of Disabilities among Older Adults		
Disability	55+	85+
Hearing impairment	31.6%	62.1%
Vision impairment	11.7%	26.9%
No teeth	19.0%	35.6%
Difficulty walking one mile	25.0%	56.1%
Difficulty walking up 10 steps	20.0%	45.2%
Difficulty stooping or bending	30.3%	53.1%
Difficulty shopping	13.3%	34.1%

Source: "Health Characteristics of Adults Aged 55 Years and Over: Untied States, 2004-2007"; National Center for Health Statistics.

For many, the scariest disability is dementia, which increases in lockstep with advancing age. The most devastating form of dementia is Alzheimer's disease. An estimated 5.3 million Americans have the disease today; as the number of Americans surviving into their 80s and 90s grows, so too will the incidence of Alzheimer's. In 2000, an estimated 411,000 new cases were reported. When the Boomers begin reaching their 80s, the number of new cases is expected to hit 615,000 a year.[45]

Given the number of chronic diseases and the severity of the medical conditions, the health care burden for Americans 85 and older is 75 percent higher than that of Americans between the ages of 75 and 78, and nearly six times as high on average as that of Americans between the ages of 50 to 54.[46] The surging number of "old old" citizens guarantees that Medicare expenses will increase at a staggering rate in the 2020s when Boomers begin hitting their 80s in large numbers.

Sex, drugs and rocky road ice cream. Not long ago, actuaries found some solace to these gloomy numbers in a phenomenon they labeled the "compression of morbidity," a term used to describe the fact that the current cohort of "old old" Americans has fewer chronic diseases than did previous generations at a comparable age. That's good news, for it means that older adults are living longer before the really big health care expenditures kick in. If that trend persists as Boomers reach "old old" age, better health will allow Boomers to live even longer with less medical and nursing care, thus providing a partial financial offset to their greater numbers.

Unfortunately, a study published in late 2009 dashed those hopes. Boomers, it seems, have reversed the trend. Despite the advance of medical science, they are experiencing more disabilities than previous generations at the same age. The data show improvements among people now 80 and older. But there is no change in disability rates among people now in their 70s, and disability rates are actually 40 percent to 70 percent higher among people now in their 60s.

"Our results have significant and sobering implications," wrote lead author Teresa E. Seeman and her colleagues in the *American Journal of Public Health*." To the extent that persons currently aged 60 to 69 years are harbingers of likely disability trends for the massive baby-boomer generation, the health care and assistance needs of disabled older Americans could, in the not-so-distant future, impose heavy burdens on families and society."[47]

If you surmised that the increasing incidence of obesity is responsible for the reversal of fortune, give yourself a slap on your big, fat Boomer booty. Packing on those extra pounds not only increases the odds of contracting a chronic disease, it interferes with daily living. The extra weight puts pressure on the joints — one orthopedic surgeon says the average age of his knee- and hip-replacement patients is around 56 or 58, down from 78 when he started his practice more than two decades ago[48] — reduces endurance, limits flexibility and generally puts a damper on mobility. Boomers may feel psychologically like they're 10 years younger than their chronological age, but their self image is severely out of joint with their physical reality.

Seeman's findings were not a fluke. The Rand Corporation showed similar results among Boomers in a study released in April. Between 1997 and 2007, an increasing number of Americans between the ages of 50 and 64 reported disabilities stemming from back or neck pain, diabetes, arthritis, rheumatism, depression, anxiety and emotional problems. The authors said it wasn't clear if more people were experiencing these disabilities, if the numbers reflected better diagnosis and reporting of the problems, or if there was some other explanation. But they found the trend disturbing.

"Although the overall rate of needing help with personal care among this group remains very low — less than 2 percent — this rise in disability is reason for concern," said Linda Martin, the study's lead author. "It does not bode well for future trends for the 65 and older population, plus there are substantial personal and societal costs of caring for people of any age who need help."[49]

Who knows what other nasty surprises Boomers may spring upon society as they age? Hepatitis C, which has an incubation period of 20 to 30 years before it actively attacks the liver, is being diagnosed with greater frequency, especially among Boomers. A widely accepted theory is that those affected acquired the disease while experimenting with intravenous drugs decades ago. Treatment requires a month-long regimen of shots and pills that is not guaranteed to work. Patients who can't lick the disease have to live with it as a chronic condition. One study estimated that total annual costs for treating Hepatitis C patients will nearly triple, from $30 billion to $85 billion over the next 20 years.[50]

While most Boomers abandoned the experimentation with drugs years ago, a few didn't get the memo. An estimated 4.3 million adults over 50 — overwhelmingly Boomers, not members of older generations — have used an illicit drug in the past year, a much higher number than previous generations did at the same age. The most common drug is marijuana, although a large number of Boomers abuse prescription drugs and a tiny percentage uses harder drugs like cocaine, heroin and hallucinogens.[51] Boomers' demand for substance abuse treatment may double by 2020, says the Substance Abuse and Mental Health Services Administration. Also, physiological changes make older adults more vulnerable to the harmful effects of drug abuse, so the Boomers' taste for mood-altering substances may require increased medical treatment as well.[52]

And let us not forget that Boomers ushered in the sexual revolution. Some four decades after the "summer of love," Boomers, thanks in part to Viagra, are still fooling around. As a consequence, public health officials, who never considered older adults an "at risk" group for sexually transmitted disease, are suddenly concerned. The deadliest STD, and most expensive to treat, is HIV/AIDS. It probably comes as no surprise to anyone that Boomers are the leading edge of a wave of HIV/AIDS cases among older adults. In 2007, 12,400 Americans in the 54-to-64-year-old Boomer demographic were diagnosed with the virus. The total for Americans 65 and over was a mere 800. Even Generation Y (ages 28 and younger), at the peak of sexual activity and risk taking, had far fewer new HIV/AIDS cases than the Boomers did.[53]

In this instance, the cost of Boomer hedonism is extremely high. As of 2006, Americans diagnosed with AIDS could expect to live another 24 years. The average cost of care ran about $25,200 annually. The average AIDS case was expected to cost more than $600,000 over a lifetime. As new antiretroviral drugs become available, the cost of the treatments will increase, life expectancy will improve, and the lifetime cost of treatments could soar. Meanwhile, the cost of treating the disease will be socialized as Boomers cross the 65-year-old boundary and enroll in Medicare.

(While sex and drugs are causing significant medical complications for Boomers, it appears that rock 'n' roll is not. A study of 5,300 people in Beaver Dam, Wis., has found that hearing is improving with each generation — and that applies even to rock-addled Boomers. Experts attribute the improvement to fewer noisy jobs, better ear protection at work, and the advent of immunizations and antibiotics that prevent hearing loss from disease.[54])

In summary, longer life spans mean that all Americans will be drawing upon Medicare for longer periods of time. The Boomer age wave means millions more Americans will be enrolling en masse in Medicare over the next two decades. The number of "old old" people is increasing at an extraordinary rate, meaning that millions of Americans will be living with chronic and complex medical conditions that need continual treatment. Last but not least, Boomers are simply less healthy than previous generations. The medical costs arising from their life-long self-indulgence — if it feels good, do it! — will be significantly higher than they were for those who came before them.

The Bottomless Pit

Imagine yourself standing on the rim of the Grand Canyon. You pick up a stone and hurl it with all your might. The stone takes flight, climbing a paltry twenty or thirty feet as it arcs across the chasm, and then begins its downward path. The momentum of your throw carries the stone halfway across the ravine, but gravity finally grips it and pulls it straight down. Into the mile-deep abyss the stone plunges, where it disappears into the shadows.

The trajectory of your throw pretty well matches the budget curve of the Medicare Hospital Insurance (HI) program. The largest of Medicare's four main components built a modest surplus in earlier years, but spending now is drawing it down. The trust fund will be drained by 2017 — just a reminder, that's only seven years away — and revenues will be sufficient to cover only 81 percent of the program's costs. If that were the end of it, the story might not be so bad. We'd come up with the money somewhere. But year after year, expenditures will outpace revenues by ever wider margins, and there is no bottom in sight. Either Medicare beneficiaries will have to eat the difference or the federal government will have to make up for it out of general revenues.

It is an iron law of American politics that elected officials follow the path of least political pain. Cutting Medicare benefits to retirees is unthinkable — at least it is if the U.S. can still borrow money and avoid making the tough decisions. We can safely assume that, barring a major legislative change to the Medicare funding stream, Uncle Sam will continue to pay for seniors' benefits by selling more Treasury securities. As the Medicare funding gap plunges deeper and deeper into the hole, reaching $79 billion in 2017, $97 billion in 2018, and successively larger sums in the years that follow, the cumulative impact on the national debt will run into the trillions of dollars.

And that's just one component, Part A, of Medicare. There are four parts in all. Part B pays doctors, testing and laboratory expenses; Part C covers the Medicare Advantage Plan, in which enrollees enjoy benefits of a privately managed plan; and Part D provides prescription drug benefits. Those plans are financed by a combination of fees and government funding. The government's obligations for Parts B and D are expected to increase dramatically in the years ahead. (Obamacare will decrease spending for Medicare Advantage but will divert the money to pay for expanded health care coverage for the under-65 population, not to bolster the fiscal integrity of Medicare.)

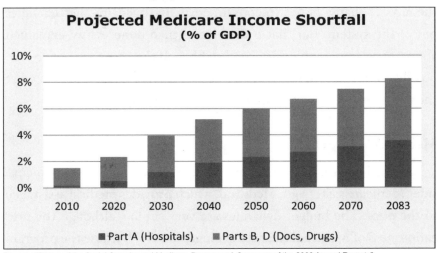

Projected Medicare Income Shortfall
(% of GDP)

Part A (Hospitals)　Parts B, D (Docs, Drugs)

Source: "Status of the Social Security and Medicare Programs: A Summary of the 2009 Annual Reports"

The income shortfall — the gap between expenditures and revenue — of Medicare programs will run around 1.5 percent of the Gross Domestic Product this year, exceed 2.3 percent in 2020 and brush up against 4 percent in 2030. Another four decades out, assuming all trends continue on the same path, the Medicare budget shortfall will be piling up deficits equivalent to 8 percent of the economy every single year. That scenario need not detain us — the system will have collapsed long before then. Indeed, as I plan to show, the system will collapse well before 2030.

One reason the system will disintegrate sooner rather than later is that the funding gap is actually worse than commonly portrayed. The Medicare trustees don't even believe their pro forma projections. As they say in their 2009 report, cost projections for Medicare Part B (covering physicians and outpatient procedures) are understated by 18 percent to 21 percent in 2015, and by up to 10 percent in 2030 and beyond! How so? The official forecast incorporates tens of billions of dollars of reductions in physician fees that are required under current law but are deferred annually by Congress on the very plausible grounds that doctors would drop like gumballs out of the Medicare tree if the pay cuts took place. In the understated words of the trustees, those cost cuts are "very unlikely to occur."

There is not much that can be done to reverse Medicare's slide into the abyss. Obama hopes to contain costs by squeezing inefficiencies out of the system. But that is easier said than done. As we explained above, the demographics driving roughly half the cost increase are impossible to reverse. In the next chapter, we'll examine the limits of what the newly enacted health care legislation can achieve.

Medicare's Mini Me

As if Medicare weren't reason enough to despair, we have to consider Medicare's alter ego, Medicaid, which provides medical assistance to the poor. The budget dynamics are very similar, although the precariousness of Medicaid finances get less publicity because the program has no trust fund to fall back upon and it has no trustees to issue dire warnings. Also, the states assume 43 percent of the cost of financing the program, so the impact on the federal budget isn't as extensive as Medicare's. On the other hand, the program does contribute to chronic stress in state budgets.

Before the passage of Obamacare, which will expand Medicaid enrollments, the government expected to spend $271 billion on Medicaid in Fiscal Year 2011.[55] That sum would benefit more than 40 million people falling into three main groups: the blind and disabled, non-disabled children, and poor adults, a majority of whom are seniors receiving home care or nursing-home care.

While the program covers millions of children, the kiddies rarely incur big medical bills — they haven't reached an age where they suffer from chronic disease. The big ramp-up in expenses will occur among the blind/disabled and among the aged populations. The Obama administration's 10-year projection assumes that Medicaid enrollments will grow modestly but that spending per enrollee will chug along at a quick clip, much faster than economic growth. Add it all up, and federal Medicaid spending should climb 80 percent over 10 years.

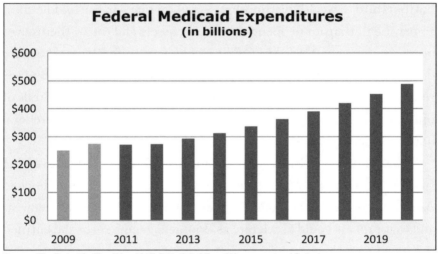

Federal Medicaid Expenditures
(in billions)

Source: "The Budget for Fiscal Year 2011"; Table S-3; Office of Management and Budget

By 2020, Medicaid will be sucking half as much money out of the federal treasury as Medicare does. (The enactment of the Patient Protection and Affordable Care Act, the aim of which is to move the country closer to universal health care coverage, will expand Medicaid enrollment. Those figures are not included in the chart above.)

At the risk of sounding like Dr. Doom, I must point out that the "Federal Medicaid Expenditures" chart doesn't show the full magnitude of the problem. To get a feel for what awaits the nation in the second decade ahead, when Boomergeddon most likely will occur, refer to the chart on page 65 that shows the Medicare income shortfall over a 70-year period. You'll see that the biggest jump in Medicare spending (measured as a percentage of GDP) takes place between 2020 and 2030. That's when the huge Baby Boomer generation completes its migration into retirement. By then, older Boomers will be hitting an age when they not only require more medical care but also Medicaid-financed assisted-living and nursing-home care in growing numbers.

Now, recall from our introduction what Alicia Munnell with the Center for Retirement Research said about how large numbers of Boomers have failed to save enough money to last them through retirement. She argued that the optimal "strategy" for Boomers in the bottom third of wealth distribution — and for many in the middle third — may be to transfer or spend down their assets and throw themselves upon the mercy of Medicaid. What would happen to Medicaid expenditures if Boomers actually followed through with that strategy and enrolled in Medicaid in unprecedented numbers? How many hundreds of billions of dollars a year would Medicaid add to the annual federal budget deficit by 2030?

That is no mere hypothetical concern. Medicaid is fast evolving from a safety net for the indigent into a vehicle to help middle-class Americans preserve their middle-class standard of living in retirement, and that process could accelerate as Boomers, members of the entitled generation, reach an age where they require nursing home care.

The AARP magazine recently profiled a Massachusetts couple that faced a terrible choice. Roberta and Alex had been married 40 years and were nearing the end of their careers when Alex was diagnosed with early-stage dementia. He took early retirement and Roberta cared for him at home. She got by for a while by hiring help for about $1,000 a month, but as the dementia worsened, Alex required full-time adult day care. Then a medical problem left him needing full-time, skilled nursing care. That expense depleted their savings at a rate of $7,500 monthly and threatened to leave Roberta with nothing.

Roberta consulted a local eldercare attorney in Springfield. After analyzing all of the options, none of them attractive, the attorney recommended divorce. He explained how the divorce settlement could be structured to leave Alex indigent so he would be eligible for Medicaid. Following the attorney's advice, they dissolved the marriage. Roberta continued wearing her wedding ring and visited Alex every day. To her mind, they were still married in every way except in the eyes of the law.[56]

It was a tragic situation and anyone with a heart would empathize with the couple's plight. AARP quoted James Firman, CEO of the National Council on Aging, a nonprofit with the mission of improving the lives of older Americans, as saying: "Requiring people who have worked hard and saved all their lives to become impoverished before they qualify for long-term care through Medicaid is draconian, demeaning, and disempowering. It is also terrible social policy and can't be sustained."

Unfortunately, morphing Medicaid from an entitlement for the poor into an entitlement for the middle class cannot be sustained either, at least not financially. The temptation always exists to expand the entitlement to cover people on the margins like Roberta and Alex. In a welfare state, someone always falls between the cracks or just barely fails to qualify, creating a sense of inequity and injustice. As William J. Voegeli observes in his book, "Never Enough: America's Limitless Welfare State," no criteria exist for drawing the line. Entitlements expand with no logical limit.[57]

To its credit, Obamacare tries a different approach with its CLASS program, a type of long-term care insurance into which employers are required to enroll employees unless they opt out. Unlike the open-ended Medicare and Medicaid programs, the program creates a means to provide long-term care coverage that is to some degree self-funding. Critics raise concerns, however, that the program will experience "adverse selection," meaning that the healthiest members of the workforce will opt out, leaving the sickliest in the program, with the end result that the coverage will cost far more than the revenue it generates. Eventually, the program will require taxpayer funding. An option would be to create more affordable, home- and community-based settings for the disabled who may not require round-the-clock nursing care. But the powerful nursing home lobby works to ensure that most of Medicaid's funds are funneled into nursing homes, not cheaper, alternative settings. The practitioners of home and community care are too unorganized politically to apply any meaningful countervailing political pressure.

Government forecasters build their Medicaid spending forecasts by projecting past patterns into the future. But if the pattern changes — if, for instance, Boomers do a poorer job than the Silent Ones of saving for their retirements and wind up falling back on Medicaid in far greater numbers — the government forecasts are suspect. Medicaid spending could well be far greater than anyone now anticipates.

No Surprises as Far as the Eye Can See

So, what do you get when you add it all up — Social Security, Medicare, Medicaid and "discretionary" spending that includes such optional items as national defense, urban renewal, transportation and infrastructure, education and the environment? The Obama administration crunched the numbers for the decade ahead as part of its proposed Fiscal Year 2011 budget, as seen on the next page. According to OMB calculations, the U.S. budget is on course to run deficits exceeding $1 trillion a year on average for the next 10 years. The Gargantua-sized deficits of 2010 and 2011 shrink as economic growth gains momentum, bottom out in 2014, and then drift higher over the rest of the decade. Cumulative deficits for the 10-year period are $8.5 trillion. (These numbers include Obamacare, which is projected to reduce the deficit by $153 billion.)

Running the same forecast based on slightly different budget assumptions, the Congressional Budget Office was somewhat more pessimistic. By the CBO's calculation, deficits will total $9.8 trillion.[58] To

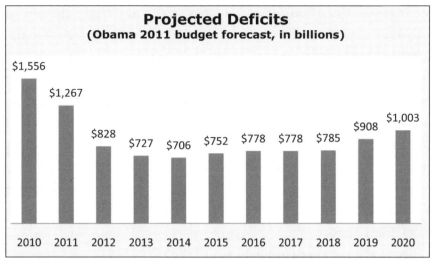

Projected Deficits
(Obama 2011 budget forecast, in billions)

$1,556
$1,267
$828
$727
$706
$752
$778
$778
$785
$908
$1,003

2010 2011 2012 2013 2014 2015 2016 2017 2018 2019 2020

Source: "The Budget for Fiscal Year 2011"; Table S-3; Office of Management and Budget

re-work the famous quip by Sen. Everett Dirksen, "A trillion here, a trillion there, pretty soon it adds up to real money."

Unfortunately, the Obama administration makes a number of optimistic — indeed, one might say heroic — assumptions. First, it imagines that real, inflation-adjusted economic growth will average 3.3 percent annually over 10 straight years, never dipping into an inconvenient recession that would drive the deficit numbers higher. No recession in ten years? What are the chances of that? Second, the budget assumes that the Treasury will never be called upon to make good on massive loan guarantees for trillions of dollars of homeowner mortgages, student loans, under-funded private pensions, energy projects and other pet causes of the political class. If you believe that, I have some Collaterized Debt Obligations I would like to sell you.

There are ample grounds to question the assumption that our nascent economic cycle can either maintain a 3.3 percent annual growth rate or that it can deliver 10 years of uninterrupted growth. As I will discuss in detail in Chapter 5, gone is the economic jet fuel of massive consumer borrowing and spending that drove the long Reagan and Clinton expansions. As consumers boost their saving, they will spend even less, depriving the economy of a major source of growth. Meanwhile,

71

Boomers will begin retiring in large numbers this decade; the loss of skilled and experienced workers will hinder productivity gains. On the global front, energy prices have dipped during the recession, but economic revival, particularly in China and India, will push the price of oil and other critical commodities higher, transferring wealth from oil-consuming nations like the U.S. to the oil-producing nations. Finally, and most critically, the economic recovery has been frightfully dependent upon fiscal and monetary stimulus. As the Treasury and Federal Reserve scale back their stimulus measures, the economy will lose a major source of strength. Bottom line: The economic growth rate will be slower than the O Team projects.

As for the notion that the decade of the 2010s will never be marred by recession, I cannot believe that the OMBots put any credence in their own numbers. We know from centuries of history that capitalism is prone to booms and busts, and there is no basis in current economic conditions to think that the pattern will change. According to the National Bureau of Economic Research, the average U.S. business cycle since World War II, measured peak to peak, has lasted five-and-a-half years, or 67 months to be precise.[59] The OMB budget model has economic growth in the new business cycle lasting ten years, or 120 months — nearly twice as long as the average.

The question then arises: What would deficits look like if economic growth were slower and more short-lived than the numbers embedded in Obama's 2011 Budget forecast? To get an answer, I approached my friends at Chmura Economics & Analytics, a Richmond, Va., economic consulting firm, for help. Dr. Christine Chmura, who has become increasingly concerned herself about the sustainability of the U.S. debt, graciously assigned the job to Dr. Xiaobing Shuai, Senior Economist. To avoid the appearance of trying to "stack the deck," we agreed that Shuai should work with the Obama administration's own 10-year budget numbers and economic assumptions as found in the proposed Fiscal 2011 budget, as opposed to the Congressional Budget Office forecast, which projects a higher deficit, or any number of even bleaker private-sector projections. We then conducted a sensitivity analysis to see what would happen: (a) if growth were one percentage point per year slower than assumed, and (b) if there were a mild recession in the 2010s, roughly equivalent to the recession that followed the 1990s Internet bubble, not a repeat of the debilitating crisis just past.

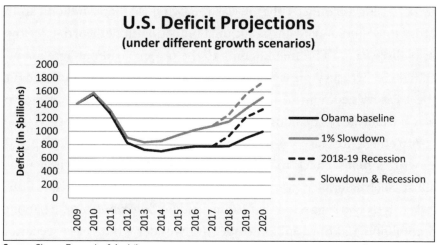

Source: Chmura Economics & Analytics

The chart above is not a forecast. It simply shows what would happen to the O Team projections if different economic assumptions were used.

Depending upon the growth scenario — pick the one that best suits your predilections — the budget deficit by the year 2020 could range anywhere from $1 trillion to more than $1.7 trillion. The total national debt (private plus government-owned debt) could climb above $29 trillion. Thus, under a different set of plausible assumptions, the deficit could grow at twice the rate posited by the Obama administration.

What Shuai's model did not try to replicate is the effect of an economic slowdown on the trillions of dollars of loans guaranteed by the federal government. Never before has the government been so directly exposed to the gyrations in market values of mortgage debt, student loans, private pensions and energy projects. If the loans go sour, the losses will be made good with money that the government does not have — in other words, money that the government will borrow.

On Christmas Eve last year the Obama administration slipped a little surprise past the American people, knowing that the news would be overlooked in the holiday festivities. Having already taken Freddie and Fannie into conservatorship, pumped $112 billion into them, and promised to provide as much as $200 billion in subsidies each, the Treasury Department announced that it was removing the $200 billion cap in order to accommodate any additional reduction in net worth over the next three years. The amendments to the original bail-out agreement, stated the Treasury press release, "should leave no uncertainty about the Treasury's commitment to support these firms as they continue to play a vital role in the housing market during this current crisis."[60]

In effect, Treasury was telling financial markets that it was prepared to write a blank check to keep the two mortgage-finance companies afloat. Such assurances were needed. Earlier that month a Barclays Capital analysis had suggested that Fannie and Freddie would require about $130 billion and $100 billion respectively under a base-case scenario, and Fannie would need up to $180 billion under a more stressful scenario. Keefe, Bruyette & Woods suggested that Fannie could require as much as $279 billion in backing.[61]

Whatever the final tally of Freddie and Fannie's bad bets, financial markets are predicting that the damage could total a lot more than the $112 billion officially acknowledged so far, and the Treasury Department's Christmas Eve action validates those fears. However, the potential liability for more bad debt doesn't appear anywhere in the official U.S. budget. It's considered an "off-balance sheet" liability. (Remember what got Enron in trouble? It was off balance-sheet financing.) In a January background paper, the CBO argued that now that Fannie and Freddie are controlled directly by the federal government, depend upon Uncle Sam for low-cost financing, and are acting to "fulfill the public purpose of supporting the housing and mortgage markets," policy makers should treat them as public entities and include their finances in the budget. If the CBO's logic were followed, $291 billion should be added to the estimate of the Fiscal Year 2009 budget deficit, and another $99 billion projected for 2010 through 2019.[62]

While Freddie and Fannie may be the most notorious users of government-backed debt, they aren't the only ones. Washington's political class has a penchant for diverting capital to favored causes through the expedient of backing up private loans with the implied faith of the federal government. Assured that any losses will be made good, creditors are willing to advance loans to favored borrowers at lower-than-market interest rates. Seemingly, everybody wins. The special interest gets its money. The lenders are assured they'll be repaid. And the politicians help out constituents without running up the budget deficit. It all works... until loans start going bad and the government has to make good, or unless you're one of the orphan categories, like small business, that gets crowded out.

As of late 2009, the situation wasn't looking so hot at the Federal Housing Administration, which insures mortgage lenders against defaults. A November audit showed that the FHA's reserves had been depleted much faster than anyone had anticipated, falling by nearly three quarters from a year earlier and leaving only 0.53 percent of its capital as a bulwark against the $685 billion in total loans insured.[63] The FHA had avoided the sub-prime disaster by enforcing more stringent lending requirements than Fannie or Freddie. But its share of the mortgage-insurance market soared in 2009 as the Obama administration sought to shore up the housing market. Because the agency insures loans for mortgages up to 95 percent of the home's value, FHA is very vulnerable to continued slides in housing prices. If home prices stabilize, the Obamanauts' bet may pay off. If not, FHA could become the next Fannie or Freddie.

Then there's the Pension Benefit Guaranty Corporation (PBGC), a federal corporation that insures the under-funded pensions of 44 million private-sector employees and retirees whose employers are bankrupt or nearly bankrupt. Last year was not kind to the PBGC. The entity's financial condition declined by $10.8 billion, bringing its total deficit to $22.0 billion.[64] The outlook could improve when the economy gets moving again. Until then, taxpayers are potentially on the hook for billions of dollars more.

That's not the end of it. The Federal Family Education Loan Program backs hundreds of billions of dollars worth of student loans made by private lenders: $54.7 billion in the 2007-2008 year alone. The Obama administration expects to save up to $6 billion a year by cutting out the private-sector middlemen and making the loans directly. The middlemen have made huge profits, but they also have provided an important function: filtering out loans to students with lousy credit histories. Student loan programs have experienced low default rates as a result. If the federal government hands out loans indiscriminately, bad loans are likely to increase, and the program could become another money sink.

Meanwhile, the U.S. Department of Energy (DOE) supports alternative fuels and other favored projects with loan guarantees. These often are large, highly leveraged projects that expose the federal government to considerable potential risk. In December 2009, for instance, DOE announced a $245 million loan guarantee to Red River Environmental Products LLC to build an activated-carbon manufacturing facility in Louisiana. The technology removes mercury from coal-fired power plant emissions, undoubtedly a worthwhile activity. But is DOE competent to evaluate the viability of energy projects employing cutting-edge technologies? If the project makes economic sense, why aren't private investors funding it? The same question could be asked of other DOE-backed loans in 2009 to a manufacturer of solar photovoltaic panels, a manufacturer of wind turbines, and an energy storage company.

Guaranteeing loans to students and alternative-fuel projects may look like safe bets now. Of course, guaranteeing loans to mortgage lenders was a respectable activity until the social activists and progressive politicians got involved with housing policy. Under political pressure to increase home ownership among the poor and the working class, lending standards eroded and risk-taking increased. There is no evidence whatsoever that the prime malefactors or their Congressional enablers have learned their lesson. But taxpayers have gotten the message: Greater government involvement = politicization of lending standards = more bad loans = more big budget surprises.

The Mathematician's Chess Board

You may recall the tale of the mathematician in long-ago India who invented a new game, chess, and showed the creation to his ruler. So pleased was the potentate that he told the inventor to name his own prize. The clever fellow asked to receive a single grain of rice for the first square of the chess board, two grains for the second square, and so on for all 64 squares. The ruler agreed, but his treasurer came back a week later with a calculation of how much rice he would have to hand over: about 18.4 quintillion grains. (That's a lot of rice. It would take a warehouse of about 20 cubic miles to hold it all.) Thus, the ruler learned an object lesson in the power of geometric progression.

The ruler was clever as well. He told the mathematician he could have the grains — as long as he counted them all first to make sure he was getting his full prize. Thus, the mathematician learned an object lesson in the value of a politician's promises.

As we contemplate the fiscal fate of the United States, we encounter the phenomenon of geometric growth, albeit on a milder upward slope than the mathematician's chess board, in Medicare spending, Medicaid spending and above all in the snowballing size of the national debt. We are in the early stages of a vicious cycle: Higher deficits beget a higher national debt, a higher national debt begets higher interest payments on that debt, and higher interest payments beget higher deficits.

As the deficits pile up, so does the national debt. By OMB's calculations, debt owed to the public will soar to $18.6 trillion in 10 years.[65]

(The "public" debt counts only money owed to the investing public. It is not the same as "total" debt, which today includes $4.4 trillion in intra-governmental holdings, such as money owed to Social Security, Medicare and the Federal Reserve system.)

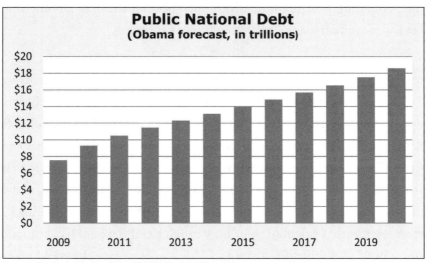

Public National Debt
(Obama forecast, in trillions)

Source: "The Budget for Fiscal Year 2011"; Table S-3; Office of Management and Budget

As the national debt grows, so do interest payments on the debt. The chart on the next page shows the O Team's 2010 forecast for interest payments on the national debt over the decade ahead. Despite massive deficits, the debt burden actually declined during the Global Financial Crisis as investors seeking safety in AAA-rated Treasuries drove the cost of borrowing for the U.S. government to the lowest levels in decades. The steep ascent in interest payments beginning in 2011 reflects two things: the growing debt and rising interest rates on that debt as the global economy recovers. (Note: The CBO forecast for interest payments on the debt runs about $1 trillion higher for the decade.)

The graph looks serious, but not as bad as it could. It shows debt payments increasing at a steady arithmetic rate, not at a geometric rate, suggesting that the situation is serious but not spinning out of control. Don't panic, say the deficit doves, debt as a percentage of the GDP may be rising, but even by 2019 it still won't be as high as it was after

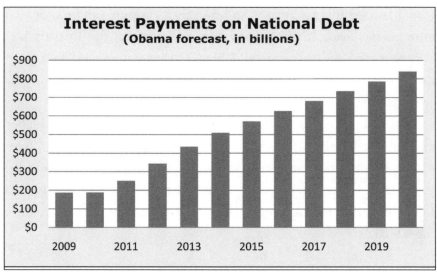

Interest Payments on National Debt
(Obama forecast, in billions)

Source: "The Budget for Fiscal Year 2011"; Table S-3; Office of Management and Budget

World War II -- and it's about one-third the level of Japan's ratio today, and Japan isn't falling apart. Sure, we need to get long-term deficit spending under control, they say, but not at the expense of stifling the economic recovery.

This view is dangerously misguided. For starters, the comparison with Japan is simplistic and misleading. Japan's saving rate, though declining, is still higher than America's, which allows the government to finance 95% of its debt internally. Also, the Japanese people are willing to accept lower yields on their investment savings than Americans are, which allows the government to borrow at lower cost. Most significantly, the Japanese have come to see their Godzilla debt as unsustainable. Naoto Kan, who assumed office as prime minister in June, has warned that the country is near financial collapse. To avert disaster, he has proposed a hike in the country's consumption tax. If anything, Japan is a warning to the U.S., not a reassurance.

The dismissive attitude toward indebtedness is reckless for another reason. When the U.S. national debt blows past the $20 trillion mark sometime around 2020, the single-most important assumption that anyone can make in a budget forecast won't be the rate of economic growth, or spending increases, or how much revenue can be collected from tax increases. It will be the rate of interest that the Treasury Department pays on the national debt. Get that wrong, and your year-ahead forecast will be off by hundreds of billions of dollars. Your 10-year projection will be off by trillions of dollars.

The O Team gets it wrong. Interest rates will be significantly higher than assumed in the official 10-year forecasts. As we shall see in Chapter 4, higher interest rates will leverage the growth rate in interest payments from an arithmetic progression, like that shown previously, into a devouring, geometric progression like the Indian mathematician's chess board.

Chapter 3
Health Care Deform

Bending the Cost Curve

ON FEB. 25, 2010, PRESIDENT OBAMA MET CONGRESSIONAL REPUBLICANS in the Blair House, the president's guest residence across the street from the White House, with the putative goal of finding common ground on health care. As Democrats had announced only a few days previously their intention to pass health care legislation through budget reconciliation, effectively excluding the Republicans from the process, expectations were low that the "summit" would reach a bipartisan deal. But the political show went on nonetheless. And quite a show it was.

President Obama achieved his aim of looking presidential and in command, but the event was not without mishap. Perhaps the most telling encounter of the summit was an exchange with Rep. Paul Ryan, a Republican congressman from Wisconsin. In his prepared remarks, Ryan laid waste to the budgetary underpinnings of the Democrats' proposed legislation. Among the many tricks in Obama's proposals, Ryan explained, was the use of 10 years of tax increases and 10 years of Medicare cuts, about $1 trillion all told, to pay for only six years of expanded spending.

That sleight of hand allowed the president to claim that the legislation was deficit neutral — indeed that it would cut the deficit — within the 10-year time frame of the Congressional Budget Office scoring methodology. The CBO limits its forecasts to 10 years because uncertainties and inevitably arbitrary assumptions make lengthier projections of dubious value. Deeming it politically necessary to win the CBO's clean bill of health, the congressional architects of Obamacare had gamed the CBO methodology to win the politically crucial finding that the legislation would pay for itself within that 10-year period. Of course, in the second decade, 10 years of revenue enhancements would have to pay for ten years of spending, not six. Strip out additional budgetary hocus pocus — using Social Security revenues as offsets, taking money from the CLASS Act long-term-care insurance program without counting future liabilities, and raiding a half trillion dollars from Medicare — and "the full 10-year cost of the bill has a $460 billion deficit," Ryan contended. "The second 10-year cost of this bill has a $1.4 trillion deficit."

Rather than dispute the congressman's points, the president lamely changed the subject. It was the Republicans' most effective performance that day. A video clip went viral on the Internet, and a transcript made it onto the pages of the *Wall Street Journal.*[66] It took more than a week for the Obama administration to respond, but respond it did, in the op-ed pages of the *Washington Post.*

OMB Chief Peter Orszag and Nancy-Ann DeParle, director of Obama's health reform initiative, defended against the charge of budgetary hocus pocus:

> *Now, it's certainly a time-honored Washington budget gimmick to pay for just a few years of costs with many years of savings. But if that were the course being taken, we would expect to see a large hole at the end of the first decade and ever-larger deficits in the second. Instead, the savings in the president's plan grow faster than the costs over time, generating greater deficit reduction with each passing year — roughly $1 trillion, all told, in the second decade. . . .*
>
> *. . . By bundling payments and creating accountable care organizations, as well as by imposing penalties for unnecessary re-admissions and health-facility-acquired infections, physicians and hospitals will be induced to redesign their systems, coordinate care to keep people healthy and avoid unnecessary complications. . . . With the addition of invest-*

ments in health information technology, research into what works and
what doesn't, and an Independent Payment Advisory Board of doctors
and other medical experts making recommendations to improve the
Medicare system, the legislation under consideration would create a vir-
tuous circle in which more information becomes available, different de-
livery system reforms are tested and successful reforms are scaled up
quickly as we learn more.[67]

While Democrats have refused to fess up to budgetary sleights of
hand, Republicans have refused to engage in serious debate over the
very real cost-containment provisions contained in the legislation. The
measures are worthy of discussion, if for no other reason than that they
attempt to get to root causes of out-of-control health care costs: the
rampant inefficiencies in the delivery system. Broadly speaking, there
are only two ways to curtail costs. One is to ration health care. The
other is to increase productivity and boost quality by focusing on improving medical outcomes. The latter is a major thrust of Obamacare,
whose designers drew upon a large academic literature and record of
experimentation in the private health care sector.

Thus, the proper way to frame the debate is this: Will the productivity gains from Obama's cost reforms be sufficient to offset the additional budgetary burden, eventually exceeding $100 billion a year, of
his expanded entitlements? If so, if Obama and Orszag are right, the
legislation will help, to use the wonkish phrase du jour, "bend the cost
curve downward." If they are wrong, then it will hasten the country's
pall mall rush to Boomergeddon.

Reform or Deform?

Obama and Orszag are counting on the Patient Protection and Affordable Care Act to do something that the federal government has never
managed to do before for any length of time: control health care costs.

Ever since taking responsibility for insuring millions of Americans through the Medicare and Medicaid programs, Congress has taken an active interest in health care. Legislators have had to balance three political imperatives: expanding the scope of government coverage, which pleases constituents and wins votes; containing the ensuing cost of health care programs in order to limit deficit spending, which voters don't like; and catering to the special interests with their lobbyists, PAC money and television ad spending. Since the 1960s, the nation has endured spasm after spasm of "reform," some driven by the private sector, most by the public, the end result of which has been to transmogrify the health care system into the budgetary disaster that it is today. Our privately owned but heavily regulated and highly politicized system has little of the vitality and innovation that animates other private-sector industries. It lacks even the static efficiencies, such as low administrative overhead and economies of scale, that characterize government-run systems. What we have is a hybrid that provides world-class care to many Americans and inadequate care to others for the highest price tag in the world.

Far from making the situation better, past reform movements have made the system worse. Layer upon layer of administration, procedure and review have driven what economist Donna Arduin calls a "wedge" between hospitals and doctors on one side and patients on the other.[68] The American way of medicine imposes a massive administrative burden on all parties, diffuses accountability and stifles innovation. Rather than working to provide value (the best medical care for the price), contend business professors Michael Porter and Elizabeth Teisberg, government, health plans, doctors, hospitals, employers and other players in the system are engaged mainly in an effort to shift costs to someone else.[69]

The modern health care system began to emerge in 1929 when Baylor University Hospital offered school teachers a prepaid plan providing up to 21 days per year of hospital care. For the price of a modest subscription, the teachers were insured against the risk of a lengthy hospitalization. The Baylor plan, which also had the virtue of providing a more predictable income stream for the hospital, became the model for Blue Cross, which rolled out its first hospital-insurance plan in 1932 in Sacramento, California. The first Blue Shield plan, which covered physician care, was introduced in 1939, also in California. There were no tax breaks, and there were no employers as intermediaries.

That changed in World War II. Wage-and-price controls made it impossible for employers to compete for workers by paying higher wages, so some circumvented the intent of the law by heaping on fringe benefits like health insurance. The Internal Revenue Service ruled in 1943 that employer-provided health benefits were tax deductible for employers and need not be treated as income for employees. The ruling did not extend to privately purchased health care plans. Not surprisingly, employees preferred to pay for health benefits with pre-tax dollars through their employers rather than after-tax dollars out of their own pockets, and by the 1950s most Americans obtained health insurance coverage through their employers, not the open market. Employer-based medical insurance became the national standard.

The development of employer-funded health plans inserted the first wedge between doctors and patients. There were two baleful consequences, the full impact of which would not be apparent for years. First, employer-based health plans restricted choice. Rather than allow employees access to the full range of plans available in the marketplace, one of which might best suit their needs, employers limited their options to a handful of standardized, easy-to-administer plans. Second, third-party insurance blinded employees to the full cost of their care and encouraged them to treat health care as an entitlement. As long as "someone else" was paying the bill, employers relinquished their role as consumers seeking the best trade-off between cost and quality.

In 1946, the Hill-Burton Act helped finance construction of community hospitals and expanded the health care safety net by requiring any hospital that received federal funds to offer free treatment to anyone who was uninsured and could not afford to pay. The wedge was driven deeper. The obligation to provide uncompensated care gave rise to cost shifting: Hospitals raised rates for paying patients to cover the cost of free care to non-paying patients.

In 1965, Congress created Medicare and Medicaid to provide public health coverage for the elderly and the poor. This wedge had a sledge hammer behind it. Americans paid into the Medicare system through an employer-matched tax currently valued at 2.9 percent of payroll. Employees never saw that money; it went to pay for someone else's care. Then, when employees retired, someone else was paying for their care. Once again, with "someone else" paying the bills, Americans had no incentive to shop for better value.

As night follows day, the cost of Medicare routinely exceeded projections, creating a strain on the federal budget. Congress and successive presidential administrations became determined to rein in expenses. Over the years, Medicare has implemented a variety of strategies to slow the relentless spending increases. One positive change was updating in 1983 the traditional fee-for-service payment system, which encouraged providers to conduct more tests and procedures so they could bill more, by reimbursing providers a predetermined fee based on a patient's diagnosis, falling into one of roughly 500 DRGs (Diagnostic Related Groups). The DRGs were a step in the right direction because they bundled multiple charges into a single payment for treatment of a medical condition. But the new arrangement fell short of true reform: DRGs covered only discrete episodes, not the entire cycle of care for a medical condition. Health care costs kept rising.

Locked into a "cost containment" mindset, federal overseers tried controlling physician fees and hospital charges. In 1984, Medicare tried freezing physician fees, but doctors gamed the system by charging extremely high rates for physicians entering the system, thus raising revenues overall. When private insurers tried imposing fixed fees, some doctors began billing patients for the difference. The practice left patients baffled and irate, and the practice was banned in many states. As wage limits on doctors became more pervasive, doctors compensated by spending less time with patients or by buying into the test laboratories to which they referred their patients.

Understandably, health plans and regulators were concerned by stories that physicians were referring patients for tests they really didn't need or could obtain less expensively elsewhere. In response, Congress passed the Stark law in 1989 to prohibit doctors from referring patients to facilities in which they had an ownership interest. This additional layer of administrative control did prevent some abuses, but it also inhibited physicians from taking equity stakes in potentially innovative business models for delivering care.

Parallel with these developments was the managed care movement. The original idea, as epitomized by Kaiser Permanente, was to assign every patient to a primary care physician whose job was to ensure that the patient received neither too little care nor too much. The approach had its merits. Gatekeepers discouraged patients from obtaining unnecessary care. The practice achieved some early successes, such as reducing the length of time that many patients spent in hospitals, with few adverse results. In the early 1990s, the academic theorists were so enthralled with the idea of managed care that Hillary Clinton made it a centerpiece of her ill-fated health care initiative.

Soon after "Hillary care" met its legislative demise, competition between HMOs took a destructive turn, morphing from providing value (superior price-quality trade-offs) into winning contracts on the basis of submitting the lowest bids. Rather than distinguishing between hospitals and doctors that delivered superior outcomes and those that delivered sub-par results, insurers built networks of providers who acceded to demands for price discounts. Furthermore, HMO gatekeepers became more restrictive in providing patients access to care. Stories of heartless HMOs denying coverage to dying patients filled the news. Within a decade, "managed care" had become synonymous with private-sector rationing. Patient dissatisfaction skyrocketed.

The rise of HMOs and their kindred Preferred Provider Organizations (PPOs) also set into motion the consolidation of the hospital industry, as hospitals sought to increase their negotiating clout in contract talks. Hospitals justified the mergers on the grounds that they would benefit patients by providing "integrated" care in place of fragmented care distributed between multiple organizations. But the efficiencies rarely materialized, or if they did, they did little to slow the relentless increase in hospital charges. By consolidating control over a regional market, however, "health care systems" in many metropolitan areas did gain more leverage to resist price discounts when negotiating with the health plans. Charges headed higher.

Other would-be reformers set their sights on the problem of over-investment in technology. Hospitals competed with one another by investing in the latest, greatest high-tech equipment like CT scanners, PET scanners and lithotripters. In the minds of critics this "medical arms race" contributed to the escalation of health care charges: In order to pay for the expensive equipment, providers were tempted to keep them fully utilized by prescribing tests that patients didn't always need. The solution to the problem was a new law creating medical review boards to approve the purchase of new equipment and construction of new facilities. Inevitably, the dominant players soon corrupted the "Certificate of Public Need" (COPN) process. Hospitals used the bureaucratic hearings to hinder their competitors from expanding services, in effect walling off geographic markets from intruders. In many states COPN laws protected the big, multi-service hospitals from competition from smaller, specialty facilities whose focused attention on particular procedures or medical conditions might allow them to operate more efficiently with superior results.

Meanwhile, Americans' increasing agitation about the growing wedge between doctors and patients gave rise to the so-called patients' rights movement. The aim was to curb unpopular HMO practices and

give patients more legal rights to sue health plans for problems stemming from decisions to withhold or limit care. The impetus behind the
movement was understandable, but the Patients' Bill of Rights law
passed in 2004 served mainly to encumber the health care system with
another layer of regulation and administration.

The cumulative effect of these top-down reforms served mainly to
ossify the health-care delivery system, make it even more dysfunctional,
drive prices higher and spur cries for yet more "reform." As Porter and
Teisberg put it, "Each new layer of regulation adds more costs unre-
lated to actual health care value. Inevitably, new loopholes, omissions,
and distortions in behavior are created that need to be addressed with
yet more regulation."

Another movement, Consumer Driven Health Care, approached
health care reform from a more market-driven perspective. The idea was
to empower patients as consumers and give them incentives to utilize
health care resources more carefully. The most visible manifestation of
this movement has been Health Savings Accounts (HSAs), in which employees make pre-tax contributions to medical-spending accounts set
up in their names. They can use money from the account to cover the
first $3,050 in medical expenses ($6,150 for a family). Whatever they
don't spend, they can roll over to the next year. Experience has shown
that individuals do shop for better value, they don't skimp on preventive
care, as feared, and they do slow the rise in medical spending.

But there are limits to consumers' ability to shop around for better
health care. It is exceedingly difficult to find out what different procedures cost, especially for more complex conditions, and there is very
little quality data. A free market in health care requires information
transparency, and that transparency does not exist. Consumers can shop
for simple, discrete procedures like childbirth or flu shots, but for more
complex medical conditions, they can easily wind up comparing apples
and oranges. Imagine trying to buy a car without knowing how much
the different models cost, how fast they go, what mileage they get, how

safe they are, how often they require repairs, or what their re-sale value is. That's what it's like trying to buy medical care.

By the 2000s, the attention of health care reformers turned to the high rate of medical errors in U.S. health care. This new wave represented an advance from the traditional focus on cutting reimbursements and reducing inputs. Putting into place processes to eliminate medical errors and the spread of secondary hospital infections does have the potential to improve medical outcomes and save money that would have been spent on prolonged hospitalizations and remedial care.

While there are positive aspects to pay for performance, there are limits to what it can accomplish, contend Porter and Teisberg. The focus is on hewing to processes, not measuring and improving results. Because health care entails so many variables and exceptions that depend upon individual circumstances, uniform compliance to standard processes is not always a good idea. Standardization also discourages the experimentation and innovation from which new insights and more effective treatments arise. Moreover, pay for performance represents one more layer of managerial oversight. Warn Porter and Teisberg: "Attempting to micromanage hospitals and doctors by specifying processes is a difficult task that will only become a morass."

Government-driven reform invariably gives more power to government. The reason is that the ideas emanate mainly from academics who seek systemic solutions, not entrepreneurs bubbling up from the health care industry itself. The academics, or "elite policy makers," to borrow a descriptor from Harvard Business School professor Regina Herzlinger, tend to share an anti-business bias and to favor top-down government solutions that put smart people like them in charge. In Herzlinger's assessment, the academic experts are as much to blame for the parlous condition of American health care as are giant insurance companies, monolithic health care systems, short-sighted employers and a meddling U.S. Congress.[70]

By the mid-1980s, the health care system was clearly broken. That's when health care inflation detached itself from the general rate of inflation and launched into its own moon-shot trajectory. The utter failure to vanquish rising health care costs only spurred the academics to greater exertions — and the situation continued to deteriorate. The rising cost of medicine priced millions of Americans out of the insurance marketplace, giving the policy elites yet another reason to intervene. As convinced as ever of their brilliance, they managed earlier this year to once again foist their policy fashions upon the American public. The academics called upon the only group in the nation even more assured of its infallibility, the U.S. Congress, to implement their theories. Where everyone else had botched reform, the politicians and policy wonks were convinced that this time they would get it right. They called it "fiscally responsible health care reform." Foes called it "Obamacare."

Two Acts, Two Acts, Two Acts in One

President Obama and his Congressional allies had two major preoccupations in approaching health care reform. First, they wanted to extend medical coverage to the 15 percent of the population that lacked it, a liberal Democratic priority since World War II. Second, they had a keen understanding that the nation could not long afford medical care if the cost steadily outpaced the rate of general inflation for the next 40 years.

The tumultuous debate that ensued revolved mainly around the question of how to achieve universal insurance coverage, how to pay for it, and what impact the legislation would have on the federal budget. Congress spent months identifying one group after another — the rich, the young and healthy, beneficiaries of high-cost health plans, consumers of soft drinks, cosmetic surgeons, tanning parlors — that could be shaken down for enough money to make the initiative budget neutral. But lawmakers faced a hard political reality in this zero-sum game: For every winner (someone who gained access to medical insurance), there was a loser (someone else who paid for those benefits). And the losers raised hell.

Democrats cut deals with Big Pharma, Big Insura, Big Labor, the hospitals and doctors to buy their acquiescence. Health reform sputtered as Congress tried to reconcile the competing visions of the Senate and the House of Representatives. After the January election of Republican Scott Brown to the Massachusetts Senate seat previously occupied by Teddy Kennedy, the initiative appeared to collapse. But a final bout of deal making and arm twisting pushed the legislation across the finish line.

The Patient Protection and Affordable Care Act is really two bills jammed together. One bill is a wealth-transfer mechanism that extends health care benefits to a broader cross-section of the American people by overhauling the insurance industry, expanding Medicaid and imposing a variety of fees and taxes. The other bill seeks to reform the efficiency of the system, primarily by disseminating best practices and by moving Medicare from a fee-based system focused on short-term cost controls to a program focused on improving medical outcomes. If outcomes improve, the logic goes, patients will have fewer complications and suffer fewer medical errors, which will translate into fewer readmissions to the hospital. As countless manufacturing companies have demonstrated, efficiency and quality go hand in hand. There is so much waste in the U.S. health care system, argue the Obamanauts, that boosting productivity and improving outcomes can corral runaway health spending, even as the expansion of health care entitlements drives up costs. For purposes of gauging the trajectory of federal spending, then, it is imperative to understand the efficiency measures that Obamacare proposes and assess whether they can accomplish what the budget meisters say they will.

Under the Obama plan, the commitment to efficiency and quality will start at the top. The Secretary of Health and Human Services (HHS) will develop a national strategy to measure results, identify best practices and goad hospitals, doctors and other providers into changing the way they practice medicine. To carry out the strategy, the president will convene a working group, the Interagency Working Group on Health Care Quality, to coordinate the activities of some two dozen federal agencies and departments and work with the private sector.[71]

In place of the current fee-for-service system, which reimburses providers on the basis of how many procedures they perform, regardless of the outcome, Medicare will endeavor to reward providers on the basis of how successfully they prevent and treat disease. Superior results will get more money; sub-par results will get less. The program will pioneer the "bundling" of payments so that teams of medical specialists with different disciplines can be paid for delivering coordinated care over the course of a patient's cycle of care, from prevention and diagnosis to treatment and recovery.[72] These ideas are similar to those propounded by Michael Porter and Elizabeth Teisberg, the business school professors whose analysis I have quoted extensively above.

In the same vein, the national health care plan will tackle the problems of costly medical errors, infections acquired in hospital settings, and the all-too-frequent problem of patients being readmitted to the hospital for the same medical episode. The strategy also will address chronic conditions, which account for more than half of all medical spending.

Sounds great in theory. Now, let's get into the weeds.

The Department of Health and Human Services will establish a hospital value-based purchasing system.[73] Each hospital will be assigned a hospital performance score based upon its cost and quality metrics. Medicare payments will be raised or lowered in tandem with the score, rewarding excellence and punishing failure. Scores will be posted on a website where it will be accessible to the public.

In a new quality-reporting system, physicians will be required to submit quality data to HHS. The department will massage the data and then inform physicians how their patterns of resource use compare to that of other physicians. To avoid punishing docs who take on the hardest cases, the data will be adjusted for the severity of the patients' conditions as well as demographic factors such as income and ethnicity.[74]

A Center for Medicare and Medicaid Innovation will create cutting-edge payment and service-delivery models that hold out the potential to improve the quality of care for patients at less cost. Doctor-nurse teams will visit elderly patients at home rather than wait for them to arrive in the emergency room. Medical homes will focus on women's unique health needs. Primary care physician groups will take lump-sum or salary-based payments in lieu of fee-for-service reimbursements.

Yet another idea, Healthcare Innovation Zones centered around teaching hospitals, will deliver a full spectrum of integrated and comprehensive health care services while incorporating novel methods for training future health care professionals.[75]

The legislation also endorses an innovation called "accountable care organizations" (ACOs), which are comprised of a hospital, primary care physicians, specialists and other medical professionals. Accountable for the cost and quality of care for Medicare populations of 5,000 patients or more, ACOs will employ quality and cost measures along with new technologies such as remote patient monitoring to continually ratchet up the quality of care. As an incentive, ACOs will be eligible to receive payment for shared savings.[75]

In a similar vein, Obamacare will create a Center for Quality Improvement and Patient Safety, to gather, conduct and synthesize research on the effectiveness of different ways to prevent, diagnose, treat and manage medical problems. The center will identify best practices for quality improvement in the delivery of health care services with an eye to reducing unintended health outcomes, improve patient safety and reduce medical errors. Where research does not exist, the Center will be empowered to grant awards for original research. Reports will be posted online and disseminated widely to relevant members of the medical community.[77]

Finally, the law establishes an Independent Medicare Advisory Board to keep Medicare spending from running over budget. The Advisory

Board will submit recommendations to Congress to improve the quality and efficiency of the health care delivery system by such means as integrated care, coordinated care and prevention and wellness. To address Republican charges early in the debate that the Advisory Board would lead to rationing, the final bill explicitly excludes any measure that would "ration health care, raise revenues or ... beneficiary premiums."[78]

These draw from the best thinking of the medical establishment. Ideally, Medicare will evolve over time from a fee-for-service system, which reimburses doctors and hospitals regardless of results, toward a system that pays providers based on results over the full cycle of care. Research and quality data will be collected, massaged to identify best clinical practices, and spit back to the doctors, hospitals and health professionals to guide them in improving their results and their public standing.

The Limits to Top-Down Reform

The reforms described above will bring real improvements to the U.S. health care system. But they do not represent a dramatic breakthrough. Many of the ideas embodied in the legislation are being implemented by forward-thinking hospitals and physician practices already, even without the carrot/cattle prod of Medicare reimbursement reform. The emphasis, for once, is on the right place: productivity and quality. The problem is in how the ideas get implemented. Obamacare puts the Department of Health and Human Services in charge. Reform will be top-down, it will unfold at the same pace at which the federal government does business, and it will be subject to lobbying and gaming by health care special interests.

Appointing Health and Human Services as the driver of health care reform inevitably politicizes the very process of change that the legislation seeks to enable. The text of the Affordable Health Care Act contains many vivid illustrations of how the government intends to micro-manage the $2.3 trillion health care industry. Just one example:

HHS is called upon to conduct a study regarding bone-mass measurement to evaluate Medicare payment rates for such services as "computed tomography, dual-energy x-ray absorptiometry." The study will take into account the costs of acquiring the equipment, professional work time and practice expense costs. The report will then be submitted to Congress no later than nine months after the enactment of the Act.[79]

Is the federal government really, truly the organization best suited to make such decisions? Why does Congress need to be involved in the selection of bone-mass measurement technology? Putting such decisions into the political sphere invites the manufacturers of x-ray absorptiometry to sell their products by hiring lobbyists in lieu of persuading patients and/or doctors of their value. Remember the chart in Chapter 2 listing the top contributors to the 2008 Congressional campaigns? Health care professionals pumped more money into the system than any other industry except the legal profession — $13.6 million — and that doesn't even include the vast sums donated to the presidential campaign. By expanding the scope of government control over the health care sector, Obamacare will compel health care businesses to spend more on lobbyists and PACs to advance their interests in Washington, D.C.

One of the advantages of being an established player like a multibillion-dollar health plan or a Fortune 500 pharmaceutical company is that you have lots of money to hire lobbyists and spread around PAC donations. Start-up entrepreneurs who might challenge your market dominance don't have big bucks to throw around — they plow every penny they've got into growing their business. So, when it comes to translating the law into the fine print of rules and regulations, whom do you think will dominate the process? The little guys trying to meet payroll on Friday or the big guys with offices in Washington?

But there's an even bigger problem. It is not enough to collect quality metrics for the nation's hospitals and doctors, as necessary as that is for building a transparent, market-driven health care system. It does not suffice to identify best clinical practices, as much as that would help improve the delivery of medicine. It takes more than redesigning Medicare's payment system, although that, too, is an important step forward. Missing from Obama's health care reform is any recognition that transformative economic change is best driven by entrepreneurial innovation.

As I shall explain in Chapter 9, the only hope we have of "bending the cost curve" fast enough to avoid Boomergeddon is to radically restructure the health care industry. To achieve dramatic gains in productivity and quality, the industry must jettison the notion that hospitals and physicians should organize their practices around functional areas like oncology, nephrology, orthopedics and the like. Providers must reorganize around multi-disciplinary teams that focus on medical conditions, providing treatment across the full cycle of care. These teams must be supported by dedicated facilities geared to carrying out treatments with maximum efficiency and attention to quality. These teams must be learning organizations, continually monitoring their quality outcomes and dedicating themselves to continual improvement rather than waiting for research to be handed down from on high. Reorganizing health care in this manner will require disruptive, entrepreneurial change, not the incremental reform of a large, lumbering private health care system prodded by an even a larger, even more unwieldy federal bureaucracy.

Here are some of the barriers that block the adoption of new, entrepreneurial business models in U.S. health:

Lack of price transparency. The Obama plan will make performance data available. That's half the value equation. But it's only half. There is no price transparency in U.S. health care. Without quality and price transparency, patients cannot make fully informed consumer decisions. Instead, they rely upon referrals, usually from other doctors who base their recommendations on vague criteria such as a doctor's "reputation" in the local medical community. Did someone go to the "right" medical schools? Does he play a good game of golf?

Monolithic health care systems. The players with the most to lose from specialty hospitals are giant hospital systems, which provide a broad spectrum of health care services, usually excelling in only a few of them. As demonstrated repeatedly around the U.S., they will use their bargaining power with physicians and insurers to freeze specialized competitors out of the market.

Certificate of public need. Hospital giants can block new competitors in this bureaucratic forum by making the case that there is no "public need" for "duplicative" and "redundant" hospital facilities.

The Stark law. The law prohibits physicians from referring patients to a medical facility in which he or she has a financial interest. That could stymie physician/entrepreneurs from taking an equity position in a specialty hospital they set up.

Medicare certification. Obamacare imposes onerous new regulations on physician-owned hospitals, including limits on new construction, restrictions on the expansion of existing facilities, detailed reporting requirements, and fines for hospitals that fail to abide by them. Within days of the law's enactment, developers across the country cancelled plans for 24 physician-owned hospitals. Another 47 were threatened with the possibility of losing their Medicare certification.[80]

Tort law. Indiscriminate lawsuits against physicians impose many costs on the health care system, the least of which is the cost of paying for medical malpractice insurance. A larger cost, as is commonly observed, is the cost of defensive medicine. The biggest cost may be the chilling effect that fear of lawsuits has on the corporate culture of health care organizations. Knowing that a plaintiff's attorney could use the data to crucify them in court does not encourage doctors or hospitals to systematically collect data on misdiagnoses and medical errors for the purpose of continual quality improvement.

American research scientists have pioneered awe-inspiring breakthroughs in genetics, cell chemistry, medical imaging, non-invasive surgical tools and related technologies. But innovation in business management and delivery models has slowed to a crawl. Labor productivity has stagnated. Despite the massive amount of information that exchanges hands in the course of medical care, implementation of information technology lags that of other industries. Perhaps most disappointing, quality control techniques remain in a state of barbaric simplicity compared to best practices like Six Sigma, Lean Production and Total Quality Management in the manufacturing sector.

The corporate culture of the health care industry desperately needs to change but, as a rule, large entrenched organizations find it exceedingly difficult to bring about that change. It will be far easier to create a new medical culture through the innovations of start-up enterprises than through the reinvention of old organizations. Diktats handed down by the U.S. Department of Health and Human Services can drive change but not very rapidly. Only an entrepreneurial revolution can transform the system in time to prevent Boomergeddon.

No Quick Fixes

In the short-term, Obamacare will drive up health care costs by feeding tens of millions of new patients into the system, adding layers of bureaucracy and insulating patients from the consequences of their lifestyle and health care choices. Over the long term, top-down productivity and quality reforms may nudge the cost curve, but they will not bend it. Sooner or later, it will become evident to all that expenses are higher than predicted, that savings are not materializing as fast as fantasized, and budget deficits are raging unabated. The baying will begin anew to "do something."

If there were any easy, painless solutions to perfecting America's flawed health care system, we would have stumbled across them by now. But that won't stop people from peddling the idea that if only we adopted one nostrum or another, we still can stem the tide of rising health costs. It is my sad obligation to strip away such delusions. There is no warding off Boomergeddon.

Single payer. Predictably, progressives will say that Obamacare did not go far enough. What the country really needs is a single-payer system. Progressives tend to view the insurance industry as the bane of U.S. health care: Not only do insurers burden the system with layers of administration and review, they pay their senior executives unconscionable compensation, and they run up unconscionable profits. By adopting a government-run, single-payer system like those in Canada and the United Kingdom, some say, Congress could strip tens of billions of dollars from the nation's health care costs in one bold stroke.

Comparing the administrative expenses of Medicare with those of private insurance companies delivering services through the Medicare Advantage Plan, Jacob S. Hacker, a UC Berkeley professor, says that administrative costs for Medicare run less than two percent of expenditures, while the comparable burden for the private plans runs around 11 percent.[81] A difference of nine percentage points is a princely sum of money. If extrapolated across the entire privately insured health care sector, it would amount to roughly $100 billion.

The idea of cutting out the insurance middleman has broad political appeal because insurance companies do encumber the health care system with red tape. Their petty-fogging rules can be impenetrable. Nearly everyone has had an encounter with endless paperwork and insufferable, uncaring claims adjustors. Insurance company bureaucrats have accomplished the seemingly impossible: giving government bureaucrats a good name. Nobody likes "Big Insura," to borrow a columnist Peggy Noonan's play on Big Pharma.[82] Few can see the value, if any, it brings to the health care system.

Insurance companies also are castigated for restricting medical coverage for those who need it the most, often for arbitrary and unjust reasons. In an August 2009 town hall meeting, President Obama singled out for special condemnation the insurance industry practice of discriminating against Americans with pre-existing conditions. A recent report, he told the audience, had found that insurers had mistreated more than 12 million Americans. Said the president:

> *Either the insurance company refused to cover the person, or they dropped their coverage when they got sick and needed it most, or they refused to cover a specific illness or condition, or they charged higher premiums and out-of-pocket costs. No one holds these companies accountable for these practices.*
>
> *Under the reform we're proposing, insurance companies will be prohibited from denying coverage because of a person's medical history. Period. They will not be able to drop your coverage if you get sick. They will not be able to water down your coverage when you need it.... And we will place a limit on how much you can be charged for out-of-pocket expenses, because no one in America should go broke because they get sick. Insurance companies will continue to profit by discriminating against people for the simple crime of being sick.[83]*

Perhaps it's like asking sympathy for the devil, to borrow a phrase from the Rolling Stones, but there is another side to the story. Medicare's low administrative costs are "a mirage," argue Grace-Marie Turner with the Galen Institute and Joseph R. Antos with the American Enterprise Institute. If all Medicare costs were accounted for, including revenue collection, personnel, enforcement and extra services such as taxes, nurse hotlines, decision-support tools and fraud detection, Medicare administrative expenses would be higher.[84]

I would be willing to wager that Mr. Hacker, the Berkeley professor who unfavorably compared the overhead costs of private insurers to Medicare, is not himself enrolled in Medicare. If he were, it would not have escaped his attention that the level of customer service in the monopolistic Medicare program suffers by comparison to that of most insurance companies. Indeed, the idea of Medicare treating enrollees as "customers" is a ludicrous one. Medicare is the ultimate monopoly.

Americans are given no choice in the matter — they must enroll at the risk of severe penalties.

My mother, a feisty 81-year-old, flays incompetence and ineptitude wherever she encounters it, whether in the public sector or private. Mr. Hacker should hear what she has to say about the difference in public quality between Medicare and her AARP-sponsored Medicare supplement plan. When calling Medicare for answers to routine questions, she often spends an hour wending her way through an impersonal telephone tree, stuck on hold for much of the time, only to hear a prerecorded voice tell her that, due to heavy "call volume" (never "insufficient staffing"), there is no one available to take her call, and could she please call back at another time? By contrast, she reports, she can always connect with a real human at United HealthCare, administrator of her Medicare supplement plan, within a few minutes. How much of Medicare's lower administrative fees is achieved by shifting costs (time spent on hold is a cost, even for retired people) to customers? How much would the cost gap shrink if Medicare took customer satisfaction seriously?

Meanwhile, because Medicare invests so little in fraud detection and enforcement, the program bleeds tens of billions of dollars per year in fraud. No one knows for sure how extensive the problem is, but the HHS Office of the Inspector General estimated that overpayments and other errors amounted to 4.3 percent in 2007.[85] If the 2007 rate still holds true, that implies a loss of $19 billion a year. The Association of American Physicians and Surgeons cited an estimate that Medicare fraud ran around 10 percent, so the figure could well be higher. Regardless, if Medicare were serious about combating fraud, it would have to ramp up its spending on auditing and enforcement closer to private-sector levels, closing the apparent efficiency gap.

As for the fairness issues, insurers do frequently discriminate against people with pre-existing medical conditions, and they sometimes do decline coverage for certain medical conditions. Let's see how

% Claims Denied		
Insurer	**2008**	**2009**
Aetna	6.80%	1.81%
Anthem BCBS	4.62%	4.34%
Cigna	3.44%	2.56%
Coventry	2.88%	3.99%
Health Net	3.88%	NA
Humana	2.90%	2.03%
United Health Care	2.68%	2.02%
Medicare	6.85%	4.00%

Source: "2009 National Health Insurer Report"; American Medical Association.

the biggest insurers stacked up against the single payer for folks over 65, that paragon of mercy, Medicare. (The data on the left comes from the American Medical Association, which has no obvious interest in slanting the data in this particular debate.[86])

Medicare denies a higher percentage of claims than the big private insurers do? President Obama didn't mention that.

What the purveyors of a single-payer system overlook is that a United States running $1 trillion-a-year budget deficits will not be in a position either to pay for everyone's care under all circumstances. Someone still has to say, "No, you are not entitled to a limitless claim on society for all the health care you want under any and all circumstances." The government might make different choices than an insurance company would, but it would have to make choices just the same — just as Medicare already does. Does anyone seriously think that shifting from a system dominated by a big, insurance-company oligopoly to a system dominated by a big government monopoly would represent a triumph for compassion and justice?

There's an even bigger reason to fear a single-payer system. In the words of Porter and Teisberg, a single-payer system would amount to "a government monopoly with absolute bargaining power." Instead of doing the hard work of boosting productivity and improving quality, the faceless bureaucracy would find it easier to hit budget goals by shifting costs to hospitals, doctors and patients. "It simply strains credulity," say Porter and Teisberg, "to imagine that a large government entity would streamline administration, simplify prices, set prices according to true costs, help patients make choices based on excellence and value, establish value-based competition at the provider level and make politically neutral and tough choices to deny patients and reimbursement to substandard providers."

Humans will be arguing about insurance reform until the sun goes supernova and burns the earth to a crisp, and even then someone will be kvetching that the government refuses to rectify injuries sustained from super-heated streams of solar plasma. For our purposes in tracking the trajectory toward Boomergeddon, it actually matters little if a single-payer system would do a better job or worse than private insurers. What matters most is the impact of a single-payer system on federal government spending. A single-payer system would have no impact on public programs. In its market niche serving citizens 65 and older, Medicare is already a single-payer system. Extending the monopoly to the private sector will not slow Medicare's march to its fiscal doom.

Big Pharma. Another favorite whipping boy is the pharmaceutical industry. Drug makers are somewhat more sympathetic characters than insurers because they at least manufacture something tangible — life-saving drugs — that people can appreciate. As a consequence, no one pretends that we can live without pharmaceutical companies or that government can do their job better. But that does not absolve the industry of its many purported sins. Big Pharma spends billions of dollars on advertising and pumping up demand for its products, say the critics. More to the point, they aggressively jack up their prices to sustain profitability that is the envy of most other industries.

There is some truth to these accusations. The drug companies exert amazing pricing power in the marketplace. In 2009, a recession year that drove the Consumer Price Index into negative territory, the pharmaceutical companies managed to raise prices charged under Medicare for brand name drugs by 8.7 percent on average — about 10 percent in inflation-adjusted terms.

Pharmaceutical companies respond that they must raise prices to maintain the profits needed to fund the R&D of new drugs.[87] The need to boost prices never seems to abate, however. As the AARP found in

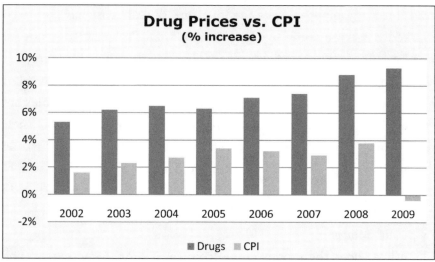

Drug Prices vs. CPI
(% increase)

Source: "Rx Watchdog Report"; AARP Public Policy Institute.

its examination of prescription drug prices under Medicare, drug prices consistently outpaced the general inflation rate over the eight years covered by the study.[88]

It is also true that drug makers are one of the most profitable industries in the United States. In 2008, the industry as a whole managed to maintain a 19.3 percent profit margin, making it the third most profitable of the 53 industries represented in the Fortune 500.[89] Worldwide profits for the 41 drug companies tracked by the Value Line Investment Survey amounted to $63 billion on revenues of $330 billion.[90]

It's less clear what we should do about it. Big Pharma argues that developing new drugs is expensive and risky. According to a widely cited study, the average cost of successfully developing a New Molecular Entity (as opposed to modifying an existing drug) ran around $800 million back in 2000. Developing the drug took 4.3 years on average, while conducting clinical trials and winning FDA approval took another 7.5 years — almost 12 years in all. The $800 million figure included not only cash outlays but the cost of tying up capital for more than a decade, as well as money invested in drugs that never made it to market.

The number of NMEs (industry jargon for New Molecular Entities) approved by the FDA bounces around from year to year but has stayed remarkably level over the long run. But the cost has increased markedly. A 2006 study by the Congressional Budget Office cited a number of possible reasons. First, a higher percentage of drug projects are failing in clinical trials: Only 8 percent successfully run the FDA gauntlet, compared to 14 percent traditionally. Second, companies are conducting larger, more elaborate trials in order to differentiate their drugs from competing products. And third, companies are emphasizing research on drugs that treat chronic and degenerative diseases, which, due to the slowly unfolding nature of the maladies, take longer to yield measurable results.[91] These cost drivers are not subject to manipulation by public policy.

Where does the money come from to pay for the research? The major drug companies don't raise money from the stock or bond markets, they fund R&D out of their cash flow. Therefore, a reduction in profitability would reduce private-sector investment in drug R&D, states the CBO study. In turn, lower investment would reduce the number of drugs coming out of the development pipeline.

The question then is this: Would it make sense for government to undertake legislative efforts to lower pharmaceutical costs for the Medicare and Medicaid programs even if it meant reducing drug makers' profits, R&D investment and the development of new drugs in the future?

That's a difficult question to answer. As the CBO study notes, anecdotal and statistical evidence suggests that drug-related R&D has contributed to "major therapeutic gains." When a new drug replaces an older, less effective drug or a medical treatment, it can represent a net savings to society. Say, for purposes of illustration, that someone invented a drug that effectively treated Alzheimer's disease. Let's say that the company charged $10,000 a year for the drug. Let's also assume that the drug was suitable for one million Alzheimer's sufferers. Our hypothetical blockbuster would reap $10 billion in revenue yearly and would be massively profitable until the patent expired or a competitor came up with a competing drug. Despite the immense cost of the drug, society would be better off. According to "2009 Alzheimer's Disease Facts and Figures," the nation spent $33,000 per patient in 2004 in Medicaid payments and other expenses. The drug would be a bargain by anyone's definition. When the patent expired, allowing competition by generics, it would be a screaming bargain.

That's an extreme example, of course. The point to remember is this: Pharmaceutical companies can introduce a new drug into the marketplace, but the compound won't gain widespread acceptance unless it (a) delivers superior medical outcomes, or (b) is cheaper than alternative methods of treatment. Drug companies can run all the television ads they want, and they can ply doctors with box seats to the Super Bowl, but unless they can persuade Medicare, Medicaid and the private insurance companies to put the drug on their formularies, few people will buy it if insurance doesn't help pay for it.

Interestingly, while the U.S. has the highest health care costs in the world, in 2005 Americans spent less on pharmaceuticals as a percentage of health care expenditures than did many other countries with advanced economies.[92] France, Italy, Canada, Japan and Germany all spent a higher percentage, and even the United Kingdom was on a par with the U.S. Insofar as other nations get more health care bang for the buck by substituting drugs for other forms of medical care, their experience suggests that pharmaceutical spending in the U.S. could be a slightly bigger share of the mix.

One of the favorite policy prescriptions endorsed by the anti-Big Pharma crowd is to allow the re-importation of prescription drugs from Canada to the U.S. That idea might have worked for a while, but it wouldn't have generated savings for long. First, pharmaceutical companies have already adjusted their pricing to Canadian retailers to lessen the price disparities. And second, a stronger Canadian dollar has made retail Canadian products more expensive when purchased with American dollars. When calculated on a purchasing power parity basis, the average retail price of pharmaceuticals in Canada was actually a bit higher in 2005 than it was in the U.S. Unless the U.S. dollar regains its strength, re-importation will lead nowhere.

For purposes of averting Boomergeddon, here's the bottom line: Targeting pharmaceutical prices or drug company profits might save Medicare and Medicaid some money in the short run. But any measure that constricts the new-drug pipeline will likely make it more difficult to control health care costs several years out.

Preventive care. In making the case for health care reform, President Obama contended that the legislation would pay for itself in part through preventive care. Expanding health care coverage to all Americans would enable poor people to seek treatment in the doctor's office when health problems are easily treated rather than the emergency room when they've become critical. The idea makes intuitive sense: An ounce of prevention is worth a pound of cure. As the president made the case in an address to Congress in September 2009:

> *Insurance companies will be required to cover, with no extra charge, routine checkups and preventive care, like mammograms and colonoscopies - because there's no reason we shouldn't be catching diseases like breast cancer and colon cancer before they get worse. That makes sense, it saves money, and it saves lives.*[93]

But it turns out that the economics of preventive medicine are more nuanced than the president let on. In some cases, preventive care makes enormous sense — giving children polio vaccines, for instance. In other cases, like cancer screenings, the benefits are ambiguous. And sometimes, it's a waste of resources. As CBO Director Douglas W. Elmendorf explained in an August 2009 letter to Congress: "To avert one case of acute illness, it is usually necessary to provide preventive care to many patients, most of whom would not have suffered that illness anyway."[94]

Obama's supporters criticized Elmendorf's findings on the grounds that the CBO considers the budget impact of legislation over a 10-year time horizon. If preventive care were scored over a longer time horizon — 30 years, say — the budget impact would be positive, the Obamanauts say.

Well, maybe. Michael O'Grady, a University of Chicago professor tested that logic using data from long-standing clinical trials to project the cost of caring for people with Type 2 diabetes. Enrolling federally insured patients in an aggressive program to control the disease would cost $1,024 per person per year. Initially, the preventive program would cost the government more money than it saved. But the costs would be recovered after 25 years through lower spending on dialysis, kidney transplants, amputations and other procedures.[95]

That argument might appeal to people who have no concept of the time value of money, but it would never fly in the private sector. No corporation would invest money if it meant waiting 25 years to break even. There are too many alternative investments that would earn back the money far more quickly. A national roll-out of O'Grady's protocols for Type 2 diabetes would cost billions of dollars up front. The savings would come 25 years from now — in the year 2035. Unfortunately, the federal government will be broke long before then.

Not only is the payback for much preventive care far in the future, recent history shows that the utilitarian logic of the technocrats is often trumped by political considerations. Nowhere was the power of pressure groups more evident than in the debacle late last year when the Task Force on Preventive Service recommended dialing back breast cancer screenings for women under 50. The logic was coldly rational: To avert one death from breast cancer among women in their 40s, it was necessary to screen 1,900 women. The screenings would generate numerous false positives, causing great distress to the women involved and running up tremendous bills for follow-up X-rays, biopsies and physician time.[96] It was not a sound use of finite resources.

Some radiologists criticized the Task Force recommendations on medical grounds, but the issue became politicized and the debate morphed into dueling sound bites quicker than you can say, "Aaah." First, women's health advocates lambasted the decision. Then Republican foes of Obamacare piled on, asserting that the Task Force action foreshadowed the kind of rationing that would take place as government increased its control over the U.S. health care system. Congress quickly amended the Senate health care reform package to instruct insurers to disregard the findings.

Preventive care is one strategy among many for improving in the U.S. health care system. Where the evidence for preventive medicine is strongest, it is widely practiced already among the 85 percent of the population that is covered by insurance. Most private plans cover the preventive tests and procedures that have been documented to have the greatest benefit, as does Medicare. That's not to say that further investments in prevention and wellness are unneeded, but the programs offering the greatest return on investment have already been made. Any future gains will be incremental in nature, not transformative.

Tort reform. The favorite magical solution proffered by Republicans is medical malpractice reform. The argument normally goes like this: Frivolous lawsuits and crazy jury awards are driving up the cost of malpractice insurance and spurring doctors to conduct more diagnostic tests that minimize the potential for lawsuits but do little for the patient. This phenomenon, known as "defensive medicine," is widely acknowledged to be real, but there is considerable controversy over how much it costs.

One widely quoted study, written in 1996 by Daniel P. Kessler and Mark B. McClellan, suggests that malpractice reforms could lead to reductions of five to nine percent in medical expenditures without increasing mortality or the rate of medical complications.[97] In 2010 dollars, that translates into reducing Medicare expenditures by some $22.7 billion to $40.5 billion.

But those numbers are probably a mirage. According to data published in a 2008 Towers Perrin study, medical malpractice simply isn't the problem today that it was in the 1960s and 1970s, when malpractice costs were out of control, or even in 1996 when Kessler and McClellan published their study. As you can see in the chart on the next page, the increase in malpractice costs plunged in the early 1980s, and leveled off for a decade and a half, roughly tracking medical inflation. Since 2000, the increase in malpractice costs has fallen even further behind medical inflation. By the mid-2000s, one could make the case that malpractice costs were acting as a damper on medical inflation![98]

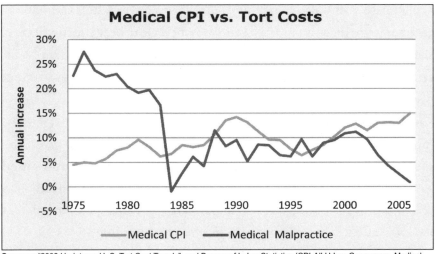

Sources: "2008 Update on U. S. Tort Cost Trends"; and Bureau of Labor Statistics (CPI-All Urban Consumers, Medical Care, 1975-2005.)

What is going on? The apparent explanation is state-level tort reform. Beginning in the early 1980s, states began reacting to skyrocketing malpractice costs by implementing a number of the strategies contemplated in federal reform, such as capping punitive damages, capping pain-and-suffering damages, limiting attorney's fees, and modifying legal rules that favor plaintiffs. While these strategies are by no means universal, they have been increasingly widespread among the 50 states, including states where lawsuit abuse was the most notorious.[99] In other words, the states have stolen the federal government's thunder. While it still may be worthwhile to make the tort reforms national in scope, much of the savings postulated by Kessler and McClellan back in 1996 have already been reaped.

Bottom line: Medical malpractice is not the problem that it used to be. Enacting national reform probably would save money, but not nearly as much as Republicans would hope.

Digital records. Tucked away in the 2009 American Recovery and Reinvestment Act (ARRA), more commonly known as the $787 billion "stimulus" bill, was a measure that funneled $20 billion into funding health care technology, including incentives for physicians to adopt electronic medical records systems. It's not clear how much stimulus the initiative will provide in the short run, but it does represent an investment in the productivity and efficiency of the health care system over the long run.

The U.S. health care industry has been notoriously slow to embrace information technology, which is all the more remarkable given the technology-intensive nature of the diagnostic and surgical tools used so widely in the industry. IT investment per worker in the health care sector averaged about $3,000, compared to a private-sector average of $7,000, and an average of $15,000 in a information-intensive field such as banking, wrote Porter and Teisberg in 2006.

ARRA's goal was to accelerate the health care sector's shift from paper-based records to Electronic Health Records (EHRs in bureaucrat speak). In a 2008 report, the CBO noted several advantages to EHRs, such as reducing the duplication of diagnostic tests, eliminating errors from physicians' messy handwriting, saving the clerical labor of pulling patient charts from office files, and alerting doctors to potentially harmful drug interactions and allergic reactions. CBO cited studies indicating that widespread adoption of IT potentially could wring as much as $80 billion in costs from the health care system. Even in a $2.3 trillion health care economy, that ain't chump change.[100]

Here's the question the architects of the stimulus package apparently never bothered to ask: If IT offers such a tremendous payback, why has the health care sector been so slow to embrace it? Is it because doctors, who dearly love their arthroscopes, gamma knives and PET scanners, are technophobes? Is it because hospitals have corporate cultures that are uniquely resistant to change? Or is it because the fee-based reimbursement system adopted by Medicare, Medicaid and private insurers provides minimal incentives for cutting costs?

The estimate of $80 billion in savings from EHRs was contingent upon "appropriate changes in health care" being made. Wrote the CBO: "Health care financing and delivery are now organized in such a way that the payment methods of many private and public health insurers do not reward providers for reducing costs — and may even penalize them from doing so."

For example:

> *The use of health IT could reduce the number of duplicated diagnostic tests. However, that improvement in efficiency would be unlikely to increase the income of many physicians because laboratories and imaging centers typically perform such tests and are paid separately by health insurance plans. In cases in which a physician performs certain diagnostic tests in the office, reducing the number of duplicated tests would reduce his or her income. As a result, the capacity to avoid duplicating tests might not spur many physicians to invest in and implement a health IT system.*

Ironically, the man who wrote the letter of introduction to that CBO report was none other than Peter Orszag, who was then CBO director under the Bush administration. If the problem stems from skewed incentives, then one must wonder why the Obama administration didn't focus on fixing the incentives rather than dumping $20 billion into a broken system. It will be interesting to see if that money was well spent or whether it was poured down a black hole. We can only hope that Congress will ask for an accounting.

If there were a silver bullet that could slay runaway health care costs, it would be harnessing the power of IT to use data to guide hospitals and doctors toward better medical outcomes. As the Dartmouth Institute, publisher of the Dartmouth Atlas, has amply documented, the cost of providing health care to Medicare patients varies enormously across the United States — from more than $14,000 per Medicare enrollee in Miami, Fla., to $5,300 per enrollee in Honolulu.[101] Patients in high-cost regions have access to the same technology as patients in low-cost regions. Patients in high-cost regions receive no better care than patients in low-cost regions, assert the Dartmouth researchers. Indeed, the low-cost care is often better. The difference in cost, the researchers say, is due to regional differences in medical practice.

Imagine this: If identifying, adopting and disseminating best practices could bring down Medicare costs from the national average of $8,300 (2006 numbers) to Honolulu levels, we could strip 36 percent of the costs out of the Medicare system. But why let Honolulu define the best practices? Even Honolulu has something to learn from other regions. If we could improve the performance of Honolulu providers and use that as the new national standard, we could really bend the cost curve!

That, of course, is one of the things that Obamacare hopes to accomplish. But effecting such changes will take a lot more than dumping "free" federal money onto hospitals and doctors' offices to upgrade their IT systems. Digitizing health records and building medical databases must be part of a broader strategic vision to redefine U.S. health care delivery around evidence-based medicine, revamp the Medicare reimbursement system to encourage the pursuit of productivity and quality, and eliminate regulatory barriers to medical entrepreneurs who want to do things differently.

Rationing in the Health Care Future

In the absence of transformative reform, back-door rationing seems inevitable. There is a severe and growing doctor shortage that neither political party seems willing to address. As the shortage intensifies and doctors find themselves with more patients than they can possibly handle, they will tend to favor the patients who pay the most. That means drop-ping Medicare and Medicaid patients in favor of privately insured patients.

In a rare instance of agreement, health care analysts concur that a doctor shortage is imminent. The only question is how severe it will be: crippling or catastrophic. There are widespread signs of a shortage already. The Mayo Clinic, praised by President Obama as a national model for providing quality care at costs below the national norm, an-nounced in December that some 3,000 senior patients at one of its family clinics in Glendale, Ariz., would have to start paying cash if they wanted to continue seeing their doctors there. Company-wide, the Rochester, Minn.-headquartered Mayo Clinic, which treated more than a half million patients last year, lost a stunning $840 million on its Medicare patients. At the Glendale clinic, Medicare payments covered only half the cost of treating its elderly, primary-care patients.[102]

Glendale is illustrative of an entire profession under pressure. Ac-cording to an extensive 2008 survey by The Physicians' Foundation, more than 78 percent of all physicians believe there was a shortage of primary care doctors in the U.S. Half said they planned to reduce the number of patients they see or stop practicing entirely. Four out of five said that health care was "no longer rewarding" or "less rewarding" than it once was, and 45 percent would retire today if they had the means to do so.

Lousy pay was the biggest impediment to doctors' practices, ac-cording to the survey. Sixty-five percent of responding doctors said that Medicaid paid them less than their cost of providing care, while 36 per-cent said that Medicare did. One-third of physicians had closed their practices to Medicaid patients, while nearly one out of eight had cut off Medicare patients. Eighty-two percent said that their practices would be "unsustainable" if proposed cuts to Medicare reimbursements were ever enacted.[103] Since that poll was taken, anecdotal evidence sug-gests that physicians are acting on their frustrations. According to a study conducted by the *Houston Chronicle,* 300 Texas doctors, mostly primary care physicians, have dropped out of the program in the past two years. Said Dr. Guy Culpepper, of Dallas: "You do Medicare for

God and country because you lose money on it. The only way to provide cost-effective care is outside the Medicare system, a system without constant paperwork and headaches and inadequate reimbursement."[104]

That was the situation two years ago. Looking ahead, the shortage gets much worse. At present, there are approximately 750,000 doctors practicing in the United States. In a 2008 study, the American Association of Medical Colleges (AAMC) projected that, under a plausible set of assumptions, the U.S. faced a shortage of nearly 160,000 physicians by 2025. In other words, there will be enough doctors to serve only 82 percent of the population.

Why does the shortage get so severe? The population is growing: The U.S. Census expects the country to add an extra 50 million people by 2025. Meanwhile, the Boomer population will hit the 75-year-old threshold at which people visit doctors with increasing frequency, thus driving up demand. While demand soars, supply is not growing to meet it. Indeed, a retirement wave among Boomer docs will make it exceedingly difficult to grow the ranks of physicians without a massive and immediate expansion of medical schools. Making matters worse, there is a shortage within a shortage — the paucity of geriatricians and other health professionals trained in the complex medical problems of the elderly is getting even more acute.

The AAMC calls for increasing medical school enrollment by 30 percent. That would reduce the 2025 shortage by about 54,000 physicians — assuming enough qualified students can be induced to attend three grueling years of graduate school, endure three to eight years of indentured servitude more commonly known as internship and residency, and take on an average medical school debt of $155,000, all for the privilege of entering a profession where income levels are under intense pressure, job satisfaction is declining and many in the profession urge young people not to enter. Equally discouraging, the medical college study evinces little hope that increasing "productivity" (usually defined as doctors working longer hours or spending less time with individual patients) offers a way out. The complexity of older patients' medical conditions will require spending more time with patients, not less. A third option offers some promise: Allow physician assistants and nurse practitioners to assume the doctors' role for some routine procedures. But even that palliative would make up for only 15,500 or so physicians. In the AAMC's estimation, the prognosis is grim.[105]

Remarkably, the AAMC study did not factor into its projections the potential impact of a spreading movement, concierge medicine, which could aggravate the physician shortage. In concierge medicine, primary care doctors charge patients monthly retainers in the range of $150 per month, creating a revenue stream that allows them to take on 1,000 or fewer patients — as compared to 2,000 to 4,000 patients per doctor in a normal practice. The idea isn't for doctors to make more money, it is to develop a more rewarding relationship with patients by spending more time with them, even to the extent of making themselves available by cell phone and email. Advocates of concierge medicine contend that it leads to greater patient satisfaction and, often, to superior outcomes.

A very close friend of mine, Linda Nash, owns a concierge medicine practice, Partner MD, in my home town of Richmond, Virginia. My wife belongs, as do several of my friends. Everyone is impressed by the detailed health profiles they get, the customized health improvement plans, the short waits, the doctors' responsiveness, and the easy access to support staff such as dieticians and exercise therapists. Patients especially appreciate the ability to set health goals knowing that someone will monitor their progress and provide advice and encouragement every step of the way.

Partner MD happens to be one of the most successful concierge medicine practices in the country. Venture capitalists and health systems routinely call Linda to urge her to expand her business model to other cities. She may do so, but only if she can maintain the quality of the company's services. She is extremely particular about hiring doctors who have the right motives for making the change and who will fit in with her corporate culture. If Linda does choose to expand, I have no doubt that she will find a receptive market. The frustration level of both physicians and patients with conventional medicine is very high. People are desperate for an alternative.

But there's a downside to concierge medicine. For every primary care physician who makes the switch from a regular practice (3,000 patients on average) to concierge medicine (fewer than 1,000 patients on average), some 2,000 patients find themselves out in the cold, medically speaking. Some physicians feel really badly about letting old patients go. My primary care physician is one of them. He tried a variation on the concierge theme: easing into a concierge practice over time. As old patients die, move away or otherwise stop seeing him, he doesn't take on new ones — instead he converts a percentage of remaining patients to concierge medicine. He continues treating some patients, like me, with whirlwind visits. (I am too cheap to pay for concierge service, and still in good enough health that I don't need it... yet.) Those who are willing to pay for the privilege get preferential scheduling and more of his time. Eventually, my doctor will reach his goal of a 100 percent concierge practice — it'll just take him longer to get there.

At present, only 5,000 doctors practice concierge medicine nationally, according to the Society for Innovative Medical Practice Design. But the numbers are growing. For every 500 primary care physicians who make the switch, roughly one million patients (order of magnitude estimate) have to seek primary medical services somewhere else, assuming they can find it at a time when the shortage of physicians grows ever more acute. If you are a Boomer expecting to retire in the next decade or so, and if you think you'll be needing a primary care physician at some point, you need to hang onto dear life to the doctor you already have and hope he or she doesn't decide to adopt the concierge model. If you move to a new community, good luck finding a doctor willing to take on new Medicare patients. Of course, you can join a concierge practice yourself and get far better care than what you've been used to. Just be prepared to pay $1,800 or more a year for each member of the family for the privilege.

So, the impending doctor shortage is probably worse than the experts say it will be. And what is Congress doing about it? The one thing it could do — for Medicare patients at least — is to reimburse physicians at market rates for their services. But Medicare is doing quite the opposite. In 1998, Medicare implemented a formula for calculating physician reimbursements called the Sustainable Growth Rate (SGR). Each year, Washington, D.C., goes through the same elaborate charade: Based on the SGR, Medicare recommends trimming physician pay, physicians howl that Medicare underpays them as it is, and Congress enacts a one-year reprieve. The minuet repeats itself the next year, the only difference being that the gap between market payments and the SGR formula is even wider and the potential loss to the physicians even greater. In 2010, the payment gap has reached 21 percent.

Congress has postponed the cuts time after time but, as of this writing in mid-May, the pay cuts were scheduled to take place in June. Whatever Congress does, it faces a no-win choice. Following through on the pay cuts would force tens of thousands of doctors to stop taking Medicare patients, just as the Mayo Clinic in Glendale, Ariz., already has. Conversely, scrapping the SGR formula would require Congress to fess up to the fact that Medicare Part B will cost roughly $240 billion more than official estimates over the next 10 years. That money will have to come from somewhere. Most likely, it will be borrowed ... from the Chinese.

Is There No Hope?

The only hope for U.S. health care is to move immediately to a market-driven system that rewards productivity, quality and innovation that will bend the cost curve downward. The first step is removing the "wedge" between consumers and providers. In other words, eliminate the third-party payer system in which most Americans get their medical insurance through their employer or government, and instill the idea that the cost of health care is not "someone else's problem." The second step is creating market transparency for medical services. Right now, there is no consumer-driven "market" for health care because there is no price transparency, and there is no way for consumers to measure the quality of the product provided by hospitals, doctors and other providers. Third, reform the fee-based system used by Medicare, Medicaid and private insurers that punishes providers who cut costs. And fourth, dismantle the entire regulatory apparatus that frustrates entrepreneurial innovation. As we'll explain in Chapter 9, hospitals and doctors know what they must do. We simply must let them.

Whether our dysfunctional political system under Obamacare will let them is a very different question.

Chapter 4
Debt Shock

The Incredible Shrinking Debt Burden

For decades now, America has dealt with chronic deficits by borrowing money. Fiscal scolds have warned that excessive debt would prove disastrous – government borrowing would crowd out private borrowing, push interest rates higher and choke the economy — and for years the scolds have been proven wrong. Government debt has not crowded out private debt. Interest rates have fallen! Even as the U.S. deficit cracked the $1.4 trillion barrier in 2009, interest rates for U.S. Treasuries fell to the lowest levels in the post-World War II era, and the prime rate (the benchmark for private sector lending) was near the lowest point of more than fifty years. How is that possible?

It helps to recall some history. The current era of U.S. government finance commenced in 1979 with the appointment of Paul Volcker as chairman of the Federal Reserve Board. At the time, the U.S. was wallowing in the 1970s-era "stagflation" of high inflation and high unemployment. In 1981 inflation was running at 13.5 percent and unemployment at 7.5. Volcker broke the inflationary fever by jacking up interest rates to 21.5 percent the following year, and plunging the U.S. into what was, until the 2008 Global Financial Crisis, the worst recession since the Great Depression. But the economy recovered, launching into an eight-year boom marked by declining inflation and interest rates.

The victory over stagflation was followed by the disintegration of the Soviet Union and the opening up of China, India, Eastern Europe and other developing economies. The integration of some 2.5 billion people into the global trading system acted as a check on wage growth in developed countries, snuffing out any budding inflation. As investors became convinced that prices would remain stable, they ceased demanding an inflation premium to protect against the eroding value of their bonds.

The decline from the mid-1990s to the mid-2000s was reinforced by what Federal Reserve Board Chairman Ben S. Bernanke called a "global capital glut" stemming from a worldwide surge in savings. Some of the savings came from developed nations where the Boomer generation had reached the age of peak wealth accumulation, and some of it came from developing nations where government policies favored exports over domestic consumption.

Then in 2008, interest rates fell some more as the Global Financial Crisis precipitated an economic meltdown. The crisis had two effects that made it easy for the U.S. to continue issuing debt. First, it decimated the private demand for credit. Banks cut way back on lending to businesses and consumers, freeing capital to be snarfed up by the Treasury Department. Second, global panic sparked a "flight to quality," and U.S. Treasuries were still regarded as the safest, most liquid debt in the world. During the bleakest days of crisis, panicky investors snapped up T-bills and Treasury notes like beach dwellers loading up on kerosene and lamps before a hurricane. At one point the interest rate on one-year notes dipped to 0.00 percent — literally, zero percent. Basically, investors were saying, "Here, please hold our money. We don't care about the interest. We just want to make sure we can get our money back."

Despite minor swings up and down in concert with the business cycle, interest rates have trended lower for three straight decades. The world's greatest single beneficiary was the U.S. government, which, not incidentally, happened to be the world's largest debtor. By early 2010, the interest rate on 10-year Treasury bonds had declined by more than two-thirds, from 14 percent in 1982 to less than 4.0 percent in 2010. The three-month rate plunged even more dramatically, from higher than 13 percent in 1982 to less than 1.0 percent. Interest rates were so low that the financing cost of the U.S.'s record-setting deficits was virtually painless.

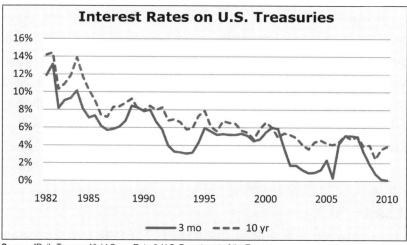

Source: "Daily Treasury Yield Curve Rates"; U.S. Department of the Treasury.

These developments — a decline in inflation, a global capital glut, a global recession and flight to safety — have insulated Americans from the consequences of their government's profligate spending. Between 1990 and 2009, the national debt increased 270 percent. Remarkably, annual interest payments on that debt increased only 44 percent over that same period — less than the economy's 65 percent nominal economic growth over the same period. In other words, interest payments measured as a percentage of the economy actually shrank — from between 4 percent and 5 percent in the early 1990s to less than 3 percent today. Debt problem? What debt problem?

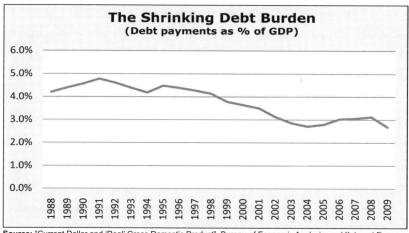

Source: "Current Dollar and 'Real' Gross Domestic Product", Bureau of Economic Analysis; and "Interest Expense on the Debt Outstanding"; U.S. Department of the Treasury.

No wonder Washington politicians are so blasé about deficits and the debt. The plain fact is, deficits aren't hurting us right now. They might cause harm in the future but at present we have an economic emergency to deal with, argue the deficit deniers. By offsetting depressed business and consumer spending, bigger deficit spending can get the economy moving again. Deficit spending also allows the government to make social, environmental and infrastructure "investments" that will help economic performance in the long run. We can tackle deficits, the apologists say, as soon as we have nursed the economy back to health.

So, what's the worry? If people want to lend the U.S. government money for almost nothing, and if the burden of carrying the national debt is no more onerous than it was two decades ago, that's like having our cake and eating it too.

We should worry because the interest-rate environment changes like the weather. At present, the U.S. enjoys the best conditions imaginable. But economic revival, renewed inflation, a shift from a global capital glut to a global capital shortage — or all three — could create a fiscal Katrina. The O Team's official 10-year forecast does contemplate an economic revival (the administration could not very well admit that its policies are leading to economic ruin, could it?), but it also assumes that inflation will remain temperate, and the possibility of global capital scarcity does not even register. Thus, if inflation picks up or if Bernanke's global capital glut dissipates, interest rates will shoot higher than the O Team projects.

It is difficult to project what interest rates will do. If anyone were consistently good at it, they would be trading bonds on Wall Street and knocking down obscene, multimillion-dollar bonuses that would get them denounced by posturing Congressmen on national television. I certainly would not venture a prediction. But I would recommend using the early 1990s as a benchmark for the purpose of sensitivity analysis. The early 1990s are relatively recent history, and it is entirely plausible to think that we could see such a financial climate again.

What would happen if interest rates did return to the 1990 level? Going back to my friends at Chmura Economics & Analytics, I asked Dr. Shuai to run a scenario, based on Obama administration numbers and assumptions, in which 10-year bills gradually rose to 8.0 percent by 2020. Upon Chris Chmura's urging, we added two additional scenarios that I had feared might make it appear that I was pushing my case too zealously, but Chris insisted she found all too plausible: a gradual increase in the weighted average of Treasuries to 10 percent, and a sharp up-turn in interest rates to 10 percent. Acknowledging the possibility that a prolonged European sovereign debt crisis could feed a lengthy flight to "quality" in U.S. Treasuries, which would hold down interest rates until the situation in Europe stabilized and investor confidence was restored, we assumed that rates would not start climbing above the Obama baseline for three years.

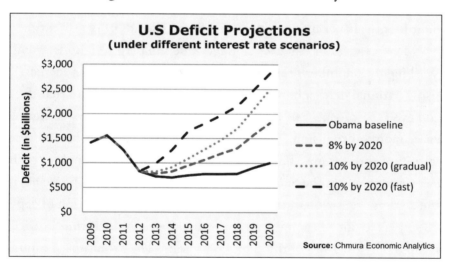

This sensitivity analysis shows vividly how vulnerable the U.S. budget is to hikes in interest rates over and above the baseline scenario — 30-day bills never to exceed 4.1 percent and 10-year notes never to break 5.3 percent — projected by the O Team. The annual deficit by 2020 could surge to anywhere between $1.8 trillion and $2.8 trillion. Under the most pessimistic of these scenarios, national debt could reach $36 trillion, nearly double Obama's projections, while interest payments on the national debt would reach orbital escape velocity, roughly 11 percent of GDP. While it seems inconceivable from our mid-2010 vantage point that interest rates could reach 10 percent in a mere decade, Chmura reminded me that we have lived through such swings before. I am not arguing that the 10 percent scenario is more likely than any other, but I agree that it is possible. If U.S. interest rates do follow this course, it's game over. Boomergeddon will swallow us before the decade is out.

(The chart on the previous page does not show the negative impact of higher interest rates upon economic growth. The masochists among you should check the chart in Appendix A, which shows what happens when we combine the effects of higher interest rates *and* slower growth, which I call the "head for the hills" scenario. I do not include it in the main body of the book because I regard it as an outlier. But I do not omit it entirely because it is not outside the bounds of plausibility.)

Many aspects of America's budget dilemma are well understood. Washington's number crunchers have anticipated spending increases, rising national debt, a hefty burden of interest payments on that debt and even the prospect of interest rates rising as they always do during an economic expansion. The OMBots may have underestimated the impact of those things, but at least they have factored them into their calculations. What the budget meisters do not sufficiently appreciate is the coming transition of the global economy from a condition of capital surplus to one of capital scarcity, perhaps because their time horizon is limited by the rules of the game to 10 years. The evolution of capital markets over the next two to three decades guarantees that the interest rates on U.S. 10-year interest bonds will far exceed 5.2 percent.

Some economists who study the future of savings predict that a decline in savings rates could materialize in the U.S. and Europe as early as 2015 and accelerate into the 2020s.[106] It may not be immediately apparent what's happening because the long-term savings drought will overlay quicker oscillations in interest rates due to business cycles. But we'll know that the era of capital scarcity is upon us when we see the peaks and valleys of each business cycle reaching higher levels than the previous cycle.

The Global Capital Glut

On September 11, 2007, Federal Reserve Board Chairman Ben Bernanke gave a speech before the German Bundesbank in Berlin, entitled, "Global Imbalances: Recent Developments and Prospects."[107] His purpose was to explain why the United States was such a large borrower on the international scene. Many pundits blamed undisciplined American consumers, who were running up credit card debts and treating the equity in their houses like ATM machines. But there was more to the story, Bernanke suggested. American borrowers were only one side of the transaction. On the other side were foreigners willing to lend Americans all that money at remarkably low interest rates. The world, he said, was experiencing a "global savings glut."

Where did the glut come from? In the 1990s and 2000s the Chinese economy grew faster and longer than any economy has ever grown in modern history. The Chinese people saved a prodigious amount of money, equivalent to half their economy by some estimates, and more than even its fast-growing industry required. One reason the Chinese save so much, Bernanke conjectured in his speech, is that the country has a weak social safety net, and households save as a precaution against disaster. Another is that China's under-developed financial institutions make less financial credit available to Chinese consumers, so they can't borrow and spend like Americans have done.

A third, and perhaps the most important, reason is that China, like many other developing nations, learned a big lesson from the so-called "Asian contagion" financial crisis of 1997 that had led to the exodus of foreign capital from Thailand, South Korea and Indonesia and the near-collapse of their debt-fueled economies. To insulate themselves from the flight of foreign capital, many countries pegged their currencies to the United States dollar. China's policy of keeping the yuan artificially low stimulated exports and allowed the accumulation of vast foreign currency reserves to guard against unexpected reversals of capital flows. By 2007, total world foreign exchange reserves amounted to $4.6 trillion. Seventy-three percent of that amount was owned by developing economies, primarily China but also oil exporters such as Russia and Saudi Arabia, which profited immensely from the run-up in oil prices during the mid-2000s but could not usefully absorb the gusher of greenbacks in their own economies.[108]

The result of the global savings glut, Bernanke told the German bankers, was a "sustained decline in long-term interest rates in many parts of the world." The yield on 10-year, inflation-indexed U.S. Treasury securities averaged four percent in 1999 but less than two percent in 2004. The yields on government bonds fell comparable amounts in the United Kingdom and Canada. Inflation-adjusted interest rates fell in Germany, Sweden and Switzerland as well.

Many Americans find massive imbalances in international trade and payments to be a cause for alarm: How long can we continue borrowing without meeting some gruesome fate? However, Bernanke did not see the imbalances as a major problem. The U.S.'s ability to borrow hundreds of billions of dollars reflected the strength of its economy and "the depth, liquidity and legal safeguards associated with its capital markets." Furthermore, American investors made their money work harder than foreign investors did. The U.S., he noted, continued to earn more on its foreign investments than it paid on its foreign liabilities.

But the Fed chairman noted that the U.S. could not continue borrowing indefinitely: "The ability of the United States to make debt service payments and the willingness of foreigners to hold U.S. assets in their portfolios are both limited." He also warned that the savings glut would dissipate "over the next few decades," reducing the supply of capital from emerging-market countries. The logical consequence would be higher interest rates.

Although Bernanke did not delve into details in that speech, there is ample evidence to support his contention that interest rates, driven by demographic changes across the developed world, will climb globally in the years to come. However, it won't take a "few decades" to notice the effects.

The Demographic Sweet Spot

Economists are in broad agreement that demographics are an important driver of national savings rates. As a general rule, children don't save money. They may deposit their Christmas checks in a bank account, but under ordinary circumstances, their function in society is to pluck mom and dad's pockets clean of every stray nickel and dime. Young adults don't save much money either. They make low wages to begin with, they often have student loans to pay off, and what disposable income they do have they spend on clothes, beer, travel... and more beer. By the time they reach the young-married stage, people are generally more serious about life, but they still are in no position to build a nest egg. They go into debt buying houses, filling the rooms with furniture, picking out draperies, and stocking up with cribs, strollers, car seats, playpens and toys... lots of toys. It's not until they reach middle age and reach their peak earnings years that most people start stashing away serious money. The "wealth accumulation" phase lasts from about age 40 until retirement. But then, in the last stage of the life cycle, all except those retirees wealthy enough to live off the income from their investments engage in what economists describe as "dis-saving." The gray hairs drain down bank accounts to pay for their Alaskan cruises, five sets of medications, subsidies to misbegotten children or repairs on their leaking roofs. At least, that's the way it works in the U.S. The specifics differ from country to country, but the patterns are the same.

The "life-cycle consumption hypothesis," as it was dubbed by economist Franco Modigliani in the 1950s, is really just common sense. While economists still fuss over the fine print, there is general agreement that the stage in a family's life cycle affects how much it spends and saves.

Likewise, there is broad agreement that a country's saving rate is influenced by the proportion of spenders and savers in its population. All other things being equal, a country with a large percentage of children and young adults will save less than a country dominated by the middle-aged. Likewise, a nation with an extremely elderly population living off pensions and accumulated assets will tend to have a lower savings rate.

The life cycle consumption theory does not explain everything about saving rates, of course. Look at our own experience in the United States. American households consistently saved 10 percent or more of their income for thirty years after World War II. Then the 1980s brought a revolution in consumer finance — Master Cards for the masses, lower down payments for mortgages, home equity loans, car leases instead of car loans, even no-interest-payments-for-a-full-year teasers on dining room sets, not to mention low interest rates courtesy of the global savings glut. Even as the massive Boomer wave hit its peak wealth-accumulation years, American household savings plummeted. So, clearly, there are other forces at work.

Notwithstanding the U.S.'s dismal track record in saving — which, arguably, would have been even worse had the Boomers not been in their peak savings years — economists have identified a demographic "sweet spot" in which predominantly middle-aged societies experience a burst of productivity, saving and economic growth. The ideal demographic profile is to have most of the population bunched in the middle of the age spectrum, with few dependent children or old people at either extreme. A society in the sweet spot is one that isn't siphoning off a large share of its resources on buying food, clothing, schooling and XBox 360s for economically unproductive munchkins, or on pensions, health care and blue-hair rinses for economically unproductive oldsters. Instead, everyone is working, paying taxes, accumulating wealth, and generating lots of money to funnel into business investment. Growth rates accelerate, deficits decline and politicians take full credit for the prosperity.

The demographic sweet spot is a glorious thing while it lasts.

The Savings Shock

Alas, the demographic sweet spot is turning sour around much of the globe. National economies enjoy a brief "demographic dividend" from lower fertility rates and a reduction in the number of little people to feed and educate. But 20 years down the road, fewer little people means fewer young adults, and another 20 years later it means fewer productive, middle-aged workers to support all those pensioners who are living longer. In the U.S., the Boomers are reaching retirement age, and they're being replaced by a smaller Generation X. For a period lasting some 15 years in the U.S., the number of retirees will surge while the number of middle-aged wealth accumulators actually will shrink.

If nations found that looking after busloads of school-bound children was expensive, it was nothing compared to the cost of looking after busloads of casino-bound old people. The large number of disabled elderly require intensive care-giving just like babies do. The difference, at least here in the U.S., is that when mama changes baby's diapers at home, society incurs no more burden than the two or three months that mama stays home from work. When a nurse changes grandma's diapers in a nursing home, grandma is costing someone up to $74,000 per year for long-term care.[109] While children may cost U.S. taxpayers some $10,000 a year on average for schooling,[110] the elderly cost $11,000 a year on average for their Medicare[111]— and in the not-too-distant future, there will be more old people than children. There's one more really important difference: Children don't collect Social Security retirement benefits averaging more than $1,164 per month on the elderly like 33.5 million elders do.[112] Add it all up and the ratio of federal benefit spending in 2000 was a seven to one in favor of seniors over children.[113] Details may vary from country to country but the basic truth — supporting old people costs more than supporting children — remains the same.

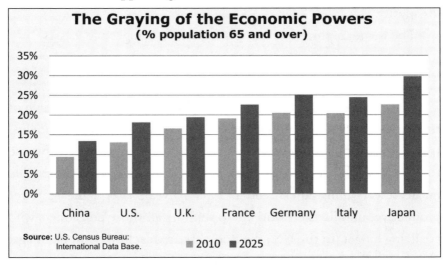

Now, let's apply that insight globally. The chart above shows how the aging will play out over the next 15 years, taking us into the mid-2020s, the period that I expect Boomergeddon to occur. Fifteen years is not a long time. Only 15 years ago, Monica Lewinsky was interning in the White House, kids were clamoring for Beanie Babies, the Macarena was the dance craze, and Budweiser was airing its "Waassssuuup!" commercials. For some of us, it seems almost like yesterday. The year 2025 will be here before we know it. And in that time, most of the world's major economies will see massive shifts of population into the wealth-consuming retirement age bracket.

Other societies have experienced similar household saving declines, most notably the United Kingdom, which dropped from 11.7 percent to 5.3 percent between 1992 and 2009, and Italy which deflated from 20.2 percent to 10.7 percent. Other nations that saw declining rates of household savings over the same period include Australia, Canada, the Czech Republic, Hungary, the Netherlands, Norway, Poland and Portugal.[114]

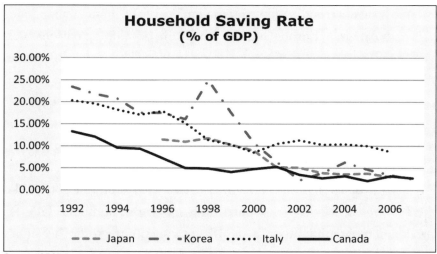

Household Saving Rate
(% of GDP)

- - - Japan   — · Korea   ······ Italy   ——— Canada

Source: "OECD Factbook 2009"; Household Net Savings Rates.

The trend to lower savings is not uniform, however. Every nation's age profile is different, and so are its institutional arrangements for providing pensions and encouraging savings. Several countries, most notably Germany and France, but also Austria, Belgium, Ireland, Sweden, Switzerland and Spain have held their saving rates more or less steady over the same 17-year period. A study that looked at the pension programs of core European nations, Germany and France in particular, concluded that their saving would continue to increase until sometime between 2015 and 2025. However, the study also noted that savings "will decline thereafter" as the populations continue to age.[115]

Although the saving rate rebounded in the U.S. last year as financial institutions tightened their lending standards and recession-battered consumers vowed to reform their spendthrift ways — households briefly boosted their saving rate to as high as six percent in 2009[116] — it may be decades before Americans resume the saving patterns of their frugal forebears. Many Boomers are determined to make up for the retirement savings they never set aside, but they will have only a few years of belt-tightening before they begin retiring in large numbers and living off their accumulated wealth. Mike Finnegan, chief investment officer for the Principal Global Diversified Income Fund, expects more money to flow out of U.S. retirement plans than into them by 2014.[117]

With saving trending lower among many of the aging democracies of North America, Europe and the Asian rim, developing nations such as China, India and Brazil are stepping in to make up the difference. (Who would imagine that Brazil now ranks as the 6th largest foreign creditor to the U.S. Treasury?) Of those, China is by far the most important. Basking in its demographic sweet spot, China's economy is bigger and growing faster than that of any other developing nation. Thanks to its one-child policy, the Middle Kingdom resembles the low-fertility European nations in having relatively few children. But unlike the Europeans, its over-65 population is modest in numbers. That favorable demographic mix is a significant contributor to both China's impressively high saving rate and its rapid economic growth.

Under an optimistic scenario, China's economy would continue growing 8.0 percent to 9.0 percent a year, its people would continue saving at the same prodigious rate, and the country would generate enough new savings to offset the decline in North America, Japan, the U.K. and parts of continental Europe. However, there are two very good reasons not to count on China rescuing the developed world. First and most immediately, China's leadership is acutely aware how dependent the nation's economy is upon exports. The Global Financial Crisis devastated China's export industries, threw millions out of work and threatened social stability. The national leadership wants to encourage consumer spending in order to grow domestic markets in place of foreign markets. If the Chinese leaders are successful in inducing such a change, consumers will spend more and save less. The less they save, the less capital they will export.

Second, China is one of the fastest-aging societies on the planet. As the authors of "China's Long March to Retirement Reform" put it, "China is being undertaken by a stunning demographic transformation" from a youthful society into an aged one. Restricted by the country's one-child policy, women are having fewer babies. (Due to lax enforcement in rural areas, women whose first child is a girl are often allowed to try for a son, so the national fertility rate of 1.8 children per women is still higher than for most of Europe. But in cities like Beijing and Shanghai, fertility is below 1.0 percent.) Meanwhile, the elderly are living longer. By the mid-2020s, the Middle Kingdom will be adding 10 million elders to its population each year, even as it loses seven million working-age adults. By 2030, China's population will be as old as that of the United States (which will be older than it is now). By 2050, there will be 438 million Chinese aged 60 and over. More than 100 million will be 80 or older.[118]

The difference between China and other fast-aging societies is that North American, European and Asian Rim countries are affluent societies with mature safety-net institutions and China is not. While China has lifted more people out of poverty faster than any other country in the history of the world, the nation is still developing. Its 2008 per capita income was less than one-fourth of South Korea's, one-sixth that of the European Union and Japan and one-eighth that of the U.S. Moreover, the transition to capitalism was accompanied by the dismantling of the cradle-to-grave protection, the so-called "iron rice bowl," of the communist era. Fewer than one-third of China's employees, mostly urban workers, earns a pension benefit of any kind. Most families will have to fall back on their children — in many cases, their one child. To make sure there was no misunderstanding about who was responsible for whom, in 1996, the National Peoples' Congress passed a law obligating children to support their elderly parents.

In China, young workers with skills adapted to the global economy make far more money than their parents did at the same age. Household wealth accumulation peaks in the late 30s, far earlier than in western countries. However, in a society where the elderly rely upon their children to support them, it will be difficult for young people to sustain their phenomenal saving rate when they have two parents — and sometimes four grandparents — to take care of.

An aging China may face capital shortages in the future, write the authors of "China's Long March to Retirement Reform." "With China now awash in excess savings ... this prospect may seem remote. Yet ... savings rates, which have risen dramatically in recent decades as youth dependency has declined and the share of the population in the working years has surged, could fall just as dramatically once elder dependency begins to climb."

Translation: Don't expect Chinese peasants and factory workers to stave off the coming global savings shock. In 20 years, they'll be part of the problem.

How about India? The world's second most populous country has a much higher fertility rate than China, and it is aging far more slowly. India's economy, although only half the size of China's, is growing nearly as fast. And its saving rate is climbing, too: from 24 percent in 2001 to a peak of 36 percent in 2008 before backing off slightly during the economic slowdown last year.[119] Could India become the next China for global capital markets?

Not any time soon. One reason that China exports so much capital is that, by the standards set by other governments around the world, its government is very frugal. China's budget deficits ran around one percent of Gross Domestic Product during the 1990s, and rarely exceeded 2.5 percent during the 2000s. Last year, total outstanding government debt amounted to only 20 percent of the GDP[120] — a fraction of the indebtedness plaguing Japan, Korea, Europe and North America. Because China's government absorbs only a tiny percentage of the nation's savings, much more money is available for investment overseas.

By contrast, India runs western democracy-style budget deficits — 8 percent of GDP in 2009 — and its accumulated debt of $2.55 trillion as of mid-2009 amounted to 78 percent of its GDP. For this and other reasons, such as capital controls, India has yet to make its presence felt as a player in global capital markets. Indians barely added anything to their U.S. Treasury holdings last year, raising their total investment to just shy of $30 billion — comparable to the holdings of Norway and

Turkey, and only four percent of what China has invested. Undoubtedly, as India's economy continues to grow, it will export more of its savings surplus. But there is no sign that it will be willing or able to take up China's slack any time soon.

"An analysis of the interaction between demographic trends and bond yields suggest that the era of low and stable long-term interest rates is over," wrote Tim Bond, an analyst with Barclays Capital, in February 2010. The current low interest rates, he said, are likely a "high water mark, to be followed by an inexorable turn in the demographic tide." He continued:

> *Over the next two decades, the boomer generation will age into retirement and run down their accumulated savings. An era of capital abundance will gradually turn into an era of capital scarcity. Government debt burdens will rise sharply, with the risk premium demanded for financing these debts increasing as private sector net savings flows dwindle. Given the broad international context for these trends, with similar developments afflicting almost all the world's major economies, the means by which the government debt burdens are eventually curtailed is unclear. As a result, government bond yields are likely to require a significant rise in risk premia to cover the eventuality of default, either outright or through inflation.*

According to Bond's analysis, long-term government yields in both the U.S. and U.K. will more than double from current levels by 2020, reaching about 10 percent.

Learning to Love Foreign Lenders

So, where does this leave the U.S. government? Under the Obama administration's optimistic budget forecast, the U.S. Treasury Department will have to borrow about $8.5 trillion over the next decade. Under Chmura's 10 percent interest-rate scenario, the feds will require between $19 trillion and $23 trillion. Who, then, will fund the federal government's debt?

The American people aren't up to the task. Last year, according to Bureau of Economic Analysis figures, American households saved $472 billion[121] — in absolute dollars, more than they had ever saved in history. Measured as a percentage of GDP, however, the sum wasn't so impressive — only four-and-a-half percent of disposable income. Moreover, it was a pittance compared to the voracious needs of the federal government. Even if American households had plowed every penny they'd saved into U.S. Treasuries, as opposed to stocks, bonds, insurance policies and other investments, they would have funded a little more than one-third of the deficit.

When the Treasury Department searches for funding sources, it will have to look elsewhere. Aside from individuals and state/local governments, the big owners of U.S. treasuries fall into three broad categories: Federal Reserve and Intra-governmental Holdings, foreign investors, and institutional investors. A breakdown of who bankrolled the U.S. government is shown below.

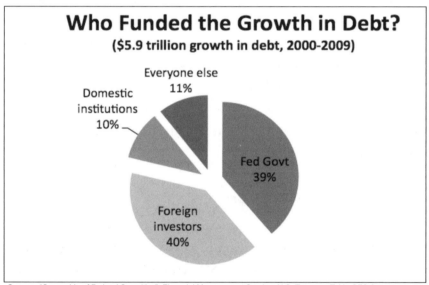

Who Funded the Growth in Debt?
($5.9 trillion growth in debt, 2000-2009)

Everyone else 11%
Domestic institutions 10%
Fed Govt 39%
Foreign investors 40%

Source: "Ownership of Federal Securities"; Financial Management Service, U.S. Treasury, Table OFS-2

Institutional investors. U.S. institutional investors such as banks, pension funds, insurance companies and mutual funds added $613 billion to their treasury holdings between 2000 and 2009, accounting for about 10 percent of the total debt. They are relatively minor players.

Government lending to itself. The federal government was the single-most important funder of its own debt, supplying two-fifths of the borrowed funds over the nine-year period mainly through two sources: the Social Security/Medicare trust funds and the Federal Reserve Bank. Social Security continued adding to the trust fund over the last decade and will continue to do so for more than another decade, although at a lower rate. But the trust funds are peaking as sugar daddies able to underwrite U.S. government debt. By 2017, Medicare will cash in its last Treasury securities. By 2025, Social Security will begin drawing down its trust fund as well, which it will proceed to exhaust within 14 years.

That debt won't disappear off the Treasury's books. Because the Treasury has no cash on hand to meet its Social Security and Medicare obligations, it will have to raise money by replacing trust fund debt with public debt. Here's an analogy. Pretend Treasury Secretary Timothy Geithner is a New York taxi cab driver, and he's in hock to his bookie, Frankie Four Fingers. He keeps falling behind on the vigorish until one day Frankie says he needs his money. Tim is still broke but he can't give up betting on the ponies, so he pays off Frankie by borrowing the money from Guido the Knife. He's in the same boat as the Treasury Department will be when it borrows from China to pay off those Social Security bonds. Guido will bust Tim's kneecaps if he fails to meet his payments. Figuratively speaking, so will China.

The Federal Reserve System also has been a major purchaser of Treasury securities. In February 2010 it had more than $700 billion in notes and bonds on its balance sheet, including $300 billion that it had purchased the previous summer explicitly to support the economy. Of course, buying Treasuries to inject money into the economy — in effect, conjuring money out of the air — is a recipe for stoking inflation. Now that the economy appears to be on the mend, such emergency measures are no longer called for. Indeed, in February testimony before Congress, Ben Bernanke stated outright that he would not allow inflation to increase, contrary to the speculation of some commentators that devaluing might be a way to ease the debt problem. Higher inflation would be harmful to the U.S. economy and living standards, said the Fed chairman. "We are not going to monetize the debt."[122]

Foreign investors. If Bernanke can be trusted, Treasury won't be peddling any more debt to the Treasury. That leaves foreign investors. Foreigners owned 29 percent of the total U.S. national debt as of June 2009. If we exclude the debt owned by Social Security, Medicare, the Federal Reserve Bank and miscellaneous organs of the government, leaving only what economists refer to as private debt, foreigners owned 52 percent. But even that doesn't fully describe the extent to which the Treasury has become beholden to foreign investors in recent years. If we focus on where the money has come from since 2000, 65 percent of it came from abroad.

It appears likely that the U.S. will owe an increasing share to foreigners on a scale unimaginable only a few years ago. As a consequence, the U.S. government increasingly will find itself at the mercy of what journalist Thomas L. Friedman called the "Electronic Herd." When he wrote his book, *The Lexus and the Olive Tree*[123] a decade ago, his focus was the impact of globalization, widely regarded around the world as a phenomenon emanating from the United States, upon other societies. Today globalization is a force by which the world impinges upon U.S. autonomy.

The Electronic Herd was Friedman's phrase for "the faceless stock, bond and currency traders sitting behind computer screens all over the globe, moving their money around from mutual funds to pension funds to emerging market funds, or trading on the Internet from their basements." The Herd knows only greed and fear. It has no sympathy for the weak, no love of country, no sense of fair play, no sentiment of any kind. The Herd wants only two things: to preserve its capital and to maximize its return on investment. The Herd enforces what Friedman called the "golden straightjacket," a set of policies that makes a country hospitable to foreign capital, such as low inflation, a stable currency, a balanced budget, minimal capital controls and other attributes associated with free market economies. Countries that embrace the straightjacket are showered with foreign investment and economic growth. Countries that slough it off, are treated like pariahs. Since the collapse of the Soviet Union, the financial history of the world has revolved around the growth in power and influence of the Electronic Herd, the blessings it bestows well-managed countries, and its chastisement of countries that break the rules, from Mexico to Russia, Argentina to Thailand.

At some point, globalization and the Electronic Herd will turn its sights upon the United States. No country is too powerful to escape its ruthless scrutiny. The U.S. dollar may be the world's reserve currency, the U.S. military may be the strongest in the world, American films, music, cuisine and popular culture may be homogenizing the world, but the Herd cares nothing for all that. Investors only want to know what

Foreign Holders of U.S. Debt						
	Dec. '09	Dec. '08	Increase		Dec. '09	Dec. '08	Increase
Japan	$768.8	$626.0	$142.8	Thailand	$35.4	$32.4	$3.0
China, Mainland	755.4	727.4	28.0	Mexico	31.1	34.8	-3.7
United Kingdom	302.5	130.9	171.6	Norway	29.7	23.1	6.6
Oil Exporters	186.8	186.2	0.6	India	29.6	29.2	0.4
Carib Bnkng Ctrs	184.7	197.5	-12.8	Turkey	28.3	30.8	-2.5
Brazil	160.6	127.0	33.6	Egypt	24.8	17.2	7.6
Hong Kong	152.9	77.2	75.7	Netherlands	19.8	15.4	4.4
Russia	118.5	116.4	2.1	Sweden	19.1	12.7	6.4
Luxembourg	99.9	97.3	2.6	Italy	18.7	16.0	2.7
Taiwan	79.6	71.8	7.8	Colombia	15.8	11.1	4.7
Switzerland	76.0	62.3	13.7	Israel	15.3	18.8	-3.5
Germany	52.7	56.0	-3.3	Belgium	15.2	15.9	-0.7
Canada	48.3	7.8	40.5	Australia	14.1	9.3	4.8
Ireland	39.3	54.3	-15.0	Chile	12.5	15.2	-2.7
Korea, South	39.2	31.3	7.9	Philippines	12.2	11.7	0.5
Singapore	38.1	40.8	-2.7	Malaysia	11.0	8.4	2.6
France	37.5	16.8	20.7	All Other	140.7	147.0	-6.3
				Grand Total	**$3,614.0**	**$3,075.9**	**$538.1**

Source: "Major Foreign Holders of Treasury Securities"; U.S. Treasury.

U.S. treasuries are yielding, whether dollar-denominated assets like T-bills will preserve their value, and whether the U.S. government can be trusted to pay back its ever mounting debt.

The herd cannot be reasoned with. It cannot be cajoled, humored, threatened or begged for mercy. The U.S. Congress and its accomplices in the political class have many ways by which to extract wealth from their fellow citizens: taxing them, eroding their savings through inflation, binding them with regulations, expropriating value from their property by restricting what they can do with it. Congress can get away with almost anything because ordinary citizens have few options. What can they do? Renounce their citizenship? Forego their Social Security benefits? Move to another country? Most Americans can't even speak a second language!

By contrast, the Electronic Herd is beyond the reach of the Congressional writ. If Congress tries to break free from the golden straight-jacket with new legislation, the Herd will respond before the ink is dry. The Herd doesn't have to yank out its trillions of dollars in loans to the U.S. All it has to do is stop lending more money, and it will bring the U.S. Treasury to its knees.

Milestones to Mayhem

The U.S. won't go broke all at once. It will be a long, slow, painful process marked by a thousand steps. We will have years of warning with many milestones to mark our progress. The precise order and timing of these markers is unknowable. But we will pass most of them on our journey to perdition. The dates I have attached to these milestones are conjectural.

2011: Slower-than-expected growth. One of the most critical assumptions embedded in the long-term budget forecasts is the rate of economic growth. More growth means more tax revenue. More growth means less spending on Medicaid, food stamps and other social safety-net expenditures. More growth means lower deficits. From the perspective of fiscal sustainability, growth is good.

The O Team has budgeted a moderately robust economic expansion over the next ten years, with the economy (inflation-adjusted) expanding by 2.7 percent this year, 3.8 percent in 2011 and peaking at 4.3 percent in 2012, and then slowly unwinding to a 2.5 percent rate of growth after a decade. On the face of it, the economic assumptions aren't unreasonable — they represent a higher rate of growth than achieved during the anemic Bush years, but the growth rates aren't as ambitious as the Reagan and Clinton expansions. However, there are good reasons to exercise skepticism. First, the current business cycle is likely to be sickly, and annual growth rates morose, as I will explain in the next chapter. Second, as I have noted already, it takes a leap of blind faith to base budget projections on an assumption of a decade of uninterrupted growth.

By next year, 2011, enough time will have passed to evaluate whether the O Team's short-term economic forecast was optimistic, pessimistic or on target. If growth meets projections for 2010 and 2011, there is a reasonable chance that the forecast will hit close to the mark through the mid-2010s at least. If it falls short, then the U.S. probably will be on a trajectory of slower growth and higher deficits than expected.

2013: Failure to cut discretionary spending. In the 2011 budget he submitted to Congress, President Obama proposed to bring nondefense discretionary spending under control. On the one hand, it would not seem to be too difficult to do, considering that such spending increased from $437 billion in the 2009 budget to $553 billion in 2010 — a 26.5 percent increase in one year. On the other hand, a Congress that could increase discretionary spending by such an amount in the face of $1 trillion-plus deficit forecasts knows no limits to its recklessness. The O Team thinks it can beat discretionary non-security spending levels back down to $456 billion in 2013 before it starts moving higher again. If Obama sticks to his guns, Boomergeddon may arrive a year or two later rather than sooner. If he fails, it's a sure sign that the political process is totally out of control.

2017: Medicare Part A crisis. The trust fund for Medicare's hospitalization insurance policy is projected to run dry by 2017, creating a revenue shortfall of roughly $100 billion a year — an amount that will grow steadily in future years. Congress will face a major test. Will it increase the payroll tax, cut benefits to Medicare enrollees, shift costs to hospitals or finance the program through borrowing? My prediction: Congress will adopt a mish-mash of policies, of which borrowing will be one component. Deficits will run higher.

2017: Currency crisis. For the better part of the past three decades, America's balance of trade has been overwhelmingly negative. At its peak in 2005, the deficit in the "current account" — a term economists use as a scorecard for the trade in goods and services — amounted to $800 billion. It has shrunk since then, but it was still running at a $400 billion annualized rate in the third quarter of 2009. Economists argue endlessly over whether such deficits are a good thing or a bad thing, a sign of strength in the U.S. economy or a sign of weakness. But one thing seems for certain: A country cannot continue running large trade and income deficits forever. Something has to change.

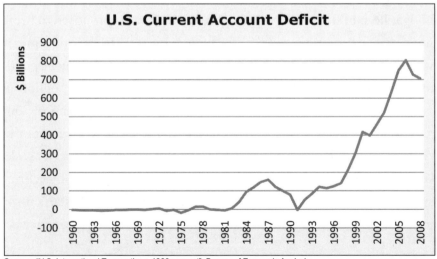

Source: "U.S. International Transactions, 1960-present"; Bureau of Economic Analysis.

In an ideal world in which currencies were allowed to float freely, these deficits would be self-correcting. If the supply of dollars increased by hundreds of billions of dollars a year, then the law of supply and demand suggests that, absent an offsetting surge in demand, the value of dollars would drop in relation to other currencies. With a cheaper dollar, American goods and services would cost less, foreign goods and services would be more expensive, the U.S. would sell more and buy less, and the current account deficit eventually would come back into balance.

Sometimes the real world conforms to theory, especially when countries are committed to market-based policies as the U.S. and the European Union are. Thanks to chronic trade deficits with the E.U., which reached $125 billion in 2005, the value of the dollar steadily eroded against the euro since its launch in 2002. As the dollar lost value, the trade deficit narrowed. Then, during the Global Financial Crisis, demand surged for U.S. safe-haven assets and the dollar regained a portion of its former prowess. The dollar continued to strengthen as the Greek credit crisis stirred doubts about the viability of the euro. For the foreseeable future, the value of the dollar and euro will reflect a tug of war between the increasing supply of dollars due to continued U.S. trade deficits and the demand for dollars stemming from fears about the viability of the euro.

Not all countries let their currencies float freely with supply and demand. Some countries, the East Asian nations especially, intervene in the market to keep their currencies weak compared to the dollar and keep exports strong. China, which pegs its yuan to the dollar, is notorious. Its below-market value currency is a contributor to the massive trade surplus with the U.S., which reached $227 billion in 2009. Because China intervenes in currency markets to prevent the yuan from rising, the imbalances persist. The strategy is not without its hazards. While China's policy does aid its export sector, the accumulation of dollars is inflationary, contributing to potentially destabilizing asset bubbles.

Here's the trillion-dollar question: How long can China hold the peg? And what happens if it allows the yuan to appreciate compared to the dollar? According to official Treasury Department figures, China owned $755 billion of treasury securities as of December 2009. But most analysts believe that is a low-ball figure. For one, it doesn't include $150 billion in securities held by Hong Kong investors. Nor does it include some portion of the $300 billion held by U.K. investors, some of whom may be acting as proxies for the Chinese. In truth, Chinese holdings could be close to $1 trillion. If the Chinese let the yuan appreciate against the dollar, Chinese holdings in U.S. assets, mostly U.S. treasury securities, will lose value. Chinese investors will demand higher interest rates by way of compensation.

The relationship between the yuan and the dollar is a critical variable in projecting long-range budget deficits because the Chinese are our largest creditors. If they insist upon higher interest rates, the U.S. debt payments will increase commensurately.

2018: The next recession. There is no reason, other than blind faith, to expect the current business cycle to be more robust or to last longer than previous business cycles. It is hardly the analysis of a doom-monger to suggest that after seven years of uninterrupted economic growth the U.S would experience another economic downturn, if not that year then soon thereafter. Hopefully, it will not be as severe as the Global Financial Crisis. According to the Chmura Economics & Analytics analysis based on Obama administration data, a mild recession could stoke deficits by $300 billion a year.

2019: Spreading fears of sovereign default. Global financial markets were roiled in the past year by the threat that Greece, a country with a population of only 11 million people, would default on its loans. Greece is a fairly prosperous nation with per capita income higher than the European Union average, but its deficit last year exceeded 12 percent of GDP, and its national debt exceeded 115 percent. As fear mounted that the Greek government would default on its obligations, speculation spread that Portugal, Ireland, Italy and Spain (which with Greece comprise the so-called PIIGS nations) could be the next in line. Suddenly, bond and currency traders are buzzing with the phrase "sovereign risk."

Japan, which may lose its status to China this year as the second largest economy of the world, runs massive budget deficits and maintains $10 trillion of debt. Bond traders are worried that a shrinking workforce, aging population and stagnant economy will erode Japan's ability to shoulder that burden. In January, citing former Prime Minister Yukio Hatoyama's lack of a plan to bring the debt under control, Standard & Poor's lowered its credit rating outlook for the country from "stable" to "negative." Japan's debt remains AA rated ... for now.[124]

In May 2009, S&P also sounded an alarm on the AAA-rated debt of the United Kingdom, lowering its outlook from "stable" to "negative" and appraising the odds as one in three that the nation would experience a ratings cut. This is the country, remember, whose currency, the pound sterling, was once the strongest in the world. But then, the U.K. under Queen Victoria didn't have a massive welfare state that kept one out of six Britons on the dole. The U.K.'s budget deficit is expected to reach 12.4 percent of GDP this year, pushing up its national debt to 67 percent of GDP and putting it on the path to exceed 100 percent within a few years. "The downgrade highlights the precarious fiscal outlook the U.K. economy faces," an RIA Capital Markets strategist told Bloomberg. "We're bearish."[125]

In the short run, the sovereign debt crisis helps the U.S. Our Treasury securities are deemed stronger and safer than the government bonds of the PIIGS and many other European nations, so scaredy-cat investors park their money in the U.S. instead. But this hardly represents a vote of confidence in U.S. Treasury securities — it means that investors regard them as less unsafe than Greek, Spanish and Italian government bonds. In the long run, a default by Greece would cast a shadow across all sovereign debt, including our own.

It is only a matter of time before the debt dominos start toppling. My optimistic conjecture is that the PIIGS will survive the current economic downturn but will fail to make the deep-rooted transformation of their economies and social-welfare programs needed to maintain long-term sustainability. Ten years from now, moreover, their populations will be even older and the degeneration of their rheumatic retirement programs will be all the more advanced. The next recession surely will topple one of the PIIGS nations, infecting sovereign bond investors everywhere with fear and paranoia. The collapse of a country like Spain, a nation of 46 million people and an economy ranked 9th largest in the world, will be felt immediately by other countries with stressed finances. Bond and currency speculators will swarm around other vulnerable nations — Portugal, Italy and Ireland — attacking their currencies like angry hornets, much as speculators weakened Russia, Thailand, Korea, Argentina and Mexico in crises past. Investors will scrutinize U.S. debt more closely than ever.

Declining confidence in sovereign debt will feed upon itself. As nations' credit ratings are downgraded, investors will command higher risk premiums. According to one 1996 analysis, the loss of an AAA rating jacks up interest rates by roughly 60 basis points (or 0.6%). Further declines to a Baa1 rating are worth another 60 basis points. Further deterioration leads to commensurately higher risk premiums: 2.5 percent for a Ba1 rating, 4.5 percent for a B1 rating, and 7.5 percent for a Caa rating.[126] In a vicious cycle, higher interest rates force governments to spend more money on interest payments, which inflates deficits and scares investors even more. It is a very quick slide down the B-level ratings to the very bottom.

2020: State defaults. The state of California, which is reeling from a $20 billion budget shortfall, is like the heavyweight fighter who gets knocked to the floor, staggers to his feet and is saved by the bell: He's still in the match, but everyone knows he can't survive another round. If the U.S. economy resumes growth this year, California may yet rise from the mat. But the structural flaws of its tax system, the power of its special interest groups and the denial of its political class run so deep that it seems inconceivable that the state can stand erect for long. A default by California, whose economy is roughly the size of Spain's, would traumatize financial markets. After all, it's the golden state, the land of dreams, home to the global powerhouses of Silicon Valley and Hollywood. If California can fail, anyone can fail.

Right behind California are New Jersey, Illinois, Michigan and perhaps New York, all once-great states laid low by out-of-control spending, dysfunctional political cultures and hobbled economies. A string of state defaults would spark paroxysms of fear that send interest rates on U.S. Treasuries shooting higher. Congress might be tempted to bail out the failed states, but doing so would create a moral hazard that would make the Wall Street bail-out of 2008-2009 seem like a dime-store transaction by comparison. Once on the dole, these states would never get off — and the U.S. would hemorrhage red ink even faster.

2022: U.S. credit downgrade. In December 2009, ratings firm Moody's said that the U.S. and 16 other countries could lose their AAA ratings if they did not do a better job of managing their deficits and national debts. While the U.S. rating was not under immediate threat, the firm raised the possibility that the rating could be downgraded if its fiscal position did not improve. Said a Moody's official: "Aaa governments with stretched balance sheets will find themselves under pressure to announce credible fiscal plans and — if markets start losing patience –– to start implementing them."

Obama advisor Austan Goolsbee dismissed the Moody's report. "The deficit in the short run is big because we confront the worst economic crisis since 1929," he said. "In the medium run, the fiscal situation is dramatically better and we need to have fiscal responsibility, but the argument that we're going to be a higher risk of default I find close to absurd."[127]

Bernanke didn't sound as confident. In his February testimony to

Congress, he dismissed concerns that the U.S. would lose its AAA credit rating. (Of course he did: Can you imagine the firestorm if he'd expressed doubt in the dollar?) But he admitted that he's so worried about the prospect for higher interest rates that every day he checks the yields on 10-year notes and 30-year bonds. He called them the "critical Achilles heel" of the economy.

Let's see what Goolsbee and Bernanke are saying 11 or 12 years from now when the U.S. national debt (private plus intra-governmental) exceeds the critical psychological barrier of 100 percent of GDP, one or more European economies have gone into default, and the bond vigilantes are betting heavily against the dollar and Treasury bonds. If U.S. debt is downgraded to AA, the repercussions will be severe and immediate. Assuming investors demand an additional 0.5 percent yield on $20 trillion in national debt, the downgrade would add $100 billion a year to U.S. interest payments.

2024: Intensifying capital scarcity. By the mid-2020s, two gale-force winds will be driving interest rates higher. First, sovereign credit risk will spill over to the financial sector. As the perception of risk in sovereign debt increases, the prices of government bonds will drop. Falling prices will generate losses for banks holding large portfolios of the bonds. Adding insult to injury, banks will find their funding costs rising, too, as investors lose faith in the value of government guarantees to the banking system. The International Monetary Fund raises the specter of international banks withdrawing from cross-border banking activities, thus spreading the virus of fear from one country to another.[128] Of course, higher borrowing costs for banks means higher borrowing costs for consumers and business, which will slow the growth of the economy and tax revenues.

Second, as the global financial system shifts from a capital glut to capital scarcity, interest rates will begin a long secular upturn that will last years if not decades. The first effects could be felt as early as 2015, although they will be modest initially. But the aging of the world's wealthiest countries will be well advanced by the mid-2020s. The underlying increase in interest rates will be masked by the oscillations of the business cycle, but the trend will be higher. Tighter supplies of capital will drive up interest rates for both the U.S. Treasury and private investors. Higher interest rates will keep a choke collar on economic growth, which will dampen the flow of tax revenues and make deficits worse.

2025: Draw-down of Social Security trust fund. In 2009 the Social Security trustees forecast that the program's expenses will exceed payroll revenues plus the interest collected on its trust fund by 2025. After some four decades of growing slowly but steadily to $4.3 trillion, the trust fund will plunge like a roller coaster into a terrifying descent. In 2039, just 14 years later, all that money will be gone. But the U.S. Treasury will feel the effects long before. Treasury won't actually have the money to pay back. It will have to borrow the money on the open market to make good on its IOUs to Social Security.

The first year of drawdown won't be so bad — the Treasury will have to borrow only $65 billion in 2025. But that number will increase with each year, reaching $300 billion in 2030 and $594 billion in 2035.[129] The good news — for Treasury — is that the trust fund's IOUs run out in 2039. Of course, that does present a problem for the Social Security Administration, as payroll taxes will cover only 76 percent of scheduled benefits. But those numbers are all academic — Boomergeddon will have knocked over the apple cart by then.

2026: Attack of the hedge funds. Throughout the long, slow demise of sovereign U.S. debt, the hedge funds will be loping alongside, like African wild dogs looking for weak prey in a herd of wildebeest. Employing derivatives, swaps and other arcane instruments that allow them to leverage their capital by 10 to one or more, speculators will sniff out weakness and run stragglers to the ground. As the dollar falters, they will find ways to profit from its fall. As worry mounts over the safety of Treasury securities, they will close in for the kill. The bulls in Congress will denounce the speculators as parasites, vermin and traitors, threatening all manner of punishment. But money can be transferred from New York to London, Frankfort or Hong Kong with the click of a button. If Congress looks like it might actually try to punish them, the wild dogs will slink back into the bush where they cannot be touched.

2027: Failed auctions. What if Treasury gave a party and nobody came? A sure sign that investors are losing confidence in the long-term integrity of U.S. finances will be when they cease purchasing 30-, 20- and even 10-year bonds altogether and start crowding the auctions for two-and three-year notes. Investors will get increasingly skittish about the Ponzi-like nature of U.S. finances, which consists of borrowing from new lenders in order to pay off the old ones. Eventually, pessimism will become so intense that the U.S. will find it impossible to borrow for more than a few months at a time. Auctions for one-year bonds will fail. Then the Treasury will find it difficult to find lenders at any price.

These are the milestones. The only real question is how long it will take us to pass them. Boomergeddon could arrive far sooner than 2027. As the meltdown of 2008 showed us, a financial crisis can unfold with terrifying speed as investor perceptions change. For all the data and all the experts at the disposal of the Treasury secretary and the Fed chairman, America's financial leaders were stunned by the sub-prime mortgage melt-down. They did not see the disaster coming, and they did not fully understand what was happening, much less know what they should do. When they finally did grasp the magnitude of the debacle, the masters of the universe truly feared that the global financial system might disintegrate.

In September 2008, Lehman Brothers, the Wall Street firm, was on the brink of insolvency. The company controlled hundreds of billions of dollars in assets, most of which were considered damaged goods. But nobody, not even Lehman's senior executives, knew which assets were bad, or how bad they were. The situation was fluid, knowledge was imperfect, and the colossi of the financial world were dazed and confused. In his autobiography, Treasury Secretary Henry Paulson recounted how his attempts to find a buyer for Lehman fell apart. Emotions were taking over the financial markets. Panic was setting in. And behind Lehman lurked the specter of insurance giant AIG. "What if the system collapses?" Paulson asked his wife at one point. "Everybody is looking to me, and I don't have the answer. I am really scared."[130]

That's how some future Secretary of Treasury undoubtedly will feel just before the U.S. government bond market vaporizes. But the consequences will be far more dire. Not only is the United States government Too Big to Fail, it is Too Big to Bail Out. If the European Union can barely muster the resources to bail out tiny Greece, there is no one strong enough to rescue the U.S. The magnitude of financial loss will be on a scale unprecedented in world history. When it comes, Boomergeddon will trigger a breakdown that will match the Great Depression in the depth of its misery, its global reach and the chain of calamities it unleashes upon the world.

Boomergeddon

The United States may be in denial today about the inevitability of Boomergeddon, but impending disaster will be abundantly clear 10 to 15 years from now. The all-consuming focus of the media will be the out-of-control budget deficits, runaway interest payments on the national debt, debt downgrades, the declining dollar, bankrupt states and municipalities, the financial collapse of other nations and the evil machinations of hedge-fund speculators. It will seem as if all the major institutions of the country are under assault. Businesses will be failing. The health care system will be breaking down. Social Security will be on the edge of insolvency. Americans will be entering the crisis of the century, and there will be no hiding it.

The trigger for the final collapse could come from anywhere. Very possibly, it will originate overseas. Perhaps the cave-in of a major nation like Japan or the United Kingdom will spark a global run on sovereign debt. Perhaps China will unload its Treasury securities in a confrontation over Taiwan, or in a dispute over oilfield rights in

Cameroon. Maybe Iran will try to incinerate Israel with a nuclear attack. Maybe the U.S. military will suffer a defeat in... who knows where
we'll be fighting then... Pakistan? South Korea? The Caucasus? But the
trigger is just as likely to come from within. Perhaps it will be another
bankruptcy of another over-leveraged, too-big-to-fail Wall Street firm.
Perhaps terrorists will attack the U.S. Capitol or assassinate the president. Perhaps Google will call off its planned acquisition of the state of
California. The possibilities are endless.

Whatever it is, something will ignite the final crisis of confidence.
Borrowers will be reluctant to lend to the United States at any price.
The failure of the Treasury auctions will spur the confederacy of dunces
in Washington to desperate action. But it will be too late. Congress will
try cutting spending, but the special interests and favored constituencies will do their best to protect their boodle. There will be endless dis-
putations over what's "fair," and why the axe should fall on someone
else. Heart-rending stories will abound: families evicted from houses,
grandmothers dying for lack of medications, factory workers laid off
from their jobs, billionaires defrocked of their limousines and third
houses in the Hamptons. Some cuts will be made, but not enough to
balance the budget. Alternatively, Congress may try raising taxes. But
the country will be in a crisis, and heaping taxes on a fragile economy
will not be an appealing idea. In the end, some taxes will be raised, but
not enough. Even if Congress could miraculously close a structural
budget gap equal to one-third of the federal budget, or 10 percent of the
economy, the anti-stimulus policy — call it "suckulus," as in giant sucking sound — would plunge the economy into a brutal recession.

As the machinery of government starts to fall apart — bureaucrats
forced into unpaid work leave, vendor payments stretched out an extra
month, or two, or three, seniors waiting an extra week for their Social
Security checks — the hysteria will intensify. The nation will have only
two broad options left: default on the national debt or monetize the
debt, which amounts to default by another name. Politically, Congress

may find it easier to renege on debt owed to foreigners who, after all, don't vote and, by that point, won't be worth coddling if they can no longer be counted upon to lend us more money. Of course, it will be years, or even decades, before any foreigner lends to the U.S. again, and it's questionable whether any American would entrust his money to the government. But Congress, focused on the bulldog biting its angle, will worry later about the Doberman down the street.

Meanwhile, the Federal Reserve Bank will do what Ben Bernanke vowed never to do: Buy Treasury securities with money created from nowhere, an action that will inject massive liquidity into the money supply and let loose a round of horrendous inflation. There will be a brief lull as the money works its way through the system, and then prices will explode. Within three or four years, a dollar bill won't be worth the paper it's printed on. Inflation will attack everyone, rich and poor, young and old, employed and out of work. But mostly it will savage older Americans who rely upon accumulated savings and fixed incomes to live. In a second round of effects, inflation will create business uncertainty, disrupt price signals, and encourage people to divert capital from productive uses into hard assets that will retain their value. Productive business investment will decline, new bubbles will arise, and only the speculators will prosper.

Depression at that point will be inevitable. Deprived of its usual Keynesian tool for stabilizing the economy — deficit spending — the president and Congress will be powerless to act. No longer supported by trillions of dollars in foreign loans, the economy likely will become mired in a super-stagflation scenario of rising unemployment, massive inflation and punishing interest rates. And that's just the immediate impact of Boomergeddon. A default on foreign debt, inflation and/or a full-scale depression will send shock waves around the globe. Foreign investors will take massive write-offs on their defaulted debt, creating overseas banking crises. Meanwhile, as the world's largest buyer of imported consumer goods, the U.S. will scale back its purchases, in effect, exporting much of its misery. Countries whose economies are built upon the manufacture of discretionary goods, from plastic toys to big-screen TVs, will suffer a debilitating loss of business.

As the economic tidal waves slosh around the globe, nations with fragile political systems could suffer social and political upheavals. In China, whose communist party depends upon the prosperity it delivers to maintain its legitimacy, there is significant risk of widespread civil disorder. Chaos in China would disrupt global supply chains, under-mining corporate profits and creating unemployment in seemingly ran-dom locations around the globe.

There will be political ramifications as well. People rarely take re-sponsibility for their actions. When Boomergeddon comes, the politi-cians and their allies in the political class will have plenty of "others" to blame. Just as Obama upbraids Bush for the horrendous economy he in-herited, Obama's successor will condemn him (especially likely if the successor is a Republican), and the president following him will blame his predecessor in a never-ending line. Some may censure the evil cur-rency speculators and hedge-fund managers who exploit the grievous flaws in the system to amass profits for themselves. Some may wag their finger at foreigners for closing off the money spigots. Generation Xers will reprimand the Boomers, labor unions will condemn the corpora-tions and everyone will be disgusted with the politicians.

The politicians are the ones we really have to worry about. In their desperate thrashing for survival, they will scapegoat anyone they can to divert the public wrath from themselves. Expect to see an endless litany of accusations and Congressional hearings full of bluster and wild ideas. Given the political imperative of all politicians to "do something," the U.S. will reenact in 21st century garb the activism of the federal gov-ernment that under Herbert Hoover converted a stock market crash and a sharp recession into a full-fledged depression through tariffs, tax hikes and monetary contraction, and then under Franklin Roosevelt prolonged the depression for a full decade by escalating the class war, expanding the scope of government and bullying business into defensive paralysis.[131] Whatever the Hoovers and Roosevelts of the 2020s foist upon the country, their legislation undoubtedly will pander to popular prejudice. It is hard to imagine the inevitable emergency measures doing any good.

Boomergeddon will be a terrible time of shattered expectations, great anxieties and widespread suffering. Like the American Revolution, the Civil War and the Great Depression, it will mark a turning point of the American civilization. The collapse of U.S. government finances will lead to a retrenchment of American power abroad: America cannot fund overseas military operations if it cannot pay the soldiers, buy the weaponry or purchase the gasoline they need to fight. Boomergeddon also will lead to a radical truncation of Social Security, Medicare, Medicaid and the rest of the welfare state. I will explore both of those outcomes in future chapters. But first I must dispense with the inevitable objections that Boomergeddon "could never happen."

Chapter 5
Boxed In

Debt Problem? We Don't Have No Stinking Debt Problem.

While some people share the alarm that I feel for the impending default of the federal government, intellectual honesty compels me to inform you, faithful reader, that other people — seemingly normal people, not homeless drifters swatting at non-existent flies or jabbering about CIA plots against them — beg to differ. Paul Krugman, a Princeton economist who won the Nobel Prize for economics and since then has taken up the banner of the progressive movement in the op-ed section of the *New York Times,* assures us that "deficit hysteria" and "fear-mongering on the deficit" has little basis in reality. It's like the groupthink about Weapons of Mass Destruction that took hold during the run-up to the Iraq war, he says. "Now, as then, dubious allegations, not backed by hard evidence, are being reported as if they have been established by a shadow of a doubt."

The federal government's humongous budget deficit is not the result of chronic, out-of-control spending, Krugman maintains. More than half of the deficit was caused by the recession, which led to a plunge of tax receipts, necessitated the bailouts of financial institutions and triggered expenditures to support the poor and unemployed. Those deficits are actually good for the economy. They act as a stabilizer to counteract the shortfall in private spending and business investment. As he writes:

> *Right now we have a fundamental shortfall in private spending: consumers are rediscovering the virtues of saving at the same moment that businesses, burned by past excesses and hamstrung by the troubles of the financial system, are cutting back on investment. That gap will even-*

tually close, but until it does, government spending must take up the slack. Otherwise, private investment, and the economy as a whole, will plunge even more.

The bottom line, then, is that people who think that fiscal expansion today is bad for future generations have got it exactly wrong. The best course of action, both for today's workers and for their children, is to do whatever it takes to get this economy on the road to recovery.[132]

Won't all that government spending push up interest rates and crowd out private spending? Not to worry. Financial markets have great confidence in U.S. Treasuries — just look at the low interest rates investors are accepting. According to Obama administration projections, interest payments on federal debt will rise to only 3.5 percent of GDP a decade from now, about the same as they were under the first President Bush. It wasn't an insurmountable problem then, Krugman says, and it isn't an insurmountable problem now.[133] He acknowledges that the U.S. can't go running huge deficits forever, but the occasional trillion-dollar deficit doesn't bother him. After all, the national debt is "basically money we owe to ourselves."[134]

Robert Reich, whom I quoted approvingly in Chapter One for his acute observations about the corruption of the political process in Washington, D.C., shares Krugman's views. Obsessing over ten-year budget projections is a waste of time, he insists. Remember third-party presidential candidate Ross Perot? "In 1992, he predicted that the federal budget deficit was on track to end the world as we knew it," Reich wrote in his blog. "In fact, the rapid growth of the economy during the following years reduced the deficit to zero."[135]

Delving a little deeper into history, Reich noted that in 1945, the federal debt amounted to 120 percent of the entire U.S. economy. "Yeegads! Yet only a few years later, the debt as a proportion of GDP had been tamed — and not primarily because of cuts in government spending.... Economic growth kicked in big time, and reduced the debt as a proportion of the economy to manageable levels."

The notion that the nation is succumbing to a "hysteria" over the budget deficit seems to be rising among liberal commentators. A Google search of the phrase "deficit hysteria" in March yielded 58,900 results. Even allowing for quotes on blogs responding to Krugman, Reich and other psychoanalysts of conservative psychosis, it appears that a lot of people are using the phrase.

One of those is a gentleman by the name of Marshall Auerback, who writes for the Seekingalpha.com financial website. "The hysteria surrounding fiscal policy has moved from the realm of rational debate and metamorphosed into a matter of national theology," he wrote. Translation: It's the deficit alarmists who are loony, not the defenders of Government As Usual.

Finally, there is a persistent theme that those who obsess about deficits are guilty of selective indignation. Where were all the deficit hawks when George W. Bush was running up the national debt? L. Randall Wray and Yeva Nersisyan in the *Wall Street Pit* put it this way: "The fact that there is a Democratic president in office and a largely Democratic congress frees the hands of conservative deficit hawks who complain about spending profligacy and growing national debt (they usually fail to recall that much of this spending and especially tax cuts have been generated under a Republican president and Congress, not to mention the $780 million bailout of Wall Street.)"[136]

Accusing partisan foes of hypocrisy appears to be a great comfort to deficit deniers. If someone is a hypocrite, their arguments can be dismissed without the necessity of confronting the facts presented. Aside from the logical fallacy of such an argument, Wray and Nersisyan also happen to be ill informed: Many fiscal conservatives were openly and vocally critical of President Bush and the Republican Congress. Now that deficits have doubled under Obama, they're doubly upset. What's hypocritical about that?

Far more disturbing is to see intellectual heavyweights of the progressive movement like Krugman and Reich provide a smokescreen for continued out-of-control spending. Interest payments on the debt will rise to only 3.5 percent of GDP by 2020? That assumes that interest rates will stay low forever. We owe the debt mainly to ourselves? Tell that to the Chinese. The U.S. grew its way out of the debt incurred by World War II? The war lasted only four years — entitlements aren't scheduled to expire ever.

Big-government progressives fear that "deficit hysteria" will inspire fiscal austerity, a withdrawal of Keynesian fiscal stimulus that will hurt the economy, and a roll-back of entitlement spending, undoing much of the progressive agenda over the past century. The fears are legitimate. Any rational person worried about the eventual default of the federal government would propose fundamental changes to the way government operates, and those changes would hurt. But deficit denial will prove even more disastrous to cherished liberal programs when the federal government goes into default in 10 to 20 years. Boomergeddon will precipitate a panicked and uncontrolled dismantling of institutions that the vast majority of Americans have come to rely upon, harming not only the poor but tens of millions of people who played by the rules, paid their taxes and put their faith in the federal government.

Politically, Boomergeddon could do to welfare liberalism what the Great Depression did to free-market capitalism. That's why I'm astounded to see so many liberals trying so hard to persuade themselves that a problem does not exist. Those who warn of impending fiscal calamity are not engaging in some right-wing, libertarian, constitutionalist, freemason plot to take away peoples' benefits so they can cut taxes for the rich. Some of us middle-class blokes want to make sure the federal government is in a position to pay those benefits, to which we have contributed all our working lives. Rather than admit this truth, which is so obvious that it borders on the banal, big-government apologists have built a phantasmagorical explanation of why trillion-dollar deficits are no big deal.

A mash-up of their logic goes like this: If we can just get the economy back on track, we will grow our way out of the deficits. Stronger growth will generate more tax revenues and, voila, half the problem is solved. Once the economy is growing and people are working again, then we can start cutting spending or raising taxes. After all, we worked down a far bigger obligation (as a percentage of GDP) after World War II. Under President Clinton, we even generated surpluses and starting paying down the debt. With a few years of spending restraint, we'll be back on a sustainable path!

It's a comforting delusion. Unfortunately, demographic, economic and political circumstances no longer resemble 1946. After World War II, the nation was demobilizing its armed services and converting its war machine back to civilian uses. Spending and borrowing plummeted. Social Security wasn't a problem because the post-war baby boom meant that there would be a massive generation of young people to support the nation's elders for decades to come. There was no entitlement crisis because there was no Medicare or Medicaid, and there was no health care crisis because the federal government had not begun to "fix" health care costs. Admittedly, a bout of post-war inflation did whittle down the size of the national debt by some 20 percent as a percentage of GDP, but the debt became manageable primarily because of vigorous economic growth — the longest, most robust economic expansion in U.S. history. Measured as a percentage of GDP, the national debt shrank just by standing still.

The U.S. is a very different country today. Ensconced in the nation's capital is an insatiable political class — the same crowd that Reich writes about in "Supercapitalism" — which did not exist in 1946. A veritable army of full-time special pleaders makes the case for an endless list of "needs." With each passing year, discretionary spending gets harder to control, not easier. Furthermore, the Baby Boomers, 64 years older, are on the cusp of retirement. The smaller generation coming behind, Generation X, cannot take up the slack, either as workers, care givers or taxpayers. The U.S. is on the verge of an unprecedented entitlement crisis. There is no demobilizing Medicare and Medicaid. The deficit projections just get bigger — scarily bigger. With the national debt bloating like a whale carcass on the beach, the nation becomes increasingly vulnerable to the coming rise in interest rates.

Finally, the comparison with the post-World War II era is foolish because the economy today is far weaker than it was in 1946. If economic recovery is feeble, deficits will remain in the danger zone and the time may never come when liberals deem it appropriate to cut spending. The economy always will appear to be in need of a stimulus. The more addicted the nation becomes to the Keynesian cocaine of government spending, the more painful — and politically impossible — will be the withdrawal.

The trillion-dollar question, then, is how strong will economic growth be? Can the U.S. grow its way out of its deficit malaise?

The Long Hangover

On the surface, the O Team's 10-year budget forecast seems fairly cautious. This year, 2010, will resume economic growth at a tepid rate, but the expansion will gain momentum over the next few years and then settle into a slow-but-steady mode for the rest of the decade. However, a comparison with previous business cycles shows that the O Team is predicating its optimistic budget forecast on the strongest, longest economic cycle of the past 40 years.

First, compare the Obama forecast (seen on the next page) for the first four years of the business cycle: Under an Obama presidency, the U.S. will outperform the first four years of the Clinton and Bush II business cycles, lagging only the turbo-charged expansion of the Reagan years. Moving into the middle years of the business cycle, Obama expects U.S. economic performance to match Reagan and Clinton. Then, in the final stages of the expansion, Obama expects the economy to keep going... and going... and going — the Energizer Bunny of American business cycles. While the Bush II's business cycle lasted only eight years, Reagan/Bush's nine and Clinton's ten, Obama projects economic growth into the indefinite future in a state of never-ending bliss.

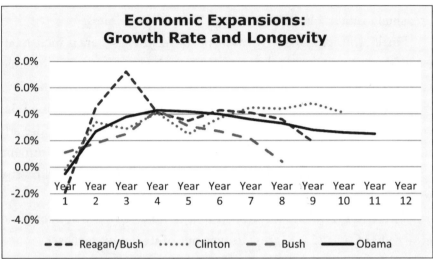

Sources: "Economic Assumptions, Table 2-1", Budget of the United States Government, Fiscal Yasr 2011; "Current Dollar and 'Real' GDP, Bureau of Economic Analysis.

Needless to say, not everyone expects to see such a strong expansion. Some, like U.S. Chamber of Commerce President Tom Donohue, have warned of a double-dip recession brought on by a wave of new taxes, regulations and mandates.[137] I happen to share Donohue's concerns but one need not heed him to think that the current economic expansion will be weak for reasons that predate Obama's elevation to the presidency and have nothing to do with his political agenda. Let me emphasize: Republicans could win control of Congress this fall, Obama could lose re-election in 2012, a new team could enact a new economic policy, and the political pyrotechnics would not change the underlying economic trends.

U.S. consumers are de-leveraging. Consumers account for roughly 70 percent of the U.S. economy, and their spending is the driving force behind economic growth. Over the past three business cycles, consumers increased their buying power through borrowing: running up credit cards, purchasing automobiles and houses on easier credit terms, and tapping their home equity. This trend was particularly pronounced during the Bush II expansion, a period in which incomes stagnated but consumers, buoyed by the rising value of their houses, borrowed more than ever. In the United States, consumer debt grew from about 60 percent of GDP in 1990 to 96 percent of GDP by 2008, according to a McKinsey Global Institute report.[138] A simple arithmetical calculation suggests that debt accumulation added an average of roughly 1.4 percent per year to economic growth over that period.

Not only will the U.S. economy lose the propellant of consumers getting into hock up to their eyeballs and spending with wild abandon, consumers will actually cut back their borrowing. In economist-speak, they will "de-leverage." Although consumers have increased their saving in the past year or two (no mean accomplishment when joblessness and underemployment approach 18 percent of the workforce), they still have a lot of de-leveraging to go. The chart below, based on Federal Reserve Board data, shows that service on mortgages, credit cards and other forms of household debt peaked at 18.9 percent of after-tax income in the 1st quarter of 2008 before falling to 17.5 percent by the end of 2009. That implies that consumers have accomplished less than half of the de-leveraging needed to get back to indebtedness of under 16 percent experienced in the early 1980s before the credit binge began.

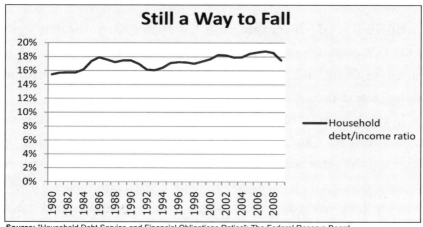

Source: "Household Debt Service and Financial Obligations Ratios"; The Federal Reserve Board.

Economists debate whether the "new frugality" represents a fundamental shift in American values, or if consumers are just making a virtue of necessity as financial institutions curb their lending for their own reasons. Evidence suggests that a little of both is occurring. Boomers have awakened to the fact that they will retire soon and that they have done too little to prepare for life after the paycheck. Although some Boomers will put their faith in God or the U.S. government, others are trying to spend less and save more. Similarly, there is evidence that the U.S. population generally has come to see the pitfalls in a life dedicated to the accumulation of material possessions and status symbols. As part of the nation's greening consciousness, people are increasingly aware that buying more "stuff" sends economic and environmental ripple effects across the globe, from the decimation of rain forests to the emission of greenhouse gases. In a parallel trend, market research tells us that people are more likely to say that the most important priorities in life are friends and family rather than earning money and getting famous. It is unknowable how long this cultural shift will last, but when reinforced by badly burned financial institutions imposing stricter lending standards, it's a good bet that consumer spending will remain depressed for years.

But it gets worse.

Business is de-leveraging too. Consumers aren't the only sector of the U.S. economy in the process of de-leveraging. The commercial real-estate sector and the private equity sector still have a lot of unwinding left to do.

In the U.S., $1.4 trillion in commercial real estate loans will come due between 2010 and 2014. Due to excessive prices paid during the boom and the subsequent collapse in demand, nearly half of commercial properties are underwater, as in, they are worth less than the money owed on them, according to a Congressional Oversight Panel report published February.[139] Rising vacancy rates since 2007 have driven rents 40 percent lower for office space and 33 percent lower for retail. Many developers will go belly up, triggering a new wave of bank defaults. The financial stress tests conducted last year for major financial institutions examined the banks' financial reserves only through 2010 — and they never subjected small and midsized banks to the tests, even though their commercial real estate losses could be proportionately larger in many cases. Things could get very ugly, very fast.

Meanwhile, the U.S. has yet to see the worst of the residential real estate debacle. While the Obama administration has pumped incalculable sums into the housing sector via Freddie, Fannie, the FHA, TARP and the Federal Reserve, it is not clear that prices have hit bottom. Housing has ridden out the wave of defaults on sub-prime loans and "Alt-A" loans (lesser credit quality than prime loans but better than sub-primes), but it is bracing for a tsunami of bad Option ARM (Adjustable Rate Mortgage) loans. During the peak of the housing bubble, financiers kept mortgages flowing by relying upon Option ARMs, which enticed buyers through ultra-low teaser rates and the ability to defer payments by adding to the mortgage balance. Typically, these loans reset after five years, at which point the payments could jump by 60 percent or more. Roughly $750 billion of these mortgages were written, and they are coming due. As Option ARM homeowners go into default, they will dump more houses into a sagging market, which will exert more downward pressure on housing prices. In a downward spiral, more homeowners will find themselves underwater, owing more on their mortgages than their houses are worth. If they walk away from the loans in large numbers, they will put even more pressure on housing prices and the financial institutions left holding the bag.[140]

Indeed, as of this writing in May 2010, there was no sign that the foreclosure crisis was abating. Monthly year-to-year comparisons between 2009 and 2010 showed that mortgage foreclosures may have peaked, but at a very high level. RealtyTrac Inc. reported more than

334,000 default notices, scheduled auctions and bank repossessions in April, a two percent decline since the previous April. Said RealtyTrac CEO James J. Saccaccio: "April was the first month in the history of our report with an annual decrease in U.S. foreclosure history. We expect a similar pattern to continue for most of this year, with the overall numbers staying at a high level."[141]

Similarly discouraging was a report by Neil Barofsky, special inspector general for the Troubled Asset Relief Program (TARP), who concluded that the Obama administration's $75 billion Home Affordable Modification Program (HAMP), which aimed at reducing the number of foreclosures by subsidizing the restructuring of troubled mortgages, was having little effect. Wrote Barofsky:

> *The program risks helping few [homeowners], and for the rest, merely spreading out the foreclosure crisis over the course of several years, at significant taxpayer expense and even at the expense of those borrowers who continued to struggle to make modified, but still unaffordable, mortgage payments for months before succumbing to foreclosure anyway.*[142]

Aggravating the downturn, the real estate market appears to be undergoing a profound shift that will leave many recent projects stranded in locations that are no longer considered desirable. John K. McIlwain, a fellow with the Urban Land Institute, predicts that a "new mode of metropolitan development" will emerge in response to changing demographics. Empty-nester Boomers will prefer suburban town centers with a walkable, urban feel over traditional cul-de-sac neighborhoods. The young adults of Generation Y are less interested in home ownership than previous generations; they, too, prefer walkable communities, though they like to be closer to the urban core. Meanwhile, immigrants tend to cluster in neighborhoods where they can form multi-generational households. In sum, there will be rising demand for pedestrian-friendly, transit-oriented, mixed use development and less demand for scattered, low-density auto-centric development. In-fill is in, sprawl is out. "The suburban century is over," says McIlwain. "This is the urban century."[143]

While emerging human settlement patterns will be more energy-efficient and a net positive to the economy in the long run, the transition will be wrenching in the short run. Demand for projects located on the periphery of most metropolitan areas, the high-water mark of sprawl during the last business expansion, will find themselves left high and dry. This structural change in the marketplace cannot be undone by mortgage loan subsidies or renegotiated loans. The failure of Obama's efforts to revivify the housing market in these circumstances is foreordained. The administration is pouring good money after bad.

Outside of the real estate and banking sectors, U.S. businesses were mostly restrained about taking on more debt during the 2000s Bacchanalia of Borrowing — thank goodness, or losses would be far more widespread and unemployment even worse than it is now. But there were pockets of excess in the private equity sector. The growth of private-equity financial companies, which structure debt-heavy buyouts, led to a surge in highly leveraged acquisitions during the 2000s. According to McKinsey, companies acquired through such buyouts were 2.7 times as leveraged on average as publicly listed corporations. The use of leverage is a wonderful thing for investors if the companies prosper and pay off their debt — big fortunes can be made in a hurry. But if the economy stalls and companies have difficulty paying off their loans, investors and debt-holders can take a beating. By McKinsey's estimate, roughly $434 billion of such loans in the U.S. are scheduled to come due between 2010 and 2014.

Add it all up, and the U.S. economy could experience another $1 trillion or more of write-offs over the next three or four years — and that's just from the problems we know about. Banks, which have barely recovered from the sub-prime loan fiasco, will take another round of hits. To avoid the prospect of more Wall Street-style bailouts, regulators are requiring banks to set aside more loan-loss reserves and strengthen their balance-sheet leverage, which leaves them no choice but to restrain lending. That they will do by tightening their lending standards. No more sub-prime mortgages. No more liar's loans. Lower lending limits on home equity loans. Fewer credit cards issued. More collateral demanded of small businesses. Predictably, the politicians will rail at the banks for taking bailout money only to turn around and curtail their loan volume, but banks cannot simultaneously bullet-proof their balance sheets and ramp up lending. It is a financial impossibility that only a grand-standing congressman could fail to grasp.

% Change in Bank Lending						
	2005	2006	2007	2008	2009	2010(1Q)
Total	6.5	6.1	2.0	-6.4	-15.6	-9.9
Consumer	5.1	5.6	8.0	-5.7	-16.3	-7.2
Real estate	12.9	9.0	-6.7	-15.4	-5.6	-12.2
Business	2.6	3.7	2.9	1.1	-19.2	-11.6

Source: "Finance Companies: Owned and Managed Receivables Outstanding"; Federal Reserve System.

The chart above, based on Federal Reserve Board data, shows the contraction in bank lending across the business, real estate and consumer sectors since 2007. Large, publicly traded corporations have alternatives to bank loans: They can issue stock and sell bonds. But small businesses, the job-creating locomotive of the U.S. economy, depend heavily upon banks and finance companies. Obama's plan to pump up small business lending by $30 billion may help, but it can't make up for the $110 billion decline in bank lending to business last year alone. If the banks can't lend, small businesses can't hire, and the economy can't grow. Especially worrisome for the prospects of a strong economic rebound this year, lending continued to shrink in the 1st quarter.

State and local government under siege. State and municipal governments, which constitute nine percent of the economy, will be another drag on economic recovery. While they suffer declining tax revenues like the U.S. government, they can't print money and they are far more restricted in how much they can borrow. Unlike the federal government, they are making painful cuts, laying off thousands of employees, tightening routine spending, and delaying capital construction projects. State and local governments will recover eventually — they always do. But in this economic cycle, it may take years to see a revival in revenues, and recovery will be slow.

The Center of Budget and Policy Priorities estimated that budget shortfalls just for the states (not including municipalities) amounted to $196 billion in fiscal 2010. Next year will show little improvement: Shortfalls will reach $180 billion. Two years from now, states still will be feeling the pain, with another $120 billion in shortfalls.[144] States will close the budget gaps primarily by cutting spending and raising taxes, both of which will depress economic activity, or by issuing long-term debt, which will defer the hard choices.

The long-term outlook for state and municipal governments does not look any rosier. At some point they will have to come to grips with their massive unfunded pension liabilities, the ever-escalating cost of Medicaid and the high cost of delivering government services to communities prone to scattered, low-density, auto-centric growth. Although states cannot borrow money to balance their budgets, they can underfund their pension plans, which, when you think about it, is akin to borrowing from their workers' retirement funds... but without the workers' permission. All told, state and local governments have pension assets totaling about $2 trillion and, depending on the accounting assumptions used, have liabilities totaling $3.1 to $5.2 trillion, contended Robert Novy-Marx and Joshua D. Rauh in a 2009 paper.[145] If state/local governments begin funding their pensions properly, they will remain stuck in fiscal purgatory for years to come. If they duck their obligations, they will face their own mini-Boomergeddons when their Boomer employees retire and outlays spike higher.

Withdrawing the federal needle. The United States, like other advanced economies, staved off a global financial meltdown and quite possibly a global depression through historically unprecedented stimulus action, from one-time emergency spending programs like the Troubled Asset Relief Program (TARP) and the American Recovery and Reinvestment Act (ARRA, aka the "stimulus bill") to the injection of massive liquidity into financial markets. Few financial commentators dispute the idea that desperate measures were called for to combat the massive loss of confidence in financial markets. But even Keynesians like Krugman acknowledge that countries cannot deficit-spend themselves to prosperity forever. At some point, when the economy is judged to be capable of self-sustained growth, the country must go off the needle.

Among the major U.S. stimulus actions, TARP seems to be faring the best. The capital infusion into the banking industry helped prevent a meltdown of the financial system. Now private capital is replacing public capital, as originally intended. As of mid-February, $170 billion of the $240 billion that Uncle Sam invested in the banking system had been repaid, and there was a reasonable expectation that billions more would be in the future. In more good news, the U.S. Treasury announced that it expects to spend only $550 billion of the $700 billion authorized.[146] Repayment of TARP money is a blessing for the taxpayer — it is money that will not be added to the deficit.

The stimulus bill — or as dubbed by Rush Limbaugh, the "porkulus" package — is more problematic. Originally spun as a quick-acting stimulus to combat the recession, the ARRA is, in practice, dribbling out its billions over three years. As of mid-March this year, only 36 percent of the $787 billion had been paid out.[147] The good news, macroeconomically speaking, is that the feds have enough un-spent money in the hopper that they can maintain the stimulus, such as it is, for another couple of years. The bad news is that the stimulus will come to an end, creating another drag on the economy. (I refrain from commenting upon the dubious merits of how the stimulus money was spent.)

The Federal Reserve Board also acted aggressively to combat the recession by reducing the discount rate (the rate at which the Fed lends money to banks) to one-half of one percent, and the federal funds rate (the rate at which banks lend their balances at the Federal Reserve to other depository institutions) to nearly zero. These actions drove down short-term interest rates. The Fed also held down mortgage rates by purchasing $175 billion in Freddie Mac and Fannie Mae debt and up to $1.25 trillion of their mortgage-backed securities. Additionally, the Fed authorized the purchase of up to $300 billion in longer-term Treasury securities.

Acutely aware that the printing of money has the potential to be inflationary, the central bank has promised that it will unwind its bank lending programs when the economy recovers. Further, it has announced that it will purchase no more mortgage-backed securities. However, the Fed is reluctant to retrench too rapidly for fear of smothering the expansion. In revealing its future intentions in March, the Fed stuck to year-old language stating that short-term interest rates will remain "exceptionally low" for an "extended period," meaning for at least several more months.[148] Bottom line: Barring an unexpected emergency, there is no more monetary stimulus to look forward to. The question is when the Fed will start tightening.

Add it all up: Consumers continue to retrench, the commercial real estate sector is imploding, the housing sector is mired in debt and foreclosures, banks are hard-pressed to increase lending to small and mid-sized businesses, local governments are still retrenching and the federal government is slowly dialing back the fiscal and monetary stimulus. It's one ferocious economic hangover. And that's before we even consider the impact of letting the Bush tax cuts expire, the cost of Obamacare, and the tremendous uncertainty created by the Democrats' activist agenda on issues ranging from financial regulation to cap-and-trade. It would be remarkable indeed for the economy to live up to the O Team's long-range forecasts. If growth falls short, as I believe it will, deficits over the next few years will mount far more rapidly than the O Team and the deficit deniers anticipate. (I refer you back to the chart on page 73 to show the impact of economic growth averaging one percentage point less than the official forecast.)

Eventually, consumers and businesses will pay down their debt, state and local governments will stabilize their budgets, and the federal government will complete the withdrawal of extraordinary stimulus measures. In time, the U.S. will have purged the excesses of the past. Then the economy will be ready to resume its traditional robust growth... won't it?

Paddling Against the Current

Our problems won't be over, not by a long shot. The U.S. economy will be paddling upstream in the face of powerful currents reshaping the global economy.

The first challenge is the demographic tide of aging populations in the U.S. and worldwide: Advanced economies, and even some developing economies like China and Brazil, are graying rapidly. Over the next two decades in leading economies, smaller percentages of the population will be working and the number of elderly dependents will grow. Economic growth will slow, especially in North America, Europe and the Asian Rim, savings will decline, the capital glut will diminish and interest rates will rise.

The second great tide is increasing resource scarcity. As millions of Chinese, Indians, Brazilians, Southeast Asians and others seek the accoutrements of middle-class living standards like electric power, modern housing, automobile and meat-heavy diets, they will bid up global prices of energy, food and raw materials.

Thirdly, the projected accumulation of debt will put the U.S. in a fiscal straight jacket that could slow the rate of economic growth by as much as one percentage point annually. At some point, U.S. economic authorities will be compelled to pursue tighter fiscal policies in order to maintain credibility with the bond investors who are keeping the government afloat.

Fourthly, the U.S. once could count on the dynamism of its entre-preneurial economy to adapt to changing circumstances through gales of creative destruction, replacing the industries of the past with the growth industries of the future. But U.S. capitalism is undergoing a shift from competing in the marketplace to competing in the political arena. The industries of the past will use their political clout to protect mar-kets, gain preferential access to capital and otherwise lay claim to soci-ety's resources at the expense of emerging industries. Creative destruction will be less destructive of the old order and less creative of the new than in the past.

There are minor eddies and back-currents that will help offset these broad trends, and we will discuss one of them. But the overall picture is grim. In the absence of some spectacular new technology on the scale of steam engines, electric power or semiconductors to give a huge pro-ductivity jolt to world economies, the economic future 20 years out does not look very promising.

Global aging. Employment growth has been a major contributor to economic expansion in all the world's advanced economies, ac-counting for 18 percent of the growth in Japan and Europe, 36 percent in the English-speaking countries, and 51 percent in the U.S. between 1960 and 2005.[149] But stagnant working-age populations portend mod-est growth or actual shrinkage of the developed world's workforce in the decades ahead. Thanks to immigration and higher fertility rates, the demographic profile of the U.S. looks better than that of other ad-vanced economies — but that's akin to saying that Hulk Hogan is bet-ter looking than Dog the Bounty Hunter. A working-age population expected to increase 28 percent in the next 45 years makes the U.S. the demographic pretty boy of the Western world. But that compares to a working-age population growth of 83 percent in the previous 45 years. We're looking at a major slowdown in workforce growth. All other things being equal, this one trend alone guarantees that long-term U.S.

economic growth will be slower by one percentage point a year than in the past.

Not only are populations getting older, workforces are aging as well. Richard Jackson and Neil Howe cite a number of reasons why productivity across the economy may suffer as a consequence. First, older workers are less mobile, which means they are less willing to relocate or retrain. Labor markets with more older people are slower to adjust to changing conditions, industries cannot expand or shrink as rapidly, and unemployment tends to last longer. Second, older managers tend to be more risk averse and less entrepreneurial. (There are indications, however, that this generality may be less true of the Boomer generation.[150]) Third, individual productivity peaks in the 40s and enters a steady decline in the 50s. Fluid cognitive abilities related to reasoning speed and learning in new environments decline the most rapidly. People can offset the loss of fluid cognitive abilities through the accumulation of structured knowledge and facts, which erode more slowly, and through cultivation of traits such as experience, patience and maturity, which may improve with age. So, although fluid cognitive abilities may peak in the 20s, productivity peaks in the 40s. But when people reach their 50s, individual productivity enters a steady decline. Unfortunately for U.S. productivity, most of the growth in the U.S. workforce over the next two decades will occur among workers 50 and older. As Jackson and Howe remark, this trend could create a serious disadvantage for the U.S. during an era of rapid technological change.

There is one other important consequence of an aging population, which I discussed at length in the previous chapter: As retirees draw down their savings, economy-wide savings rates decline. Diminished savings translate into higher interest rates, less investment and lower rates of economic growth.

One reason — not the only reason, but an important one — that the U.S. economy performed so well during the Reagan and Clinton eras is that it was basking in the demographic sweet spot. With

Boomers in middle age, a disproportionate number of all Americans were (a) in the workforce, (b) in the wealth-accumulation phase of their life cycles, and (c) in the most economically productive years of their lives. Today, our demographic glory days are behind us. The U.S. is transitioning into the demographic sour zone, moving from the demographic dividend to demographic decadence. Demography is not the only factor influencing economic growth, of course. But it is very important. Given the demographic transition, it is foolhardy to assume that we will resume past patterns of growth.

Resource scarcity. The global economy will be more sensitive to energy and resource scarcity than in previous business cycles. China, India, Brazil and other large developing nations have emerged as major consumers of oil, coal, iron and other raw materials. China, which only 20 years ago depended upon bicycles as its primary mode of urban transit, now vies with the U.S. to be the world's largest market for and second largest manufacturer of automobiles. China has become the world's second largest generator of electric power, and the world's largest producer of coal. On a massive scale, the Chinese are transforming the housing stock of peasant cinderblock huts to condominiums supplied with utilities and modern furnishings — and even a few U.S.-style cul-de-sac subdivisions. The Chinese are upgrading their diets as well, not only ingesting more calories but eating more meat, which is far more resource-intensive to produce. Indeed, the Chinese are eating so well that, based on 2000 data, 24.5 percent of all adults were overweight and 3.0 percent were obese — and the measures were rising fast.[151]

Similar trends can be seen in India, Brazil and the more prosperous nations of the developing world. This explosive demand-side revolution in the global market for energy, raw materials and food is not being matched by a commensurate revolution in supply. The most visible challenge is that of "peak oil." The vast reservoirs of oil and gas discovered in the heyday of the oil industry are being depleted. Energy companies have been extraordinarily resourceful at identifying new supplies but finds are located in deeper waters, or in more fractured geologies, or in other places where the oil is far more expensive and, as the Deepwater Horizon oil spill disaster in the Gulf of Mexico has so forcefully reminded us, environmentally risky to extract. Oil and commodity prices plunged during the Global Financial Crisis as demand in the U.S. and other advanced economies drove off a cliff. But prices will likely surge again, probably earlier in the business cycle and arguably reaching higher levels. The price of oil, trading for about $80 per barrel in the spring of 2010, could easily spike above the $150-per-barrel level of the previous expansion.

Oil selling for $150 per barrel would pose enormous difficulties for the energy-intensive economy of the United States, which relies upon imports for nearly two-thirds of its oil supply. Each $1 rise in the price of oil adds roughly $4 billion to the annual balance of payments deficit.[152] A return to the days of $150 per barrel — an increase of $70 per barrel — would add some $280 billion to the balance of payments deficit.

Talk of achieving "energy independence" is a fantasy. Successive presidential administrations since the 1973 Arab oil embargo have pushed energy independence, and the U.S. has lost ground almost every year. The much-touted shift to green technologies may bring some improvement, but the transition will take longer than the optimists expect. Most renewable fuels — wind power, solar power, bio-fuels — are aimed at replacing coal used to generate electricity, not oil used primarily for transportation. Only when electric vehicles develop performance characteristics competitive with gas-powered vehicles will the renewable energy/electricity matrix begin to compete with the oil-based transportation economy. Even then, it will take decades to re-balance electric power production, upgrade the electric grid and install recharging stations outside the home.

Developments in the energy economy have implications for the agricultural economy as well. Agricultural production around the globe is increasingly energy-intensive, substituting tractors, fertilizers, herbicides and pesticides for raw human labor. That substitution has created an agricultural bounty never seen before. But there is a downside: The energy intensive nature of food production makes it more vulnerable to increases in the price of energy.

By one estimate, the demand for food will increase 50 percent by 2030, driven by a growing world population, rising affluence and shifts to Western dietary preferences. "Between now and 2025, the world will have to juggle competing and conflicting energy security and food security concerns, yielding a tangle of difficult-to-manage consequences," says "Global Trends 2025: A Transformed World." "[The] 'fuel farming' tradeoff, coupled with periodic export controls among Asian producers and rising demand for protein among growing middle classes worldwide, will force grain prices in the global market to fluctuate at levels above today's highs."[153]

By no means am I a "limits of growth" alarmist who foresees collapsing agricultural production and mass starvation, nor do I think we are "running out" of oil. Humans are resourceful. I have confidence that science and capitalism will devise new technologies, identify new energy sources, find substitutes for scarce commodities and find more energy-efficient ways to do things. But it does not make me a fuzzy-minded One Worlder to acknowledge that a planet in which 2.4 billion Chinese and Indians are clamoring to enjoy the same middle-class living standards as one billion inhabitants of the developed world will boost demand for most commodities faster than producers can increase supply in the face of ever-tighter environmental constraints. Nor does it make me a member of Greenpeace to acknowledge that humans have consumed or degraded much of their natural inheritance: depleting the easily accessed deposits of fossil fuels, devastating the ocean's fish populations, eroding the soil of the world's most fertile farmlands, creating expanding dead zones in the world's seas and toxic no-go zones on the land, sucking the water from rivers and aquifers, denuding the coastlines of wetland buffers and pillaging the world's great forests.

In a global economy, tectonic shifts in supply and demand don't spell an end to the petroleum era or portend a crippling scarcity of food and raw materials. But they do suggest that commodity costs will experience upward pressure for decades to come. Prices still will fluctuate up and down. But relative scarcity will ignite inflationary pressures earlier in the business cycle, forcing governments to counteract with tighter fiscal and monetary policies. Two or three years into the new economic expansion, the U.S. will start feeling the pinch.

Loss of fiscal flexibility. Several years ago business school professors Carmen Reinhart and Kenneth Rogoff built a massive database of financial data, spanning 44 countries and extending back to the 19th century, with an eye to better understanding the debt crises that periodically disrupted the capitalist world. They have been mining the database for insights ever since. One of their key findings was that the accumulation of national debt, up to a point, had no negative effect on a country's rate of economic growth. However, when national debt exceeded 90 percent of a country's annual economic output, economic growth consistently began to deteriorate. On average, the median growth rates of high-indebtedness countries fell by a full percentage point.[154] In other words, a country that typically experienced three percent annual growth would see its growth rate decline to two percent after it crossed the threshold.

Reinhart and Rogoff aren't certain what happens at that 90 percent tipping point, but they hypothesize that investors get squeamish about the nation's indebtedness and start demanding a higher risk premium on the interest rates they are paid. Higher payments on the national debt crowd out other categories of government spending, including those that might stimulate economic growth, and limit macro-economic policy options such as cutting taxes and boosting spending.

According to Obama administration forecasts, U.S. Treasury debt held by the public in 2020 will exceed $18.6 trillion, equivalent to 77.2

percent of the economy at that time. If debt held by the Social Security trust fund, other federal agencies and/or the Federal Reserve Bank were included, total indebtedness would vault well over the 90 percent mark. A slowdown in U.S. economic growth would cause more budget hardship. Lower growth = lower tax revenues = bigger deficits = more borrowing, in a vicious cycle.

The rent-seeker economy. Economists use the term "rent seeking" to describe the actions of corporations utilizing the coercive power of the state to advance their narrow economic interests at the expense of the public good. Rent seekers have always existed in American history, from the war profiteers of the French and Indian War to textile manufacturers who hid behind Hamiltonian tariffs, from the railroad monopolists of the Gilded Era to agribusinesses creating government-enforced cartels in farm commodities during the Great Depression. The difference between the 19th and 21st centuries is the size and scope of the federal government and the power of Congress to dispense favors. In the 19th century, the federal government had limited powers to tax, borrow and regulate. It did control access to vast tracts of unsettled lands, which exerted a magnetic effect on railroads and land speculators, but otherwise there was little for most businesses to gain from spending time in Washington, D.C.

The rise of the progressive movement in the early 20th century, the New Deal in the 1930s and the Great Society in the 1960s ushered in a vast expansion of federal power. The rise of Washington, D.C., from a malarial town on the swamps of the Potomac River into an imperial city — the nation's fifth largest metropolitan area — is the story of the extension of government power into every crevasse of the American economy. Initially, corporations established a Washington presence to protect themselves from the meddling of reformers and do-gooders. But in time, they saw opportunities to exploit the government's powers in ways unforeseen by the reformers to benefit themselves. When the reformers passed from the scene, the corporate interests remained behind as a permanent presence, the foundation of the political class. Often, they captured the very regulators meant to oversee them.

Today, the political class exercises control over vast swaths of the American economy through direct federal expenditures, through tax subsidies, through preferential access to credit, and through the regulatory structure of entire industries such as telecommunications and health care. If government had been this large and powerful in 1860, it would not be far-fetched to speculate that the whaling and potbelly stove industries would have halted the rise of the coal and petroleum sectors. The equine, carriage and buggy-whip industries still would be a powerful economic force.

It is an iron rule of political economy: Dominant industries will utilize their wealth and power to influence the political and regulatory arenas to protect their dominance. They will manipulate the regulatory process to favor themselves over smaller, nimbler competitors. They will seek subsidies under the guise of saving jobs or advancing the public interest. They will raise tariffs and other trade barriers to limit competition from overseas. Corporations that maximize profits through rent-seeking are less likely to invest in productivity and innovation, the only true sources of economic progress. By gaining preferential access to capital, they will starve the entrepreneurial sector of the economy — as is occurring in the current business cycle. Rent-seeking economies will be more stable, but they will be less dynamic, economic growth will be slower, the tax base will be smaller, and deficits will be bigger.

America Alone

I do see one positive mega-trend affecting America's economic future. Sadly, our good luck will stem from the misfortunes of others. European nations are sliding even more rapidly than we are down the curve to institutional sclerosis and fiscal decrepitude. Their working populations are aging and soon will be shrinking. Their welfare states are even more swollen than our own, their economies are more hobbled by taxes and regulations, and the governments of many are even deeper in debt. In the past year, worries about Greece's ability to pay its sovereign debt prompted investors to dump euro-denominated investments and buy U.S. Treasuries. The emotion was a mere frisson of fear, however, compared to hair-raising developments to come.

Europe has one other drawback compared to the U.S.: large and growing minorities of increasingly radicalized Muslims. For whatever reason, Europeans have been unable to assimilate Muslims into mainstream society in the same way that the U.S. appears able to assimilate its vast immigrant Hispanic population. Indeed the secular culture of the indigenous European population increasingly seems to be at odds with the religious culture of the Muslim immigrants. An indigenous backlash is building, as witnessed by the French campaign against head scarves, the Swiss restrictions on mosques and the clampdown on immigration generally. Such measures are sure to antagonize Muslims and inspire greater assertion of cultural identity. Yet none of the restrictions are likely to reverse the fact that the one fecund demographic segment in Europe consists of people who face Mecca when they pray. While the fertility rates of Spaniards, Italians and Germans push those venerable cultures towards extinction, imams talk openly of conquering Europe in the bedroom — out breeding the native Europeans.

The Muslim population, which was negligible in the 1950s, has grown to 38 million, or 5 percent of the European Union population today.[155] Between immigration and higher birth rates — the Muslim birth rate is three times higher than that of the natives[156] — the Muslim population is said to be increasing 10 times faster than other inhabitants of the United Kingdom. Indeed, it was commonly said that mosques in the Sceptered Isle have more worshippers than does the Church of England. Comparable changes are taking place in other European countries. In France, 10 percent of the population is already Muslim. In Brussels, the most popular boy's name is Mohamed. As Libyan strongman Muammar Gadhafi told Al-Jazeera: "We have 50 million Muslims in Europe. There are signs that Allah will grant Islam victory in Europe — without swords, without guns, without conquests ... [They] will turn it into a Muslim continent within a few decades.[157]

Before the end of the century, some fear, some European nations will have Muslim majorities. But it will not be necessary for Muslims to dominate the electorate if they can command the streets. Columnist Marc Steyn makes the point that while Muslims account for only 10 percent of the population of France, they represent some 30 percent of the population under the age of 20, and 45 percent of the youth in some major urban centers.[158] Project the demographics out another generation, then think of the car-burning restiveness in Paris' banlieus magnified by a factor of three or four. Silver-haired pensioners don't make credible riot police. Either through threats or persuasion, Muslims will become increasingly assertive of their rights.

But long before Muslims seize power in the voting booth or even come to rule the rues and strasses, an increasing number of Europeans will see the drift of things to come. Educated young people will migrate to the U.S., Canada, Australia, New Zealand and other culturally hospitable nations to make a living. The wealthy will repatriate money abroad, just as the Jews secreted their money out of Germany during Hitler's rise to power. In the U.S., Europe's millionaires will purchase U.S. Treasuries, South Beach condos, Virginia horse country estates and equities of AAA-rated American corporations — enough to live in comfort if they have to flee their homelands. For the U.S. and other English-speaking countries outside Europe, and perhaps the more stable democracies in Latin America and the Caribbean, the influx of capital will buoy their currencies and drive down the cost of borrowing.

To what degree will European capital flight offset all the other forces retarding economic growth, destabilizing the dollar and downgrading the credit-worthiness of U.S. debt? It depends upon the timing. How long can European governments keep a lid on restive Muslim populations? What restrictions might they impose on emigration and capital flight? How rapidly will European economies deteriorate? If it takes 10 to 20 years before human and capital flight from Europe becomes significant enough to measure, it may not come in time to forestall Boomergeddon.

The Taxman Cometh

It is the fond hope of Paul Krugman and his ideological soul mates that at some point economic growth will resume with sufficient vigor that the federal government can begin pruning discretionary spending. That is, in fact, the very budget scenario laid out by the Obama administration for the decade ahead. I have made the case that the U.S. economy is not likely to catch fire in the current economic cycle. Growth will be tentative, unemployment will linger and deficits will stay chronically high. Even if a lukewarm recovery does take root and economic growth does become self-sustaining, what are the odds that the O Team — or any Republican administration that might supplant it — would have the fortitude to cut spending enough to reverse the head-long rush to Boomergeddon?

Budget cutters will encounter formidable resistance. Under the best-case (and highly unlikely) Obama scenario, the lowest annual deficit in the decade ahead will be $706 billion. However, the backlog of "unmet needs" will not have disappeared. The special pleaders will not have gone into hiding. There will be calls for more money for schools and student loans, for roads and for high-speed rail, for wind mills and solar power, to prosecute the war against radical Islam and to counteract China's military build-up. The list of "needs" is endless. Meanwhile, absent fundamental reform, health care will emerge again as a pressing concern. The Medicare trust fund and Social Security trust fund for the disabled will nearly be drained dry, creating new emergencies. And the cry will echo across the land, "If we can't address these problems now, while the economy is growing, when will we ever address them?"

As long as the politicians and the political class can continue borrowing, the temptation to do so will be overwhelming. Democrats and other budget busters will bolster their case for loose fiscal policy with the following logic: The economic recovery is fragile. Cutting spending by $700 billion, equivalent to roughly 5 percent of the GDP would be devastating; even if the cuts were phased in over several years, they would slow desperately needed economic growth. Now is no time to cut spending, they will say. Far better it would be to "invest" in the future — in schools, in infrastructure and in clean energy — to promote a stronger, more competitive economy. As a practical matter, Obama's promise to freeze discretionary spending for three years has as much credibility as my 12-year-old son's vow to feed, walk and clean up after the puppy he begs his parents to buy him.

Under the guise of fiscal responsibility, liberals may balance their plans for more spending by renewing calls to "tax the rich." They may get their wish, but not without stiff political resistance. Americans don't like paying more taxes. Indeed, many dislike it with such intensity that they aren't even comfortable with soaking the rich — they understand that taxing the rich means punishing the businessmen and entrepreneurs who drive innovation, create wealth and hire more workers.

Beyond Americans' skepticism that the nation can tax its way to prosperity, there is an important empirical question: Will higher taxes actually increase revenue? The level of thinking is sorely deficient on both sides of the ideological spectrum. Democrats assume that if you raise a given tax by 20 percent, you will gain 20 percent more revenue. The Dems think that no one will alter their behavior in order to reduce their exposure to taxes; people will just stand there and write their checks. Such thinking is obtuse. Even Democrats re-arrange their affairs to minimize their tax payments! But the deficits-don't-matter wing of the conservative movement isn't much smarter. Republicans invoke the mystical powers of the Laffer Curve, which posits that tax rates do alter peoples' behavior. Cut taxes, conservatives say, and people will work so much harder and become so productive that tax revenues will actually increase. There *is* such a thing as a free lunch!

While I mock the misuse of the Laffer Curve, which economist Arthur Laffer famously traced on the back of a paper napkin and inspired the "supply side" thinking that drove President Reagan's tax cuts, I do not mock the Laffer Curve itself. The concept is very helpful in understanding tax policy. In a nutshell, it can be summarized thusly: If the government sets the tax rate at zero, revenue from a tax will be (drum roll)... zero. If the government sets the tax rate at 100 percent, people will stop engaging in an activity that results in total confiscation, and revenues will be... zero. Somewhere between the two extremes is a point that optimizes the trade-offs between the tax take and encouraging/discouraging the activity to be taxed.

The important thing to remember is that the shape of the Laffer Curve varies from tax to tax, which means raising and cutting rates have different effects for different taxes. Take the capital gains tax, for instance. The optimal tax rate is fairly low. That's because people usually control when they execute a transaction that triggers the tax. Many investors hold profitable stocks for years — even a lifetime — specifically to avoid paying the capital gains tax. In the U.S., the long-term capital gains tax is 15 percent. There seems to be a gross injustice in the fact that the vast bulk of what Bill Gates earns is taxable at the rate of 15 percent — the capital gains on his Microsoft stock — while a working stiff pays up to 35 percent on a salary that constitutes nearly all of his or her income. Why does a billionaire enjoy a lower tax rate? Because Bill Gates is not compelled to sell his shares of Microsoft stock. Should he choose to, he can sit on his shares until he dies and never pay a dime. By setting the capital gains tax rate at 15 percent, the penalty is low enough that Gates might figure, what the heck, he'll cash out some of his stock. At that rate, the government actually collects more in revenue than if it set the rate at a level that seems more "fair."

More controversial is the personal income tax. For middle-class taxpayers who derive most of their income from wages and salaries, the tax is relatively insensitive. If Uncle Sam raises taxes, few Americans will quit their jobs and stop working. A few may decide to cut back to a part-time job, turn down overtime work or maybe retire early, but for the most part, middle-class Americans will suck up the higher taxes and pay. The fact is, they need the money they earn and they have few alternatives. (They may have more alternatives than they realize, however, as I will discuss in Chapter 8.)

But progressives don't overtly target the middle class because that's where the votes are. Rather, lovers of the leviathan state propose to address America's fiscal woes by taxing the rich. The difficulty they have is that the rich have far more tax-minimizing options than the middle class. For instance, if Congress jacks up taxes on salaries and bonuses, the rich, who tend to call the shots in America's corporations, will restructure corporate compensation packages to give themselves more stock equity, which is taxable at the lower capital gains rate. If the income levelers jack up capital gains, the rich will re-balance compensation packages to pay more in non-taxable perks.

The rich, by virtue of being rich, have other advantages. They can afford the services of tax planners to help them reduce net income. They have access to the creative book cookers on Wall Street who continually whip up new confections to shelter income. The rich won't blink at the cost of paying Washington lobbyists $600 an hour to drill new holes in the tax code just for them. If wheedling tax breaks out of Congress is not practicable, the rich can park their money in off-shore banking havens. America's wealthiest citizens have one more option: transferring assets to philanthropic foundations beyond the reach of the taxman. Let's face it, after the first $1 million a year or so of income, it's not easy for rich people to spend all their wealth on themselves. But they do derive psychic gratification through philanthropy, and foundations allow them to indulge that itch tax free.

In extremis, Americans can renounce their U.S. citizenship. Indeed, some 500 citizens and green card holders gave up citizenship or permanent residency in the 4th quarter of 2009, more than in the entire year of 2007 — a fact that Anthony Tong, a tax partner in Pricewaterhouse-Cooper's Hong Kong office attributes to anticipated tax increases. "At a certain point, it gets beyond peoples' pain threshold."[158]

The lamentable news for those who seek to reduce deficits by raising more tax revenue is that, in all probability, the U.S. income tax rate is very near the optimum point on the Laffer Curve. In other words, if we raise the income tax rate, we will induce so much tax avoidance that revenues will fall. On the flip side, if we cut the income tax rate, we may coax the rich out of some of their tax shelters, but not enough to make up for the lower rate.

Let us review a little tax history. In 1993, President Bill Clinton signed a tax package that included higher rates for the rich: 36 percent plus a 10 percent surcharge. Misunderstanding the Laffer Curve, the Republicans predicted calamity: The tax cuts would cripple the economy and the rich would pay less. But they were wrong. The Internet bubble gave a great boost to the economy, and the tax take from the rich increased. Then in 2003, George W. Bush cut the top tax rate for high income earners to 35 percent, and the Democrats predicted a fiscal disaster. In fact, the share of percentage of income taxes generated by the rich actually increased — the top 1 percent of all income earners paid almost 40 percent of all income taxes in 2006.[159]

As the chart on the next page shows, the rich (the top 1 percent of income earners) have been getting richer, increasing their share of national income between 1986 and 2006 from 11.3 percent to 22.1 percent, an increase of nearly 11 percentage points. But their share of income taxes has paid increased even more, from 25.7 percent to 39.9 percent, an increase of more than 14 percentage points. Interestingly, Clinton's tax hike helped boost the take from the rich, but W.'s reversal on the tax rate did not hurt tax collections. Through trial and error, it appears, the U.S. has groped its way to tax rates that are close to the optimal point on the Laffer Curve.

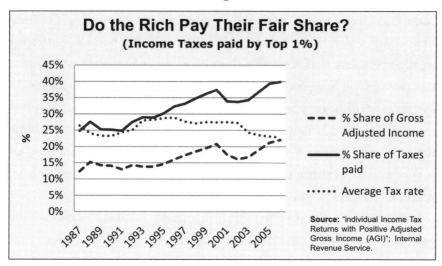

Do the Rich Pay Their Fair Share?
(Income Taxes paid by Top 1%)

- - - % Share of Gross Adjusted Income

——— % Share of Taxes paid

•••••• Average Tax rate

Source: "individual Income Tax Returns with Positive Adjusted Gross Income (AGI)"; Internal Revenue Service.

Bottom line: We're squeezing the rich for about all the money we're going to get out of them. If Americans are to find a way to avert Boomergeddon, we will have to do it some way other than by sticking it to the wealthy. The rhetoric of class warfare may feel good to some, but it solves nothing.

As it dawns on progressives (at least those who pay attention to the facts) that little more in the way of taxes can be pried out of the rich, there is increasing talk of imposing a Value Added Tax, a consumption-oriented tax widely used in Europe. Politically, it would be very hard to sell. Republicans would oppose it bitterly out of philosophical conviction. Democrats would find it difficult to gin up much enthusiasm for a tax that requires the poor to make a sacrifice. The general public, knowing that there's no way to slough the tax onto "someone else," is not likely to warm to it either. It will take a cataclysmic crisis on the scale of Boomergeddon to mobilize support for such a thing.

Theft by Stealth

The Boomers running the United States today lived through the stagflation era of the 1970s and the painful recession it took to quell inflation, so there is little appetite among the nation's leaders at this time for trying to solve the nation's fiscal problems by devaluing the currency. But, as Joshua Aizenman and Nancy Marion note in their paper, "Using Inflation to Erode the U.S. Public Debt," inflating away the debt is not beyond the realm of consideration. As the national debt grows exponentially bigger and the interest on that debt consumes the federal budget, progressives inevitably will be tempted. We don't want to become like Germany's Weimar Republic, loading up wheelbarrows of cash for a trip to the grocery store, they might say, but a little inflation wouldn't hurt very much. Just crank up the printing presses enough to work down the debt to a manageable level, and then stop before doing any lasting damage.

As Aizenman and Marion analyze the situation, a "moderate" inflation of six percent — only a little higher than the rate prevailing after World War II — would reduce the debt/GDP ratio by 20 percent within four years. However, there are two important differences between now and then, they continue. First, a much higher percentage of the public debt is held today by foreign creditors, 48 percent. And second, today's debt maturity — the average duration of the notes, bills and bonds before they expire — is less than half of what it was in 1946.[161] The higher percentage owned by foreigners, they contend, makes it more tempting to inflate away the debt. While the two economists don't put it quite so starkly, sticking it to foreigners is politically easier than sticking it to the rich because (a) they don't vote, and (b) they are forbidden to contribute to electoral campaigns. On the other hand, a four-year average maturity of Treasury securities is a disincentive to inflation. When the securities expire, the Treasury has to replace them by selling new notes to the public — presumably at much higher interest rates as investors demand protection from inflation. Shorter average maturities mean the interest payments ratchet up more rapidly.

Aizenman and Marion concede that there would be risks associated with such a strategy. Modest inflation may inadvertently turn into severe inflation, perhaps shooting into double digits. "Such an outcome often results in an abrupt and costly adjustment down the road," they write. "Accelerating inflation had limited global implications at a time when the public debt was held domestically and the U.S. was the undisputed global economic leader. In contrast, unintended acceleration of inflation to double digit levels in the future may have unintended adverse effects, including growing tensions with global creditors and less reliance on the dollar."

That's putting it mildly. Financial markets have come a long way since the 1940s. Foreigners now own $3.6 trillion in U.S. treasury securities, and they would be furious to see their holdings eroding at a rate of six percent per year — an expropriation exceeding $216 billion — especially knowing that the inflation had been deliberately engineered for the purpose of easing the debt burden. Thanks to the transparency of the Federal Reserve Board deliberations, such machinations would be impossible to hide. The Chinese, Japanese, Brits and others would regard such actions as tantamount to theft — and rightly so. Moreover, they would have no way of knowing when the theft by inflation would end. It's one thing for academics like Aizenman and Marion to suggest inflating away 20 percent of the debt. It's quite a different perspective if you're the one whose assets are being devalued. Why would the Fed stop at 20 percent, creditors would wonder. And what assurance would they have that the Fed could bring inflation back under control once they thought they'd stolen enough? The Electronic Herd today is as sensitive to inflation as wildebeest are to lion spoor. If prices rose, investors would immediately add a stiff inflation premium to the interest rates they charged for loans.

Let's envision how the engineered inflation would unfold. From the Treasury Department's perspective, the first year or two of six-percent inflation would feel great. The inflation would downsize the debt in real-dollar terms by the equivalent of $216 billion or so each year. Higher interest rates would start kicking in immediately as 30-day notes expired and had to be rolled over, but because some securities don't mature for 10 or 20 years, the increase in interest rates, and payments on the debt, would lag inflation by several years. Thus, during the early phase of inflation, the real value of the national debt would erode faster than higher interest rates would drive up payments on the debt. Mission accomplished!

Not so fast. Let's assume that after three years, the Fed met its target of 20 percent inflation and, on cue, managed the trick of dialing back inflation to one percent or so. Is that the end of the story? No. By then, much of the Treasury's obligations would consist of high interest-paying debt — and now the time lag would work the other way. Inflation would be lower, but the Treasury would be burdened with loads of t-bills, notes and bonds with high interest rates. Badly burned and resentful at the theft of their wealth, investors would not easily trust U.S. authorities to refrain from repeating their trick. They would demand a permanent interest rate premium to guard against a political risk of default by inflation that had never existed before. The U.S. would pay the price in the form of higher interest rates for years to come. Over a ten-year perspective, any gains from such monetary adventurism would be minimal.

And that's the best case scenario. Under a worst-case scenario, the Fed would be unable to rein inflation back in. The dollar would plunge, and investors would flee not only U.S. Treasuries but all U.S. investments. Simultaneously, U.S. consumers and businesses would shift their capital into speculative assets to guard against inflation, starving the productive, wealth-producing sectors. Growth would stall and tax revenues would deflate like an old beach ball.

There is a reason why Fed Chairman Ben Bernanke is committed to keeping inflation in check, and why even deficit deniers like Paul Krugman and Robert Reich are not touting the benefits of just "a little bit" of inflation. The risk-reward calculus is too unfavorable. The U.S. cannot inflate away its national debt without the risk of doing grievous economic harm and hastening the inevitable day of reckoning.

End Game

Boomergeddon is coming. We are locked into a trajectory of rising deficits, bloating national debt and spiraling interest payments. Our national leadership cannot solve the problem because our leadership is detached from reality. The Democrats seek to expand government entitlements even as Medicare Part A and Social Security disability trust funds run out of money, and they devote hundreds of billions to "counter cyclical" spending as if there were no limit on the national credit card. Republicans decry the mounting deficits, but they seem unwilling to level with the voters about what needs to be done. Paul Ryan, the Wisconsin congressman who gave President Obama an unwelcome dose of budgetary reality at the health care summit, is one of the few exceptions. His "Roadmap for America's Future" outlines a momentous overhaul of entitlements and the budget-making process, but his proposals are outside the political mainstream. As *Time* magazine reported in February, "House Republicans have conspicuously stood apart from the plan."[162] Any plan that falls short of Ryan's roadmap only tinkers at the margins of the problem.

Entitlements are stuck on auto-pilot and discretionary spending is out of control. Raising taxes on the rich won't work because the rich have too many means of hiding their income, and raising taxes on the middle class is political suicide. We cannot inflate our way out of our predicament because the Electronic Herd and sovereign wealth funds will jack up interest rates to punishing levels to protect against the devaluation of their Treasury holdings. Economic growth won't bail us out in the short run because consumers and banks are still recovering from a ferocious hangover brought on by their 30-year debt bender, or in the long run because America's producers and innovators will swim against a tide of slower workforce growth, declining global savings, increasing capital scarcity, higher interest rates, rising commodity prices, and the inefficiencies inherent in the rent-seeking political culture in Washington, D.C.

Some may dream that another electoral uprising will take over Washington and complete the work that the Reagan revolution and the Gingrich insurrection left undone. Such a hope is naive. While Republicans may make big gains in the fall 2010 elections, the chances are remote that they can take control of both houses of Congress, and even if they do, the most they can hope to accomplish over the next two years is to halt the expansion of the leviathan state, not to roll it back. President Obama will veto any legislation that seeks to undo his health care reform or to dismantle other favored spending programs.

Republicans would be as mistaken as Obama and the Democrats were last year to interpret a narrow electoral victory as a mandate. Americans threw the Republicans out of power in Congress four years ago, and then they evicted the elephants from the White House. Now they are turning on the Democrats. Voters may well throw out Obama when he runs for reelection in 2012. But disenchantment with the Dems does not translate into love of Republicans. Both parties dwell in the basement of public esteem. If Republicans take control of Congress, they will hold it only on the sufferance of voters, who will not hesitate to fire them again if conditions do not perform.

Given the conflicting impulses of the American people, it is difficult to see what Republicans can realistically accomplish. The people fear the fiscal disaster they see bearing down upon them, but they abhor higher taxes and they refuse to surrender their entitlements. Americans are not to be reasoned with — they are a maddened beast rushing at one tormentor and then another. Whoever succeeds Obama will confront the same irreconcilable demands. Making matters worse, the next president will find himself caught in the same Keynesian trap that bedevils Obama now. Closing the budgetary gap over five or six years, either through reduced spending or higher taxes, will create a huge drag on the economy. Slower economic growth will engender lower tax revenues and . . . higher deficits. Extricating the nation from its current predicament will feel like running in a bed of quicksand. But the people will not be forgiving of failure.

When Boomergeddon comes, most likely in the 2020s, the federal government will launch into emergency survival mode. If expenditures are limited to cash generated through taxes, plus whatever can be conjured from thin air by the powers of the Fed, hideous choices will have to be made. The U.S. will no longer be able to finance military outposts around world, much less to prosecute endless wars. The only question is whether the retreat of the American empire will be panicky and precipitous or deliberate and carefully executed. The money will not exist to continue funding Social Security, Medicare and Medicaid at current levels, much less whatever new entitlements Congress dreams up between now and then. Benefits will have to be radically restructured, which means cut, and most probably means tested. It will be the end of the retirement safety net as the middle class now knows it.

Chapter 6
Bye, Bye, American Empire

The American Age

As far as imperialist, war-mongering hegemons go, the United States has been remarkably benign. The world will miss us when we're gone.

I'll stack up our track record of world domination against that of any other empire. The Romans brought *Pax Romana* to the Mediterranean world, but they had a nasty habit of razing rebellious cities and crucifying the survivors. Building the largest empire ever known to mankind, the Mongols terrorized the world from Cathay to Muscovy with rapine, pillage and butchery. Hitler's Thousand Year Reich and Stalin's Soviet empire took mass slaughter to an industrial scale, slaying or starving their enemies by the millions.

By the standards of the other great empire builders, the English were pretty decent chaps. They were imperialists, to be sure: They subjugated peoples around the globe and treated some of them in a beastly manner. But they extinguished the African slave trade — no mean accomplishment — did not target civilian populations, and for the most part brought stability and increased material prosperity to the places they ruled.

But even the English can't compare to post-World War II Americans for the benefits they imparted to the world. Our early forays into empire building did us little credit — we treated the native Indians and the Filipinos especially shabbily. But by Word War II we had developed a conscience, and we managed to build an empire without permanently subjugating anyone. After defeating Germany and Japan in World War II, we did not salt their fields, dismantle their industries or saddle them with reparations. No, we converted them into democracies, nourished their economies and stood by like proud parents as they grew to become major economic competitors.

We expended blood and treasure to defend South Korea from a communist invasion, and then shielded the country as it transformed itself from a dirt-poor outpost of Japan's "Greater East Asia Co-Prosperity Sphere" into the world's 15th largest economy. The U.S. intervention in Vietnam led to a protracted and sanguinary conflict, but we never intended to conquer the country. We just wanted to keep it free from communism. Two decades later, we brought the Soviet Union to its knees without firing a shot (although we did provide a few Stinger missiles to the mujahedeen in Afghanistan). The Eastern Europeans thank us for it, even if the Russians don't.

After fighting a war to rescue Kuwait and its neighbors from the clutches of Saddam Hussein, Americans turned the country back over to the Kuwaitis, asking nothing from anyone beyond defraying some of the expense of prosecuting the war. We fought a second war in Iraq on the basis of faulty intelligence, but when we depart, we will leave behind a nation with nascent democratic institutions. And, despite calumnies to the contrary, we never tried to steal its oil.

A frequently overlooked virtue of the American empire is that the U.S. Navy rules the oceans — "the single most important geopolitical fact in the world," according to strategist George Friedman.[163] The Navy keeps the sea lanes open for everyone. We could shut down global commerce in an instant, if we chose to, but we extract no toll nor tribute. Our dedication to freedom of the seas and our exercise of diplomatic power to promote trade liberalization has created a global economic system that has lifted more people out of poverty than any other arrangement in human history. The most prosperous peoples in the world are those who are interconnected with the American economy; the poorest are those who are isolated from it.

American conduct has been far from perfect. We supported unsavory dictators during the Cold War, although they were less repressive in most cases than the leftist alternatives. We blackened our honor with episodes like the My Lai massacre and Abu Ghraib, although never in history has an army fought with such strict rules of engagement as in Iraq and Afghanistan, routinely risking the lives of its soldiers to avoid killing innocent civilians.

Perhaps most grievously, to the French at least, we exported our boorish culture, from Big Macs to Rambo movies. Say what you will about our proletarian tastes in cinema and cuisine, there is no denying that the American Age has advanced the noble ideals of political freedom and human rights. According to Freedom House's annual "Freedom in the World" survey, which classifies countries by the freedom of their elections, the pluralism of their political processes and the accountability of their governments, 29 percent of all nations were classified as free in 1972, while 46 percent were deemed free in 2009. (Peaking in 2006, political freedom has eroded somewhat in the four years since, especially in Africa and the countries of the former Soviet Union, but is still more widespread than 28 years ago.)[164]

In sum, the American empire has created a global environment where economic freedoms have proliferated, prosperity has flourished, and political freedoms have made steady gains. That setting is the basis of the world trading system, which in turn is the source of much of our wealth. If the empire collapses, the entire edifice could follow.

Freedom Isn't Free

There was nothing pre-ordained about advances in the human condition. The world enjoys the freedom it does largely because the U.S. and the other nations of the Anglo-sphere (the United Kingdom, Australia and at times Canada and New Zealand) have confronted the enemies of freedom over the past century and defeated them. The world would be a very different place if the German, Austrian and Russian monarchies survived World War I, if fascism had triumphed in World War II, or if the Soviet Union had prevailed during the long Cold War.

The political and economic systems of the good guys prevailed because the good guys prevailed militarily.

The United States has expended immense blood and treasure to expand the sphere of freedom over the past century, and it continues to do so today. President Obama's proposed 2011 budget includes $549 billion for base Department of Defense expenditures, plus $159 billion for "overseas contingency operations"[165] — the sum total of which reputedly exceeds what the rest of the world devotes to military spending. Not only is the U.S. conducting a two-front war in the Middle East, but it is modernizing weapons systems to counter emerging threats. New armaments include the F-35 Joint Strike Fighter, a new family of ground vehicles and the next generation of ballistic missile submarine. The budget also bolsters capabilities in Unmanned Aerial Vehicles, helicopters and cyber warfare.

The challenge in being the U.S. is that we must maintain the ability to defend across a wide spectrum of conflicts. As always, we must preserve the strength to defeat a conventionally armed opponent such as Iran, North Korea or China. But potential foes saw how quickly we demolished Saddam Hussein's army, one of the largest armed forces on the planet, and they have enough sense to challenge us obliquely, through terrorism, guerilla warfare, cyber warfare or other means. (Who imagined a decade ago that home-made bombs buried in the road would be the deadliest scourge of the U.S. military?) Accordingly, U.S. ground forces must be nimble enough to switch between conventional warfare, counter-insurgency mode or nation-building mode, each of which requires different armaments, tactics and training.

Until this year, it has been U.S. military doctrine to field a force sufficient to fight and win two major wars simultaneously. As a result of the 2010 Quadrennial Defense Review, the Pentagon has dropped the two-war paradigm in favor of tackling a range of missions that include defeating conventional state adversaries, combating transnational terrorist threats, engaging in nation building, and supporting civilian authorities in emergency relief missions. The challenges get more diverse and complex with each passing year.[166]

Another difficulty of being the U.S. is that we must be able to project force halfway around the world. China, which can boast of the world's second most powerful conventional force, would be hard pressed to cross the 80-mile-wide Formosa Strait and supply an invading army with enough materiel to defeat Taiwan's 300,000-man military. Take China's challenge and multiply it one hundred times to get an idea of what we are facing. A significant percentage of our military expenditures goes to support a globe-straddling network of military bases and the supply chain to keep our war fighters housed, clothed, trained and equipped in forward positions. That ocean-spanning supply chain, incidentally, must be protected against submarines and long-range missiles.

The cost of building and maintaining bases in 38 different nations (not including Iraq, Afghanistan, U.S. territories, or bases owned and operated by the host companies) is immense. Nearly 19 percent of all buildings and structures inventoried in the DoD 2008 Base Structure Report are in overseas bases.[167] The largest concentrations of facilities we own and operate abroad, ranked by Plant Replacement Value, are listed in the table below.

Largest Overseas U.S. Military Presence			
(Plant replacement value, $billions, 2008)			
Germany	$39.8	Diego Garcia	$2.6
Japan	$36.9	Marshall Islands	$2.4
South Korea	$13.6	Guantanamo Bay	$2.2
United Kingdom	$6.3	Spain	$2.0
Italy	$5.4	Portugal	$1.6

Source: "Base Structure Report: Fiscal Year 2008"; Department of Defense.

What would happen to this archipelago of defense establishments if the federal government went into default? How would it affect the functioning of the military if the U.S. suddenly found itself in a position where cash flowing in from taxes covered only two out of three dollars being spent... when hospital bills were going unpaid, pensioners were getting smaller Social Security checks, discretionary spending programs were being gutted and the Federal Reserve Board chairman was pulling money out of his sleeve, pumping up inflation and precipitating chaos in global currency markets?

At the very least, the Pentagon would find it exceedingly difficult to procure the diesel and aviation fuel that powers its tanks, Humvees, trucks, jets, helicopters and most of its surface fleet. In fiscal 2008, the U.S. military purchased 135 million barrels of petroleum products costing $18 billion, equivalent to about 1.7 percent of total U.S. consumption.[168] By the 2020s, two-ton civilian cars will be running just fine on electric batteries, but armored utility vehicles capable of carrying extra tons of payload still will require power and range that only diesel can deliver. In any case, aircraft account for the majority of military fuel consumption, and there are no renewable-energy substitutes for aviation fuel.

In the event of Boomergeddon, where will the petroleum feedstock come from? It might be possible to draw down the U.S. strategic petroleum reserve for a while, but ultimately the oil will have to be purchased on global markets with rapidly depreciating dollars — with money the Pentagon won't have. As the supply of fuel constricts, the pace of military operations will slow to a crawl. It will be difficult to sustain a conventional war of maneuver, much less a conventional war plus major counter-insurgency operations or nation-building exercises.

As the reality sinks in that the U.S. war machine is running on fumes, the U.S. will find it more difficult to deter its adversaries. The risk-reward calculus of aggression will change. Despots around the world will be tempted to take risks they otherwise would avoid. At some point, it will become obvious that our immobilized troops are exposed and vulnerable. Our diplomats will try to persuade Germany, Japan or South Korea to help defray the cost of deploying U.S. troops in their countries. But the chances of success will be remote. The average age of those countries will be so advanced by then and their social welfare burdens so heavy that they will be facing fiscal crises of their own.

Boomergeddon will bring about the end of American empire. In the financial chaos following default, the U.S. will have no choice but to shutter bases and demobilize combat units. The process may take years to complete, but our strategists will see the folly in putting our troops in exposed forward bases with no means to conduct sustained operations. They will bring the boys home.

Return of Attila the Hun

Human nature abhors a geopolitical vacuum. As U.S. power recedes, other actors on the world stage will move in to fill it. Movements like al Qaeda and the Latin drug cartels will seek to topple weak governments, or at least to create zones of ungovernable anarchy where they can operate with impunity. Cross-border ethnic conflicts will simmer as groups like the Kurds and Pashtuns seek to increase their autonomy. Competing ethnicities will prey upon one another inside their own borders, like the Khartoum Arabs who launch razzias to seize cattle, slaves and land from the tribes of Darfur and southern Sudan. Without the U.S. to prop up central governments with foreign aid, humanitarian assistance, and above all military weaponry, training and intelligence, the forces of chaos increasingly will gain the upper hand.

Even with the U.S. functioning as world policeman, much of the planet is heading in the wrong direction. Fifty years ago, in 1960, the United Kingdom and France had decolonized most of their vast empires, minting new, independent countries by the dozen. There were no failed states back then. Well, there was one, the colony formerly known as the Belgian Congo. Riven by ethnic tensions and Cold War rivalries, the mineral-rich country sprawling across 900,000 square miles of rain forest and savanna fell prey after independence to an endless succession of secessions, rebellions, coups, despots and invasions by unruly neighbors. Other than the Congo, however, functioning central governments held sway around the globe, buttressed by the U.S., the Soviet

Union, the United Nations, former colonial powers and any number of humanitarian organizations.

There have been a number of individual success stories, most notably in the Asian Rim, but otherwise, the world's nation-states have made remarkably little progress in building legitimacy and power over the past half century. Each year *Foreign Policy* magazine and The Fund for Peace compile a Failed States Index that ranks the world's countries by the central government's ability to maintain core government services and a monopoly on violence. The bottom 20 on the list are deemed to be in "critical" condition. In one of those, Somalia, the central government has passed beyond the critical stage into a state of total collapse. In other failed states, the central governments are unable to deliver essential services or monopolize the use of force. In many such countries, the government writ extends little farther than the capital, major cities and revenue centers such as oil wells, diamond fields or copper mines. While the rulers may be recognized by world organizations as representatives of a legitimate government, they do not exercise meaningful control over large chunks of their own territory.

The condition of the Bottom 20 failed states has materially worsened in the past four years since *Foreign Affairs* started keeping a comprehensive list. Some nations have graduated from a "failed" classification to merely "in danger," but they have been replaced by others in even worse condition, as shown in the chart on the next page, which compares the worst scores of 2006 with those of 2009. (A score of 120 would indicate a state in a state of utter and total collapse.)[169]

There may be a cyclical element to the deterioration. The Global Financial Crisis has depressed the export markets of developing countries, battering fragile economies and adding to the populations' grievances. But in country after country, familiar and depressing patterns transcend temporary economic hardship: corruption, disenfranchisement of minority ethnic groups, destructive economic policies, and/or civil war. In most instances, "failed state" status was self-inflicted, not the result of outside economic forces. Zimbabwe is a classic example: The Mugabe regime's eviction of its highly productive white farmers, widespread corruption and hyper-inflation have transformed what had been one of the most prosperous nations in Africa into an economic basket case.

Thomas P.M. Barnett, best known as the author of "The Pentagon's New Map," sees the world divided into two zones: the "Integrated Core," by which he refers to the countries participating in the global trading system, and the "Non-Integrated Gap," by which he means those countries that are largely isolated from it. All the failed states in

Failed States (Rated "Critical" in the Failed States Index)			
2006		**2009**	
Sudan	112.3	Somalia	114.7
Democratic Republic Congo	110.1	Zimbabwe	114.0
Ivory Coast	109.2	Sudan	112.4
Iraq	109.0	Chad	112.2
Zimbabwe	108.9	Democratic Republic Congo	108.7
Chad	105.9	Iraq	108.6
Somalia	105.9	Afghanistan	108.2
Haiti	104.6	Central African Republic	105.4
Pakistan	103.1	Guinea	104.6
Afghanistan	99.8	Pakistan	104.1
Guinea	99.0	Ivory Coast	102.5
Liberia	99.0	Haiti	101.8
Central African Republic	92.5	Burma	101.5
North Korea	97.3	Kenya	101.4
Burundi	96.7	Nigeria	99.8
Yemen	96.6	Ethiopia	98.9
Sierra Leone	96.6	North Korea	98.3
Burma/Myanmar	96.5	Yemen	98.1
Bangladesh	96.3	Bangladesh	98.1
Nepal	95.4	East Timor	97.2
Average	**101.7**	**Average**	**104.5**

Source: "The Failed States Index: 2009"; Foreign Policy and the Fund for Peace.

the list above fall within the Gap. Gap countries are economic failures. They seethe with turmoil, and they exude disruptive influences such as terrorism, drugs, crime, piracy, refugees, disease and other ills that make life unpleasant for the countries of the Integrated Core. The great foreign policy challenge of the U.S., Barnett suggests, is to integrate the Gap countries into the global economy, engender enough prosperity to give rise to a middle class, and support each country's middle class in indigenous efforts to develop the rule of law, pluralistic institutions and eventually democracy. In his latest book, "Great Powers: America and the World After Bush," Barnett illuminates how the U.S. might induce regional powers, most particularly China and India, to assist in that effort.[170]

By nature an optimist, Barnett takes on the "doom mongers" who forecast Armageddon. He does, in fact, make a highly persuasive case for realigning U.S. foreign policy, which I will draw upon in Chapter 9. Upon reading his book, however, one may come away with the feeling that the shrinking of the Gap is an all but inevitable result of globalization — only the timing and the details remain to be worked out. In his optimism, he neglects to examine the many ways in which the Gap can spread.

As Barnett readily acknowledges, globalization is a highly destabilizing force, not only because Western secularism, female empowerment and sexual freedom threaten core values of traditional societies, but because throughout the history of the world economic progress has been uneven. Some regions, by virtue of geography, are better located to participate in global trade than others. Some cultures are more open to innovation, others more closed. Invariably, the integration of traditional societies into the global trading system creates winners and losers. The losers may, in fact, be no worse off than they were before their countries opened up, but their standing may decline in comparison to others. The sense of relative deprivation fuels tensions between different ethnic, tribal and religious groups, especially if dominant groups use the coercive power of the state to magnify their advantages. In turn, those tensions breed instability that threaten to undermine integration into the world trading system.

I see at least three additional avenues for functioning states to devolve into failed states and spread the Gap: terrorism, criminality and leftist revolution.

Terrorism. Al Qaeda and its allies in militant Islam have elevated terrorism as a strategy for conquest to a new state of the art, far sur-

passing in effectiveness the random violence of the 19th century anar-
chists, the Basque separatists, the Irish Revolutionary Army and the
Baader-Meinhoff gang. The Islamists have shown how to use assassina-
tions, Improvised Explosive Devices (IEDs), terror-inducing car bomb-
ings, and the sabotage of vulnerable infrastructure to render a country
ungovernable, thereby destroying the legitimacy of the central authority. In Iraq they chose their targets shrewdly: running off the United Nations and the Non-Governmental Organizations, vulnerable groups that
could have played an important role in stabilizing the country, assassi-
nating key government officials, and inflaming tensions between ethnic
groups. Although the terror campaign ultimately failed in Iraq, thanks to
the presence of some 150,000 American troops, it very nearly succeeded.
Elements of the Iraqi terror template are being applied in Afghanistan,
where it is too early to tell whether it will prevail. In an especially alarming development, al Qaeda has demonstrated the ability to migrate its
terror doctrine and technical, bomb-making expertise to other countries. Islamic extremists can reconstitute themselves anywhere.

Learning through hard experience, the U.S. has developed much
more effective counterinsurgency tactics and doctrine. But that knowledge is not easily transferred to the militaries of other nations. If the
U.S. is fiscally unable to maintain a global presence, al Qaeda and its
sundry brethren movements may well find weak states where their terror tactics work.

Drugs and criminal syndicates. Drug lords represent a tremendous threat to the integrity of the Andean states of South America, the
world's leading center of cocaine production, of Afghanistan, a center
of poppy cultivation, and even of Mexico, an advanced developing nation
with a strong central government. The narcotics trade is an especially
potent force when combined with revolutionary movements — Maoist
guerillas in South America, the Taliban in Afghanistan — that provide an
ideological appeal to the local population. In at least two instances, drug-

fueled movements have nearly toppled democratic governments in South America — the Revolutionary Armed Forces of Colombia (FARC) in Colombia, and the Shining Path in Peru. For long periods of time, these movements controlled significant chunks of the interior in both countries. Like Al Qaeda in Iraq, FARC financed its activities through kidnapping, extortion, smuggling and other criminal enterprises.

Leftist revolution. Marxism is a spent force throughout most of the world, but it survives in outposts as varied as the Unified Communist Party of Nepal, a Maoist political movement that conducted a "people's war" against the Nepalese monarchy; the Sandinistas, whose leader Daniel Ortega was re-elected president of Nicaragua in 2006; and, ahem, the faculty of the University of California, Berkeley. Extreme leftists have been propelled to power in Ecuador, Bolivia and, most notoriously, Venezuela. Leftist governments are effective in direct proportion to which they abandon their Marxist radicalism, as they have done in Brazil, and disastrous to the extent they attempt to put their egalitarian ideologies into practice. Marxism in Cambodia created the Khmer Rouge, architects of the so-called killing fields that sought to transform the country into a peasant utopia. Marxism in an African context created the disaster that is Zimbabwe. Marxism in a Latin context could well turn Venezuela into the world's next failed state.

Hugo Chavez, a leftist general, won power in Venezuela by means of a democratic election but has steadily chipped away at the country's pluralistic institutions in order to undertake a massive transfer of wealth to the poor. His policies are devastating the economy. By turning over control of the oil industry to his cronies, he has crippled the country's major source of foreign exchange. Wage and price controls have created widespread shortages in everyday commodities. The failure to invest in infrastructure has aggravated the drought-induced outages in an electric system dependent upon hydro-electric power. The mismanagement of Venezuela's coffee industry, once one of its export powerhouses, has been so egregious that the country now imports coffee. Suffering from a flight of both human and financial capital, the economy goes from bad to worse.

While the Venezuelan state maintains a formal monopoly on the use of force — opposition violence remains limited to street demonstrations — criminal violence is widespread. Caracas was rated in 2008 as the most violent city in the world, with 4,160 murders the previous year. If Chavez completes the demolition of democratic institutions and then loses legitimacy himself, the country could easily plunge into civil strife that will leave the central government a shambles.

Of course, some nations have dragged themselves back from the precipice, often with U.S. help. That's the case with Venezuela's neighbor, Colombia, where the central government's power was severely compromised by drug cartels, a leftist guerilla insurgency and right-wing paramilitary groups. By the 1990s, the country had become nearly ungovernable. But with heavy U.S. military backing, President Alvaro Uribe repressed the drug lords, dealt major defeats to the guerillas, and demobilized many paramilitaries. Progress is evident in the steady decline in the number of murders and homicides.

U.S. assistance has been decisive in helping the central government of the Philippines contain the terrorist Abu Sayyaf organization as well as the larger Moro Islamic Liberation Front. U.S. aid was instrumental in Peru's defeat of the Shining Path guerillas. Likewise, the U.S. has retrained and rearmed the Liberian army in the hope of converting a criminal military that fostered chaos into a force for stability.

The chart on the next page lists the 20 largest recipients of U.S. military aid in 2007. Not surprisingly, Iraq and Afghanistan topped the list. Perennial foreign aid favorites Israel and Egypt followed close behind. Most of the rest are failed or in-danger-of-failing states, often overwhelmed by humanitarian crises. In all, the U.S. spent nearly $42 billion in economic and military aid that year.

U.S. Economic and Military Aid (2007) (in millions)			
Iraq	$8,193	El Salvador	$513
Afghanistan	$5,186	Colombia	$497
Israel	$2,508	Ethiopia	$470
Egypt	$1,972	South Africa	$393
Russia	$1,594	Uganda	$370
Sudan	$1,180	Nigeria	$338
Pakistan	$977	Mozambique	$261
Ghana	$621	Liberia	$260
Jordan	$560	Tanzania	$253
Mali	$535		
Kenya	522	**Total**	$41,941

Source: "U.S. Foreign Economic and Military Aid by Major Recipient Country: 2000-2007"; U.S. Census Bureau.

The U.S. is not the sole source of humanitarian aid, but it is the world's largest, and it is the major source of military assistance. To be sure, Russia, China and other nations eagerly export armaments. But the U.S. is one of the very few nations — the U.K. and Israel are others that come to mind — whose military has extensive experience in conducting successful counter-insurgency operations. Guns, tanks and helicopters do little good if the recipient military doesn't have the training and military doctrine to use them effectively.

In summary, vast swaths of territory in the developing world are slowly but surely slipping free of central government control, yielding to tribal militias, liberation armies, drug lords and sprawling, un-policed shantytowns. For every nation that the U.S. helps pull back from the brink, there are two that pursue spectacularly inept economic policies, squander funds slated for nation building or foment insurrection through the persecution of minorities. As the reach of effective central power contracts in weak and failing states, the lines on the map that designate national boundaries become increasingly irrelevant.

If failed states kept to themselves, quarantining their agonies, the countries of the integrated Core could ignore them. But failed states have a way of exporting their misery. Fleeing battle zones, villagers encamp in neighboring countries. Seeking havens, guerillas recruit from

refugee camps and enlarge the zones of ungovernability. One vivid example: Hutu militia, escaping the warfare in Rwanda and Burundi, ran
amok in the eastern Congo, raiding, pillaging, raping, and reducing a
California-sized area into anarchy. Another: In western Africa, the civil
war in Liberia spilled over into Sierra Leone, driving that country into
chaos and sending disorder rippling through neighboring nations.

The U.S. has been critical to the effort to prop up the system of nation-states and to slow the descent of the Gap into barbarism. As the
world's undisputed superpower, the U.S. deters some (but hardly all) nations from invading one another. By distributing economic, humanitarian and military aid, the U.S. buttresses the power of central
governments. If the U.S. turns its back on the world, as it surely will in
the aftermath of Boomergeddon, the slow-motion disintegration of
weak central governments will gain momentum.

The future of a world without a U.S. to police it will be more failed
states, more militias, more drug lords, more insurgents, more genocide,
more refugees, more economic migrants, more sanctuaries for terrorists
and more havens for pirates. The expanse of territory subject to barbarism and warlordism will expand, and the expanse subject to the rule
of law will shrink. Globalization, trade and the economic integration
of nations likewise will contract.

The Rise of Regional Powers

As the U.S. retreats, regional powers will assert their primacy lo-
cally, and they will do so for three reasons. First, they will be drawn into
destabilizing rebellions and insurgencies in nearby countries that
threaten to slop over their borders. Second, with no United States to act
as a counterweight, they will press their material interests more aggressively, laying claim to strategically important resources such as oil,
minerals, water or even revenue-producing infrastructure like pipelines.
Third, regional powers will intervene in other countries to satisfy old ir-
redentist claims or settle old scores that were impractical to pursue

when the U.S. put a damper on aggressive behavior.

Russia. The Russian Federation is bent upon expanding its sphere of influence to the old Soviet republics. This won't be easy because most of the republics do not want to be re-integrated with Russia. Moreover, Russia is undergoing an extraordinary demographic collapse — unprecedented in a country not afflicted by war, famine or plague. The old Soviet Union boasted a population of more than 290 million at its peak. Russia today stands around 145 million, and forecasts suggest that the population could decline to 120 million or lower by 2050. Moreover, it is the ethnic Russian population that is in free-fall. The head-count of Muslim minorities is increasing. The insurgency in Chechnya, whose people have resisted Russian suzerainty for more than 200 years, could foreshadow conflicts to come in Dagestan, Ingushetia and other Islamic population centers.

Russia's greatest strength is its wealth of oil and gas, which, when energy prices increase again, will prop up the economy. Meanwhile, the country is modernizing its military, making it smaller and more professional. Because the new Russian army will no longer rely upon ill-motivated conscripts, it won't need the same large population base to support it. Russia will not be a threat to Europe in the foreseeable future, but it will be the big bear in its own back yard.

The Caucasus region, an ethnically fragmented no-man's land situated between the regional powers of Russia, Turkey and Iran, will likely be destabilized for decades to come. The three independent states, Georgia, Armenia and Azerbaijan, are fragile, contending with restive minorities within their boundaries. The Armenians and Azeris, whose quarrels go back more than a century, engaged in a six-year, on-again, off-again conflict known as the Nagorno-Karabakh War after the fall of the Soviet Union. The two countries remain bitterly hostile. More recently, Russia defeated Georgia in a brief war and carved off two of its provinces. Iran's strategic interests appear to lie elsewhere, but Turkey, which has historic and ethnic ties to the region, could enter the region as a counterweight to Russia.

Turkey. Turkey may be the most under-rated geopolitical power on the planet. With a population of 74 million and an annual GDP exceeding $1 trillion, it has the most advanced economy in the Islamic world. It has a strong central government, and its armed services, numbering more than 1.3 million, are well equipped and well trained. The foreign policy of the traditionally secular Turks has long been focused on Europe. The country belongs to the North Atlantic Treaty Organization, and it aspires to join the European Union. But if Turkey is refused admittance to the EU, the government may turn its attention eastward to the Caucasus and the Middle East, where it is already active. In the aftermath of Russia's war with Georgia, for instance, Turkey called for a "Caucasus Union" to strengthen economic ties with countries in the region and to work out peaceful settlements to problems.

When America's pull-back turns the world into a geopolitical free-for-all, Turkey will be tempted to pursue interests in the Caucasus, where it will come into competition with Russia, and in the politically fractured Persian Gulf region, where it could butt heads with Iran. At the very least the Turks, who have fought a bloody Kurdish insurgency within its own borders, will be tempted to meddle in Iraq if the autonomous Kurdish provinces there continue to harbor the terrorist Kurdish Workers' Party guerilla movement.

Iran. With a population of 72 million, Iran has an economy almost as large as Turkey's. Its conventional armed forces are not as large, but Iran soon will be a nuclear power and it is building an arsenal of medium-range missiles that could be capable of delivering nuclear weapons. Its position athwart the Straits of Hormuz, the narrow opening to the Persian Gulf, gives it the ability to shut down half the world's oil supply. Furthermore, as the most powerful state in the Shiite Islamic world, Iran postures as a champion of Shiite communities in Iraq and the Persian Gulf countries. Between its nukes, its missiles, proxies like Hamas and Hezbollah, and its strategic geographic position, Iran is in a position to dominate the world's greatest petroleum reservoirs.

A withdrawal of the U.S. presence from the Persian Gulf would be extremely destabilizing. Without the U.S. to act as a counter-balance, Iran could shut down the Persian Gulf knowing that Saudi Arabia and the Persian Gulf sheikdoms lack the military capacity to keep the sea-lanes open. Indeed, a shut-down of the Persian Gulf would disrupt the Gulf states' economies and threaten the very survival of their regimes. As Saudi Arabia contemplates the possibility of a U.S. retreat, it would have little choice but to seek nuclear weapons as a counter to the Iranian threat, or to do the unthinkable such as seek a rapprochement with Israel. Anything can happen in this unpredictable corner of the world — and probably will.

India. In a post-American world, India will be the dominant power of the Indian Ocean. The nation of Gandhi already has the world's second largest armed force, with more than 1.3 million military personnel as well as an arsenal of nuclear weapons. India also has an increasingly muscular economy to support military expansion and modernization, and it is developing its own industrial-military complex.

India has two primary strategic concerns: protecting its Himalayan border with China and managing its troubled relationship with Pakistan, with which it has fought four wars. If the U.S. pulls out of the Middle East, the situation in Afghanistan and Pakistan — a failed state next door to a semi-failed state — will become India's problem. A collapse of the Pakistani central government would create horrendous headaches for India, for only a strong central government can rein in the extremist anti-Indian groups seeking sanctuary there. Islamic militants will likely continue disputing Indian rule of Jammu and Kashmir on the northern border of the two countries. That rift, like the one dividing Israelis and Palestinians, is unlikely ever to heal. India also has to worry that extremism might spread from Pakistan to its own Muslim minority, estimated at more than 160 million. Should the Pakistani central government collapse, India would have many compelling reasons to intervene. But its presence would destabilize the country even more.

China. In the estimation of most foreign affairs analysts, China will be the only nation capable of challenging U.S. supremacy in the next half century. With the world's second-largest economy — and one that is growing much faster than that of the U.S. — and a population of 1.3 billion, China is rapidly modernizing its three million-man military service. The People's Liberation Army (PLA) is no longer an army of peasant conscripts topped off with nuclear weapons. It is researching advanced technologies that include cruise missiles, laser weapons and cyber-warfare capabilities. Many in the U.S. are raising the alarm that China is already capable of contesting U.S. military power in the East Pacific, and its power will only grow over time.

Andrew F. Krepinevich writes about China's "shasoujian" strategy named after the medieval Chinese assassin's mace, designed to surprise and cripple U.S. forces in the event of a conflict. The PLA would launch massed salvos of ballistic missiles at forward U.S. bases in Okinawa and even Guam, followed by waves of strike aircraft. The attacks would target aircraft, runways, maintenance facilities, and fuel and munitions storage facilities with the goal of devastating the U.S. ability to maintain its warfighting capabilities in the East Pacific.[171]

While China's military capabilities continue to grow, the Middle Kingdom suffers enormous strategic disadvantages. First, it has attacked (India, Vietnam, South Korea) or threatens (Taiwan and Japan) nearly every country on its periphery. It has few natural allies. A pull-back of the U.S. military could well prompt an alignment of China's enemies into mutual protection arrangements. Secondly, the potential targets of Chinese aggression are protected by natural barriers, either mountains (India), jungle (Vietnam), water (Taiwan, Japan) or an intervening country (South Korea). It's one thing to thwart the projection of U.S. power into the east Pacific with missiles, it's quite another thing to project power itself. Third, China is the world's third largest importer of petroleum, after the U.S. and Japan.[172] The necessity of protecting oil imports, some 3.9 million barrels per day in 2008, would render any long-term war against its neighbors highly problematic. China lacks the capability to defend shipping on its own coastline, much less all the way to the Persian Gulf.

China is arguably building its "area denial" capability as a way to exert diplomatic leverage, not with the serious thought of ever using it. If China does deploy its military to advance its interests, it most likely will be in developing nations where it has a major commercial presence. China has emerged as a major source of Foreign Direct Investment in Africa, pumping billions of dollars into the continent, often with an eye to locking up strategic resources like oil, copper or iron ore. The Chinese have no reluctance to partner with the most oppressive regimes. Their interests are purely mercenary: to ensure access to the sources of petroleum and raw materials needed to feed its voracious industrial economy. Chinese involvement in Africa is still in its early stages but, as its interests expand, the People's Republic inevitably will become embroiled in internal politics. Because so many African states are fragile, it is only a matter of time before China is called upon to militarily bolster one or more in order to protect its commercial interests.

It would be naive to suspect that regional powers — Russia, Turkey, Iran, India and China — will be as dedicated to preserving the global free-trade regime as the U.S. has been. Russia is already notorious for using its control over natural gas pipelines to exercise leverage over its neighbors in the Ukraine as well as Europe. It is difficult to imagine Iran dominating the Persian Gulf oilfields without manipulating the supply and price of oil to its advantage. And it is abundantly clear that China, the world's leading mercantilist power, will utilize its influence to preserve preferential access to raw materials. Turkey and India are both democratic states, but they, too, will be tempted to use their power to benefit their own business interests.

The one geopolitical entity I have omitted from the discussion of regional powers is Europe. That's because Europe is a spent force on the great-power stage. It is a region in demographic decline, marked by increasing pacifism of the population and growing resistance to foreign entanglements. Furthermore, as evidenced most recently by the Greek crisis, the Europeans are flying at ram-jet speed toward their own rendezvous with fiscal calamity. In all likelihood, several European countries will precede the U.S. to a Boomergeddon-style meltdown, and those that don't will follow soon after. We can hope that Europe will maintain the means to defend itself against Russian encroachments but it will have neither the will nor the means to project power anywhere. Let me rephrase that. "Europe" won't defend anything, if it means calling upon France, Germany, Italy or other NATO members to shed blood in a foreign war. However, it is possible that Poland, the Czech Republic, Hungary, the Baltic nations and other countries fearing Russian expansion may unite to form an opposing power bloc. Indeed, George Friedman envisions the Poles becoming the dominant power in the region following a demographic and military collapse of Russia around 2020. Poland, he imagines, will project power into Belarus and the Ukraine as it did in its 16th century golden age. If Poland becomes the future muscleman of European geopolitics, the continent's role in the post-American era will be very circumscribed indeed.

As regional powers expand their spheres of influence, there is a danger that they will exercise their power to maintain preferential access to consumer markets and natural resources. Very few governments of developing nations are deeply committed to free trade, so they will willingly grant preferences to the new powers in exchange for diplomatic and military favors that cement the governments' hold on power. Think of it as a kinder, gentler form of colonialism. Free trade will give way to mercantile empires hoisted into place by rising regional powers to lock up resources and confer competitive advantage upon their own industries. The march to globalization will stumble. There will be less prosperity for all to share.

But Boomers will scarcely notice. Their all-consuming reality will not be wars in Sudan or Myanmar over natural resources but the collapse of the American social safety net and the rapid deterioration in their own quality of life.

Chapter 7
Safety Net Unraveled

The Fleecing Draws Nigh

By now, you're probably thinking, "Wow, this book is really a downer. This Bacon fellow thinks the world as we know it is coming to an end." Fair enough. Away, then, with pessimism! Let us lift the veil of gloom. Permit me to assure you that Boomergeddon will not bring about the total and utter destruction of America's old-age safety net. Medicare, Medicaid and Social Security will survive in one form or another.

Admittedly, you will feel cheated, lied to, stolen from and violated when your Social Security and Medicare benefits are cut back to a fraction of what you were expecting. You will likely compare yourself to the poor devils who trusted Bernie Madoff to take good care of their life savings. But don't slit your wrists. Unlike Madoff's investors, who should collectively recover about $18 billion of the $36 billion they put in,[173] or about 50 percent, you're likely to receive a full 65 percent, maybe even a whopping 75 percent, of the benefits that Uncle Sam promised you!

And to think that some people call Social Security a Ponzi scheme. The nerve. There is no legitimate comparison between Bernie Madoff, who gambled that he could always find new investors to pay off the old investors, and, say, Rep. Barney Frank, the Massachusetts congressman who said, "I want to roll the dice a little bit more,"[174] gambling that Fannie Mae and Freddie Mac could always find new buyers for its packages of subprime mortgages. Here's the difference: What Bernie Madoff did was illegal. He is now serving a 150-year federal prison sentence in Butner, North Carolina. What the swindlers in Congress do is perfectly legal. Barney Frank is still running loose. In fact, he is helping to run the country.

Feel better now?

Unfortunately, there is one thing I neglected to mention. While you may get two-thirds of the Social Security and Medicare benefits you counted on, there is a good chance that the inflation ignited by Boomergeddon will erode the value of your pathetic little savings down to a nub. Indeed, if you worked hard all your life, played by the rules and salted away a bit of money for your retirement instead of spending it like your spendthrift brother-in-law on booze and roulette in Vegas, then you are a sucker and a fool, and you deserve to be fleeced like a Hampshire ram in a New Zealand sheep farm. There will be no mercy or justice for the middle class because (a) unlike the rich, the middle class cannot afford to hire lobbyists to change the rules in its favor, and (b) unlike the poor, the middle class is not destitute and will evoke little compassion.

It is impossible, of course, to know some 15 to 20 years ahead of time exactly how Boomergeddon will affect your retirement finances. What I can do is list some possibilities. Mix and match them according to your own view of just how weasely, cowardly or ignorant members of Congress are likely to be two decades from now. Here is what to look for:

- The Social Security trust fund turns out to be a mirage.
- Congress jiggers Social Security and Medicare payout formulas to transfer payouts from the better-off to the poor.
- The Fed monetizes the debt and lets inflation run wild.

By my reckoning, you have until 2027 to prepare — if you are lucky. That may sound like a long time away, but Boomergeddon will get here faster, and last longer, than you can imagine. If you are 54 years old today, smack dab in the middle of the Boomer cohort, you will be 71 years old when Boomergeddon shatters your finances (and, for what it's worth, the finances of everyone else in the country).

Actuarially speaking, if you make it to 70, you probably will last another 10 to 15 years before you pass to your final reward. Think of it, 15 long years of sitting around a rickety table in a dingy kitchen with a bare light bulb and peeling linoleum tile you can't afford to replace. Overhead, a rusty fan squeaks because you can't pay for WD 40 oil, much less air conditioning. Joints aching, you shuffle over to the stove to heat up a tin of beanie-weenies for Thursday night dinner because the ground chuck is too expensive... OK, that probably won't be your life. But it could be that of many middle-class Americans who failed to save enough and entrusted their well-being in old age to Uncle Sam. It definitely won't be what they signed up for.

The Social Security Cupboard is Bare

In theory, Social Security should be able to ride out Boomergeddon in decent shape. After all, by 2023, there will be more than $4.3 trillion in the Social Security trust fund.[175] That should be good enough to last a decade or more... shouldn't it?

Not quite. Let me explain. In the 1950s the Bureau of Public Debt opened an office in Parkersburg, West Virginia, to house Social Security's Treasury bond assets in the event of a nuclear attack. The non-negotiable bonds are stored in three-ring binders, locked in the bottom drawer of a white metal filing cabinet.[176] When Social Security needs the money, it will redeem the bonds and the U.S. Treasury will hand over the funds. At least that's the plan. Unfortunately, the federal government has nothing in the till. The only way for the Treasury to pay Social Security will be to borrow the funds from someone else. But in 2027 no one else will be lending.

It doesn't matter if Congress passes reforms to make Social Security actuarially sound. All that will do is allow Social Security to build up a bigger trust fund and accumulate more non-negotiable U.S. Treasury bonds that will be impossible to redeem when the federal government goes into default. It's like when my son says, "I bet you a billion dollars that I can hang a spoon from my nose." I say he can't, and I take the bet. He proceeds to hang the spoon from his nose, and I write him a check for a billion dollars. Holding in his hands a check for a billion dollars does not make my son a billionaire. I'm not good for the money — and the federal government won't be either, no matter how fancy the filigree on the bond certificates.

Social Security recipients, most of whom will be Boomers by 2027, will be among the very first victims of government default. They are counting on Social Security to provide a significant share of their income. According to a late 2009 survey, retired 64-year-olds said that 35 percent of their income on average came from Social Security; 64-year-olds who had not yet retired expected the program to account for 44 percent of their income.[177] When the "lockbox" is vaporized in the fires of Boomergeddon, the Social Security Administration will be unable to pay out any more than it receives in payroll taxes, about 76 percent. A cut of 24 percent today would wipe out about one-tenth of older Boomers' income.

As disastrous as it would be to have one's Social Security check pared by a quarter and one's income by a tenth, the situation could get worse. Incredible as it sounds, with its dedicated payroll tax, Social Security could be on a sounder footing than the rest of the federal government. If we exclude Social Security revenues and outlays, the rest of the federal government will generate enough revenue from taxes in 2020 to cover only 71 percent of its expenditures, by the CBO's reckoning. Project another seven years ahead, with seven more years of debt accumulation and higher interest payments, and assume that an economic downturn plays a role in triggering Boomergeddon, which means depressed revenue and increased social welfare outlays, and it is possible that taxes will cover no more than 60 percent of non-Social Security outlays.

Now, imagine that you're a member of Congress in 2027 confronting the fact that the country is generating only $3 in taxes for every $5 in spending, and you can no longer borrow the difference. Constituents are jamming your email inboxes, overwhelming your voice mail messaging, and sending 3-D videos rants of themselves baring their teeth and shaking their fists for display on your newly installed Apple iHolograph. Lobbyists are pounding on your doors, threatening to cut their PAC contributions. Crowds are picketing outside the Capitol and hurling "smart" rocks through your window in the newly erected Nancy Pelosi House Office Building. It will not escape your attention that Social Security is better funded than the rest of the government. Will you be tempted to divert money from the retirement program to put out fires elsewhere? Of course you will. As a member of Generation X yourself, you probably ran on a generational-war platform of refusing to coddle the "rich Boomer retirees" who expect younger, poorer generations to bail them out. Your Boomer constituents might threaten to lynch you if you dipped into Social Security, but, let's face it, most of them are in their 70s — what can they really do?

(Just hope they never hear of the case of James Amburn, a 56-year-old American investment consultant who finagled two retired German couples to invest in Florida real estate. So outraged were the pensioners with the result that they kidnapped Amburn last year, threw him in the trunk of a car, and held him four days in a cellar, where they beat him and demanded their money back. Once when he tried to escape, the seniors assaulted him from behind and bound him up with masking tape. He regained his freedom only after being rescued by a heavily armed counter-terrorist unit.[178] If law-abiding Germans could do such a thing, just imagine what gun-toting Americans waving "Don't Tread on Me" flags could do!)

There is one other threat that the better-off Boomers had best brace themselves for: redistribution of the flow of funds within the program. Even before Boomergeddon throws government into a tumult, there will be a swelling chorus of think tank studies, op-ed columns and news articles about how poor Americans are finding it impossible to survive on Social Security and Medicare benefits alone. If Social Security is cut by 24 percent, the nation could well face a humanitarian crisis.

The quickest, easiest remedy will be to recalibrate the formula for distributing Social Security benefits. As a responsible member of society who had the foresight and discipline to save for your retirement, you will draw the short stick.

Here's how it works today: The Social Security Administration calculates your Average Index Monthly Earnings (AIME) based on how long you have paid into the system and how much money you earned. Your AIME is adjusted by a formula to calculate the "Primary Insurance Amount" (PIA), the size of the check Social Security strokes you each month.

In 2009, the formula equaled the sum of:

• 90 percent of the first $744 of AIME, plus
• 32 percent of the next $3,739 of AIME, plus
• 15 percent of AIME over $4,483.[179]

The way the formula is weighted, low-income earners get a much higher percentage of their income counted in the calculation of benefits. Higher-income earners get less. In other words, Social Security is already a mechanism for wealth redistribution. It's a modest redistribution, to be sure, but the precedent has been established.

Again, place yourself in the shoes of your Congressman when Social Security benefits are meat-axed by 24 percent. The poorest seniors will face hideous choices. What do they cut from their household budget? Their medication? The electric bill? Lottery tickets? Life won't exactly be roses for better-off Boomers, but their choices will not be as dire. Trade dinners out from the Olive Garden for dinners at Applebee's... or unsubscribe from HBO? Not so hideous. Political pressure will be powerful to support a minimum standard of living for helpless, elderly Social Security recipients, even if it means breaking the implicit bargain made with the better-off Boomers.

Congresspersons will be unhappy about being forced to adopt such a win-lose measure, but circumstances will force them to make the tough choices that were deferred for so many decades. A growing number of poor people will be living in destitution, and the only readily available source of relief will be restructuring the flow of funds generated by the payroll tax. Middle-class Boomers could well wind up receiving only 60 percent or so of the Social Security benefits they expected. If that undermines their retirement plans, tough luck. They still should have enough money to dine on better than beanie-weenies on Thursday night, and for that they will be told to be grateful.

Medicare Madness

The picture will be just as bleak in the Medicare program. Around 2017, about a decade before Boomergeddon hits, the Medicare Hospital Insurance (Part A) reserve fund will run out. If Congress does not act, the payroll tax will cover only 81 percent of Medicare's hospital expenses. With each passing year, as more Boomers retire and as medical costs escalate, payroll taxes will cover a smaller and smaller percentage. The Medicare trustees predict that the percentage of scheduled benefits payable by the payroll tax will decline to 50 percent by 2035.

The cost and quality reforms enacted with Obamacare may take some of the sting from rising Medicare costs but not as much as the O Team expects, as I explained in Chapter 3. Congress will move quickly to patch the Part A shortfall before constituents experience benefit reductions. If the 2009 health care debate was any guide, politicians will adopt a spread-the-pain approach of nudging payroll taxes a bit higher, making patients shoulder a share of hospital expenses, imposing taxes to punish the unworthy — first the tanning-bed companies, now the cola bottlers — and sticking hospitals with what's left over. If the numbers don't add up, the U.S. can still borrow what it needs.

Thusly bandaged up like a mummy from Pharaoh's tomb, Medicare will lurch forward to its next rendezvous with crisis in the mid-2020s. The least necrotic appendage of the Medicare ghoul will be the revivified Hospital Insurance (Part A) program. But Medicare Parts B and D will be looking positively dreadful. During Boomergeddon, when the feds are forced to limit spending to revenues, Medicare will have no choice but to severely pare back the 75 percent share that it contributes to defraying the cost of doctors and outpatient services, as well as its subsidies for medications.

The redistributionist logic that prevails in Social Security will likely guide Congress' approach to Medicare, too. Benefit cuts will prove financially disastrous to the less well-off Medicare recipients. Millions of Americans will lose their homes and savings. Once they are penniless, they will become wards of Medicaid — but Medicaid won't be spared from the ravages of Boomergeddon either. Because lives are at stake, Congress will likely re-channel the flow of funds within the Medicare program, taking from those who "can afford it" and giving to those who cannot. The change will be easy to legislate and administer: All Congress will need to do is adjust the formula for an existing surcharge that "the wealthy" already pay for their Medicare benefits.

The mechanism for shifting the burden of paying for Medicare Part B goes by the acronym of IRMAA, which stands for Income Related Monthly Adjustment Amount. Single Medicare beneficiaries earning less than $85,000 a year pay a monthly surcharge of $96.40 per month. (The income threshold and the surcharge are double for couples.) The surcharge varies depending on the beneficiary's income, as shown below:

Income	Monthly Premium
Less than $85,000	$96.40
$85,000 to $107,000	$134.90
$107.000 to $160,000	$192.70
$160,000 to 213,000	$250.50
More than $231,000	$308.30

It's hard for most Americans to work up much sympathy for a retired couple living on more than $170,000 a year. But that's missing the point: The means by which Congress can redistribute wealth within the Medicare program is already in place. The legal language has been written. The administrative apparatus has been set up. The kinks have been worked out. All Congress has to do is fiddle with the income brackets and the size of the premiums to get the results it wants.

The income levelers will make a powerful moral plea that poor seniors cannot be allowed to die from lack of access to basic medical care. And once again, those Americans who played by the rules for 40 or more years will find at the last minute that the rules have changed to their disadvantage. Congress will abandon the core Medicare principle that everyone pays into an insurance-like system in which the level of benefits is tied to the amount paid in. Medicare will become an overt wealth-redistribution scheme guided by the ideal of "from each according to his ability, and to each according to his need."

If the frugal Boomers were 50 years younger, they would be holding mass marches in Washington, D.C., and burning their congresspersons in effigy. But 78-year-old Boomers aren't likely to take to the streets: "I'd love to go to the Tea Party rally, but my lumbago is killing me." Even if they do attend, the protests won't play well on the evening news. It's hard to look threatening by waving your walking cane — especially when you're tipping over!

United States of Zimbabwe?

The southern African nation of Zimbabwe, once one of the most prosperous countries of sub-Saharan Africa, has the distinction of having the world's most worthless currency, the Zimbabwe dollar. In 1980, the nation's inflation rate was 7 percent. By 1990, the rate had surged to 17 percent, and by 2000 to 55 percent. Things were clearly out of hand in 2007 when inflation reached 66,000 percent. But worse was yet to come. In 2008, the inflation rate of the Zimbabwe dollar spiked to 231,000,000 percent! So useless was the currency that people abandoned it, using U.S. dollars and South African rand for their transactions.

Even in the depths of Boomergeddon, the U.S. will never become another Zimbabwe. It is hard to imagine that our economic fundamentals will deteriorate to the point where the highest and best use of the currency is toilet paper. But I mention Zimbabwe to make a point: Inflation is one potential future for any country, including the United States, that monetizes its debt. When faced with Boomergeddon, U.S. policy makers will have few options available to keep the government running. To keep government from shutting down, the Fed will purchase U.S. Treasury bonds with newly created money. Those purchases will inject hundreds of billions of dollars into circulation. All other things being equal, as more dollars chase the same number of goods and services, the price of those goods and services will increase.

Of course, all things are never equal. Each situation is different, and it is very difficult to know what impact future Fed actions will have — the experts can't even agree on what impact current Fed actions will have. Inflation hawks on the Federal Reserve Board are terrified that Fed actions — increasing bank reserves, lowering interest rates and purchasing mortgage-backed securities — will lead to inflation. But an argument can be made that the greater risk at the moment is deflation as consumers, businesses and governments around the world suppress demand to pay down debt, a fear that is supported by near-zero price increases for the past two years. Members of the policy-making Federal Reserve Board acknowledge the theoretical risk of inflation, but they are even more concerned about stifling the fragile economic recovery.[180]

The circumstances will be different in 2027, but the Federal Reserve Board will face similarly difficult choices. A government in default will call for drastic action. A sudden end to foreign loans accounting for some 10 percent of GDP will push the debt-addicted country into a severe recession. But stepping in with enough monetary stimulus to offset the loss of foreign lenders could set off an inflationary spiral the Fed can't control.

A great unknown is how much the Fed will have to borrow. That will depend largely on how the Treasury handles the debt crisis. Interest payments on the national debt could reach $1.5 trillion to $2 trillion a year by the mid-2020s, accounting for as much as one-quarter to one-third of total federal government expenditures and more than half of the budget deficit. If the Fed stopped paying interest on that debt, the budget problem would be half solved. Admittedly, a default would create tremendous economic problems of its own, but if your house is burning down today, you'll douse it with water even if there's a hurricane on the horizon tomorrow.

In 2027, Americans will become conversant with a body of economic theory that only a handful of economists and bond managers study today: the fine art of managing a default. It's not a subject that Americans have had to deal with since the end of the Civil War when the Confederate States of America collapsed and left its bond holders bereft. Many southern states had amassed great war debt, too, and debates ensued as to whether they should honor it, at great sacrifice, or repudiate it and start fresh. The circumstances of the South's pre-industrial economy were so different from today, though, that there is little useful we can learn from examining them.

More instructive is Argentina's 2001 default, the largest sovereign loan default in history until that time. The South American country was in hock to the tune of $195 billion, some of it owed to international institutions like the International Monetary Fund, some to Argentine investors and some $105 billion in principal and past-due interest to foreign investors. The central government decided to honor debt owned by domestic investors and the IMF, and to concentrate its write-downs on debt held by foreign investors. After three years of negotiations, the government imposed a take-it-or-leave-it solution that offered roughly 25 cents on the peso, repayable in tranches over 30, 35 and 42 years.[181] Investors were exceedingly unhappy, but most went along because there were no avenues of appeal.

By honoring some of its debt, Argentina left the door open to one day being rehabilitated in the minds of international investors. But the payback for default was punishing. Foreign investment fled the country; capital inflow came to a dead halt. The peso devalued severely, and inflation shot up as a consequence. Argentina's economy contracted nearly 11 percent in 2002, its nominal GDP per capital plummeted from $7,200 to $2,700, and the percentage of the population in poverty shot up from 25 percent to 54 percent. Living standards suffered so badly that the BBC ran an article on how former prostitutes, now grand-mothers, were coming out of retirement to pay the bills.[182] But growth soon resumed, and the country now runs a large enough balance-of-trade surplus that that government can support the portion of the debt it chose to honor.

The lesson for the U.S.: Going into default does not necessarily mean repudiating the entire national debt. The federal government could preserve a few shards of credibility among investors by reneging selectively on its obligations — promising to honor debts held by domestic investors, for example, and sticking it to non-voting foreigners. Alternately, the Treasury could tell investors of all stripes, "We can't pay your interest right now, and we can't pay back your principle when it matures. But we will offer to exchange your current holdings for these nifty new bonds repayable over 40 years and yielding a nice 5 percent interest rate. And we promise to pay those back. You can take a sure thing, or you can hang onto your old bonds, file lawsuits, petition Congress and hope a miracle happens."

Engaging in selective default would make it possible to ease the immediate pain of the debt crisis. The U.S. government, like Argentina's, would pick a level of debt payments it was willing to live with and tailor its default accordingly. Of course, there's no such thing as a free lunch — even if you steal it. The obliteration of half the value, $10 trillion or more, of the defaulted bonds — roughly 100 times more than the Argentine default — would be catastrophic to the investors, foreign or otherwise, who lent the money. Around the world, financial institutions would crack up on a scale that would make the recent Global Financial Crisis look like a branch bank stick-up by comparison. The economic repercussions would ripple back and forth across the globe in ways impossible to predict.

Another drawback to the partial default scenario is that foreign investors will shun us. For the foreseeable future, they will refuse to invest another dime in U.S. Treasury securities. Indeed, many will unload their securities in disgust for whatever they can get and pull their money out of the country. Foreign investment in the private sector likely will dry up, too. As capital flows out of the country, the value of the dollar will dive, the cost of foreign goods from flat-screen TVs to barrels of oil will shoot higher, and inflation will be rekindled. But inflation may seem the least of our problems at that point: As the global financial system becomes unhinged, economic anarchy will reign.

Pulling the stands together, we can discern the basic outlines of how the U.S. government might respond to the shock of Boomergeddon. The Treasury could engage in a partial default, cutting its debt obligations by a significant amount. Congress could raise taxes and slash spending to help close the budget shortfall, but not too much for fear of deepening the economic downturn. Meanwhile, legislators could reallocate existing Social Security and Medicare revenue streams from well-off retirees to the poor to prevent too many from slipping into dire poverty. Then the Federal Reserve could step in, buying Treasury bonds in a bid (1) to keep essential government services open and (2) to help offset the massive loss of fiscal stimulus. It is impossible to say now, in 2010, what effects an aggressive Fed intervention would have on the economy. A one-shot jolt might have only a mild effect if it served to offset the deflationary impact of fiscal contraction. But the public could get spooked if it appeared that the Fed would be called upon to intervene year after year. In that case, inflation could build a good head of steam.

It is futile to try to predict any particular outcome so far in advance. There are too many unknowns. But from the vantage point of 50-something Boomers planning their retirement, it is clear that higher taxes, restructured Social Security and Medicare, and a rapid acceleration of inflation will not bode well for their golden years.

If the inflationary scenario comes to pass, Boomer retirees will be disproportionately affected. Young people with long-term investment horizons can afford to take more risk, so they invest more heavily in equities, which are hurt by inflation but not wiped out by it. By contrast, retirees are advised to reduce risk by investing a larger share of their assets in fixed financial instruments. If global interest rates rise in the early 2020s but inflation remains restrained, as I have argued they will, Boomers may find that bonds offer attractive yields. The lead-up to Boomergeddon, higher interest rates with stable inflation, will benefit anyone in saving mode. But fixed investments are not the place to put your money when inflation heats up. For many Boomers, a bout of stiff inflation could be the most catastrophic outcome of Boomergeddon of all.

Chapter 8
Surviving Boomergeddon

The Boomers' Dilemma

If you're reading this book, you're most likely a middle-class Baby Boomer. I don't get a picture of you hanging around the crack house, sucking on your pipe and worrying how long the Chinese will continue buying 10-year Treasury bonds. And I don't see you shuttling between your Manhattan penthouse and *pied a terre* in the Hamptons agonizing over the future of FICA payroll taxes. No, you've probably worked hard all your life, bought a house, paid your taxes, sent your kids to college, and tried to build a retirement nest egg. You probably stood by helplessly as half the equity in your house went up in smoke and your 401(k) plan turned into a 201(k). But you consoled yourself that the Social Security and Medicare programs that helped your grandparents and parents in retirement would be there for you. Indeed, you've paid payroll taxes all your life, and you feel like the government owes you something in return, even if it's less than what you would have earned if you'd invested the money yourself.

Odds are, though, if you are who I think you are, your retirement probably won't be much fun. First of all, the actuaries say that you'll probably live longer than your parents and grandparents did — at least you will if you take decent care of yourself. That means you'll have to set aside more money than they did to cover more years of retirement. Second of all, if you make it into your 80s, there's a good chance that you'll contend with years of multiple chronic medical conditions — diabetes, arthritis, emphysema, heart disease, cancer, Alzheimer's disease — that are associated with advanced age. Even with Medicare coverage, medical bills will gnaw a big hole in your bank account. The Urban Institute estimates that out-of-pocket medical expenses and supplementary insurance for Americans 65 and older will increase from $2,600 yearly in 2008 to $6,200 (in inflation-adjusted dollars) in 2040. Put another way, medical expenses will increase as a share of retiree income from about 10 percent today to 19 percent thirty years from now.[183]

Third of all, you could well be among the Boomers who encounter a caregiver crisis they never planned on. It will dawn upon many Boomers about the time they hit 80 that vision impairment and slower reaction times make driving a dicey proposition. Disabilities also will make it difficult for many to walk more than a block and lug around shopping bags. If they can't drive, can't walk and can't tote a grocery bag, they will find it difficult living on their own. While their parents often had three or four children to help look after them, most Boomers will have only one or two — and if one of them is a daughter, odds are she's working or moved out of town. Some Boomers, never married, have no children at all. If they want care-giving assistance, they will have to pay for it themselves. And always in the back of their minds, they will be worrying, what happens if they have a stroke, or fall and break a hip? The prospect of checking into a nursing home at a cost of $7,000 a month (in today's dollars) will evolve from a distant, theoretical concern in middle age to a pressing and continual worry.

In sum, there is a good chance that your retirement finances will be disintegrating slow-motion before your very eyes, when, boom, the federal government goes into default. The flow of funds into Social Security and Medicare will jerk short like a barking dog reaching the end of its chain. The retirement programs will have no money to spend other than the revenue they bring in from payroll taxes, and that revenue will be shrinking because millions of Americans will have lost their jobs in the recession that precipitated the default. Making matters worse, Congress most likely will divvy up the payroll taxes to help out the poor at the expense of people like you who had the foresight to put something aside. You could wind up with Social Security and Medicare benefits equivalent to 60 percent to 70 percent of what you had been receiving.

You will have no way of making up the loss of income. At 75 or 80 years old, going back to work will not be an option.

It's a grim scenario. You have two ways of responding. One option is to plug your fingers in your ears and say, "La, la, la, la, I can't hear you." A lot of Boomers will do precisely that — not because Boomers are uniquely perverse or bull-headed as a generation but because the older people get, the less likely they are to respond to negative images, concepts and words. Researchers have studied the way people process information by conducting MRI scans and watching the activity of the amygdala, the neural complex in the brain that processes emotions. Older and younger adults show similar amygdala activity when viewing positive pictures, but the amygdala of older adults don't fire off when they're viewing negative images. In a word, older people subconsciously tune out the bad stuff.

The alternative is to view the world as it is becoming, as horrifying as that might be, and to adapt to it. I'm assuming you're that kind of person, despite the bad vibes this book is transmitting to your amygdala. If you want to take your future into your own hands rather than trust to fate, the solution is conceptually very simple: Save more. Build your own retirement fund. Do not rely upon government to take care of you because the government will fail you.

Start by defining your life goals and creating a long-term financial blueprint to achieve them. A sound plan develops a realistic budget to live on, adds any bequests you want to make, and accounts for risks that are widely acknowledged today to exist, such as the one-in-three chance that you will have the need for expensive, long-term care. As a final step, you must bullet-proof your plan to withstand the shocks and discontinuities arising from Boomergeddon.

Conventional retirement planning assumes a fairly steady-state world. In that world, the biggest risk for retirees is the escalation of medical costs that cut into discretionary income over the decades. That is not a challenge to be minimized, but it is one that at least can be anticipated and planned for. Boomergeddon requires your long-term financial plan to be robust enough to survive the possibility of prolonged economic trauma... and worse. Will the collapse of the market for U.S. Treasuries spread to other sovereign debt, to bond markets generally and to the stock market as well? Will the flight of foreign capital combine with a downturn in the business cycle to plunge the U.S. economy into a deep depression? Will the Fed, in a desperate bid to keep the economy afloat and government services from collapsing, ignite rampant inflation?

There are the second-order effects to anticipate, too. What happens if Boomergeddon spreads from the federal government to fiscally debilitated state governments like California? Could parts of the U.S. experience a breakdown of civil order? What impact will the retreat of the American empire, the fiscal breakdown of our major allies and trading partners, and the disintegration of fragile nation-states have upon the world trade and capital flows that support our global economic system? Such fears seem overwrought now, but anyone who has studied the fates of other countries and other periods of history, such as the era preceding World War II, knows just how frail human institutions can be.

We can speculate endlessly, but in the end there is no way to know how the interplay of complex economic and political forces will unfold. We can say safely only that the world will enter an era of extraordinary uncertainty and that the nostrums that applied to personal investing in the post-World War II era may no longer hold true. With the prospect of governments in chaos, economies collapsing, deflation taking hold here, inflation breaking out there, currencies fluctuating, the Electronic Herd shuttling its capital from one safe haven to the next, civil disorder breaking out and wars erupting, it is impossible to devise a retirement portfolio today that can survive all possible outcomes.

I am not one to dispense investment advice, so I will offer none here. Find an advisor you trust, employ him or her to set realistic goals and draw up a long-term financial plan. Calculate how much money you need to save between now and then to achieve your goals. Then seek counsel on how to insure or hedge against the kinds of disruptive, unpredictable events you see emerging from Boomergeddon.

Planning is the easy part. The hard part is executing the plan.

To survive Boomergeddon in reasonable comfort and security you need to show sustained discipline and commitment to saving. Arrange your affairs to drive your household costs as low as you can and to save as much of your income as you can. Adopt the attitude that the Social Security and Medicare programs as currently configured are living on borrowed time, and that any benefits you receive from them are a welcome but fleeting gift that some future session of Congress, panicked by Boomergeddon, may snatch from you. With all due recognition of the fact that you need to continue generating income and cannot retreat to a cabin in the Montana woods, you should move "off the grid" as much as possible. You must become as independent of the government as you can. You must become as self-reliant as you can.

The Tax-Time Treadmill

Before you take the time to set achievable long-term goals, you need to understand why so many Americans feel like they are running on a treadmill, exerting themselves and going nowhere. Americans work longer hours than do the populations of most economically advanced nations — 1,792 hours on average in 2008, a tad higher than the famed Japanese salary man (1,772 hours per year) and somewhere between the extremes of the workaholic South Koreans (2,316 hours) and the laid-back Dutch (1,389 hours). Of the 30 nations measured by the Organisation of Economic Cooperation and Development, Americans logged longer hours than 20 other nations; only nine others, all poorer, logged more.

Americans, the Boomers especially, take great pride in their work ethic. We measure our self worth largely by what we do and how successful we are in doing it. All that work pays off not only psychically but monetarily. Americans earn more money than almost everyone else in the world. Measured by per capita income, we ranked 6th highest in the world in 2009, making $47,600 for every man, woman and child. We were exceeded only by three small, oil-rich countries (Qatar, Brunei and Norway), which owe their extreme affluence to the accident of mineral wealth, the prosperous city-state of Singapore, which achieved its wealth by means of a social discipline that Americans would find oppressive, and Luxembourg. . . . Luxembourg? Who knew? The half million residents of that tiny, land-locked country may be on to something.

But, for all the money we make, we do a terrible job of saving. The Chinese, whose average incomes are one-thirteenth of ours, manage to save half of their household income. The chart below shows the net savings rates for major developed countries, based on each nation's latest data (either 2006 or 2007). The U.S. wasn't the worst back then, but we were close to it. It turns out that the Danes and Finns have a savings crisis, too. Since the recession, the U.S. savings rate has bounced back to between 4.0 percent and 5.0 percent. But for years we have ranked among the world's great spendthrifts. Why is that?

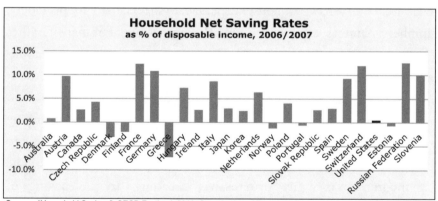

Source: "Household Savings", OECD Factbook 2010; Organisation of Economic Cooperation and Development.

There are many possible reasons. One is that American financial institutions pioneered new channels for consumer lending, such as credit cards and home equity loans. Another is a tax structure that penalizes savings and rewards consumption. Yet another in recent years has been the influx of cheap foreign capital that has driven down interest rates and reduced the monthly carrying cost of consumer debt. Then there is the interplay between work effort, income, taxes and the time famine — a complex of factors that can be summed up as servitude to the leviathan state.

Americans are stuck on a treadmill. The harder they work, the more they earn and the less free time they have. But the more they earn — at least those in the top income brackets — the more they pay in taxes. The more they pay in taxes, the less discretionary income they have. That much is self-evident.

But there is a subtler point that warrants mention: The less free time Americans have, the more their family expenses mount. Many affluent American households in which husband and wife both work suffer from what sociologists call a "time famine." Achieving a work-life balance is tough enough when you're juggling kids, housework and errands with a 40-hour-per-week job. It's even harder when you're juggling all of those things with a 50- or 60-hour-a-week job, as many managers, professionals and executives do. Families compensate by spending money to outsource domestic work: stroking endless checks to landscapers, yard boys, housekeepers, babysitters, day care providers, plumbers, painters, electricians and other tradesmen. For many families a major expense is dining out: in effect, outsourcing the work of cooking and kitchen cleanup. With the notable exception of day care, Americans pay for most of that outsourcing in after-tax dollars.

One reason so many affluent Americans feel like they are running on a treadmill is that government taxes those who employ their time to generate income, not those who employ their time to enjoy leisure. The U.S. income tax is highly "progressive," meaning that the earnings of families in higher income brackets are subject to a higher percentage of tax. The income of Americans who work shorter hours and make less income is taxed for less. Households earning more than $82,000 pay a top rate of 28 percent; those over $172,000 pay 33 percent, and those over $373,000 pay 35 percent. When the Bush tax cuts expire at the end of 2010, the top tax rate will reach 39.6 percent.

On top of the federal income taxes, taxpayers in most states also pay a state income tax. In Hawaii and Oregon, the top bracket reaches a punitive 11 percent (although that rate doesn't kick in until families have reached $200,000 and $250,000 in income respectively). Outside of Texas, Florida and a handful of other states that levy no income tax, most two-income families can count on paying an extra 5 percent or 6 percent on each additional dollar of income earned.

Top Tax Brackets by State					
		State	Top Tax Rate		
Hawaii	11.00	Delaware	6.95	New Mexico	4.90
Oregon	11.00	Montana	6.90	North Dakota	4.86
New Jersey	10.75	Nebraska	6.84	Colorado	4.63
Rhode Island	9.90	Connecticut	6.50	Arizona	4.54
California	9.55	West Virginia	6.50	Michigan	4.35
Iowa	8.98	Kansas	6.45	Indiana	3.40
New York	8.97	Ohio	6.24	Pennsylvania	3.07
Vermont	8.95	Georgia	6.00	Illinois	3.00
Maine	8.50	Kentucky	6.00	New Hampshire	*
Maryland	8.50	Louisiana	6.00	Tennessee	*
District of Columbia	8.50	Missouri	6.00	Alaska	0.00
Minnesota	7.85	Virginia	5.75	Florida	0.00
Idaho	7.80	Oklahoma	5.50	Nevada	0.00
North Carolina	7.75	Massachusetts	5.30	South Dakota	0.00
Wisconsin	7.75	Alabama	5.00	Texas	0.00
Arkansas	7.00	Mississippi	5.00	Washington	0.00
South Carolina	7.00	Utah	5.00		
* Limited to dividends and interest income only					

Source: "State Individual Income Taxes"; Federation of Tax Administrators.

Then there is the so-called Alternative Minimum Tax (AMT), enacted in 1969 to target some 155 high-income households that owed little or no income at the time. As is typical when politicians decide to play Robin Hood, there have been unintended consequences. Inflation has elevated millions of middle-class Americans into tax brackets once deemed the exclusive preserve of the "rich." Meanwhile, the "rich" have moved on, reallocating their portfolios to limit tax exposure by other means.

The ATM works by phasing out common deductions that the upper middle class uses to reduce taxable income, including the standard deduction, state and local taxes, medical expenses, interest on second mortgages, tax-exempt interest, incentive stock options and tax credits of various types. Judged by the revenues it raises, the impact of the AMT is modest, contend Daniel Feenberg and James Poterba in a 2003 paper.[184] Projecting to 2010, the two economists expected the ATM to bump up the average income tax liability as follows:

$75,000 to $100,000 income   +1.6 percent
$100,000 to $200,000 income +2.4 percent
$200,000 to $500,000 income +2.7 percent
More than $500,000 income   +0.6 percent

That may not seem like much extra money, but the phasing out of those important tax breaks has the effect of boosting the effective marginal tax rates by several percentage points more. Add it all up, and the average middle-class American family pays about 33 cents on the last dollar in wages earned. Upper middle-class families pay closer to 40 cents on the last dollar in salary earned, while upper-income families will pay an effective rate of well more than 50 percent next year.

As I shall explain, the secret to a better life — and surviving Boomergeddon — isn't working harder, buying more stuff, paying more taxes and getting more stressed out. It's simplifying your life, learning to live with less, cutting your tax load and becoming more self-reliant.

Too Much Stuff

Between taxes and the time famine, the average American family finds itself running hard just to stay even. What, then, do Americans do with their disposable income? For the past 30 years, rather than saving money, Americans have been spending it. Some of what they spend yields tangible things like bigger houses and newer, shinier cars. But a lot of it is just "stuff." By "stuff," I mean consumer products that provide an ephemeral sense of satisfaction upon purchase but are quickly forgotten, like children's toys, clothes that get pushed to the back of the closet, and gewgaws that clutter the sideboards and bookshelves.

The rich aren't the only people who buy loads and loads of stuff. Poor and working-class people do, too. The main difference is the quality of the stuff, not the quantity. One way or the other, the vast majority of Americans spend an inordinate share of their disposable incomes on stuff, not to mention bigger houses to store and house all of it.

The Bacon family is no exception. When the stuff accumulating in my garage takes on the look and feel of a junk yard, I take it down to the Henrico County dump. One day not long ago, I ran into a couple of good ol' boys, William Barker and William Nance, as they unloaded construction scrap from a pickup truck and tossed it into the county's enormous green metal bins. Both men were plumbers by trade. Barker was working on a home improvement project, and Nance was helping him.

It was amazing, I remarked, how much of the stuff we buy — stuff that at one point in time we thought we wanted — winds up in the landfill. The two men responded animatedly. "A friend of mine found a painting in that too-good-to-throw-away area," Barker said, pointing to a shed where people had dropped off some perfectly serviceable furniture, children's bicycles and barbecue grills. "She sold it on the Internet for $800. ... Look, there's a Nordic Track in really good shape! ... It's unreal what people come here and trash."

Nance picked up the theme. Rich people aren't the only ones who are wasteful, he said. Just go see what people buy at Dollar Tree. "I asked my wife, 'Show me something you bought from Dollar Tree six months ago that you still have now.' It's all junk!"

Personally, I'm a big fan of material prosperity, and I'd like to get my share of it. I'm also a big believer in consumer sovereignty, the idea that Americans should be allowed to spend their money on what they want and not have their choices constrained by a nanny state. If I want to squander my money to provide a fleeting elevation to my endorphin level, that's my business.

Still, I sense that something has gone seriously awry with our values and priorities. Collectively, we Americans buy way too much useless stuff. We get bored with it, banish it to the attic or garage and, eventually, throw it away. And we do so without giving serious consideration to what it costs us individually or as a nation.

Buying stuff costs us far more than the price we pay at the store. If we hadn't bought the stuff, we could have done something else with the money, a concept that economists refer to as "alternate opportunity cost." We could have paid down our credit cards, for instance, or put the money in savings. There is a second cost that most people overlook: the cost of storage. More stuff requires bigger houses, as I shall illuminate in a moment. Thirdly, the manufacture and transport of stuff consumes energy, which generates pollution and distresses the environment on a planetary scale — a point that activist Annie Leonard drove home with her famous Internet animation, "The Story of Stuff."

Americans are obsessed with achieving energy independence, and propose all manner of public policy solutions to emancipate ourselves from oil sheikhs and tin pot dictators whose hands are on the pipeline valve. Yet we think very little about financial independence. For the most part, we seem perfectly content to entrust our well-being in retirement to the willingness of the Japanese, Chinese and other foreign creditors to lend money to us forever. You don't have to be a hippie, environmentalist or religious ascetic to question the wisdom of pursuing happiness via the accumulation of stuff. The addiction to buying more stuff and finding somewhere to put it is at the heart of our national over-spending, under-saving and humbling dependence upon foreign capital.

Across the nation, Americans devote billions of square feet of retail space to display the greatest cornucopia of crap in the history of mankind. The mind-numbing variety of stuff on display is a testament to the power of our capitalist system to cater to consumers' every desire. I'll touch upon just two examples among thousands that could be chosen.

In a mall near where I live there is a Mikasa store. The retail chain sells products relating to dining, entertainment and "home accents." Normally, I steer a wide berth around such places, but one day I ventured inside. An illuminated display of "stemware" deemed essential for entertaining caught my eye. The shelves sparkled with all manner of glass and crystal vessels: some designed for drinking wine, some for beer, some for martinis and some for bubbly. Certain pieces were shaped to capture the taste and aromas of red wines, others of white. There were pieces of "stemless" stemware that served obscure functions I could not fathom. Evidently, the versatile, multi-functional glass — as in a "glass" of milk — is no longer adequate to carry out the full range of tasks required by the modern-day American hostess.

A similar profusion of styles and types characterized the porcelain dinnerware. In days past, young couples started out with a set of every-day plates and dishes, and, if their friends were affluent, wedding presents of china. No longer. Today's trendy household might have complete sets of everyday plates, a set of semi-formal stoneware and a set of china. Some hostesses have special sets for Christmas and other occasions. "One lady came in and said she has literally six sets of china," volunteered one helpful young store clerk in response to my queries. "She came back in [to buy another] because her husband didn't like the cups in one set."

For those who prefer paper plates to porcelain, there is always the Dollar Store. The first thing that struck me when stepping foot inside one of these paeans to plastic was the extraordinary diversity of products emblazoned with the image of Shrek, the affable ogre of movie fame. There were Shrek figurines, Shrek bubble wands, Shrek Frisbees, Shrek swimming goggles, Shrek sand molds, Shrek coloring books and Shrek lip gloss. The other inescapable impression was that virtually every object in the store was made of synthetic material: flowers and flip-flops, flimsy toy golf clubs and toy pirate guns; luau masks, fake flower leis and pink flamingo stirring sticks; glo-sticks of all colors and toy mobile phones so cheap that the hucksters at Chuck E. Cheese wouldn't even give them away as a prize.

Americans have devised a number of mechanisms to cope with all the "stuff" they accumulate. One option, as famously lampooned by comedian George Carlin, is to buy a bigger house. Creating more room for their stuff is only one reason, of course, that people buy bigger houses. Children lobby for their own private bedrooms. Americans crave dedicated "family" rooms for adults and playrooms for children. People want offices and guest rooms, laundry rooms, sunrooms and sauna closets — all examples of hyper-consumption in their own way. But a compelling motive for many a housing upgrade is to create more space to store more stuff. Stand-up attics. Three-car garages. Master bedrooms with his-and-her walk-in closets.

This craving for space has a huge impact on the economy. In 1978, the median new single-family house was 1,650 square feet, according to the National Association of Home Builders. One generation later, by 2006, the median size had reached 2,237 square feet, an increase of 35 percent.[185]

The number of new houses with four bedrooms increased from 24 percent in 1970 to 39 percent in 2005 — even though the average number of people per household in the United States had shrunk. More bedrooms means more closets to put more stuff. Meanwhile, garages have gotten bigger, too. In 1970, 39 percent of new houses were built with two- or three-car garages. By 2005, that number had reached 84 percent. Of course, garages are used for a lot more than cars these days. The wife rules the house, but the man rules the garage.[186] The garage is the manspace; it contains the manly stuff like tools and riding mowers.

Incredibly, for all the swollen garages, closets, attics and basements, today's bigger houses are not capacious enough to hold the accumulated flotsam of American families. People are carting excess belongings to off-site depositories in such numbers that the self-storage industry now claims to be the fastest-growing segment of the commercial real estate sector over the past 30 years.

Among the amazing facts reported by the industry's trade association: As of the first quarter of 2007, there were more than 50,000 primary self-storage facilities in the U.S., generating approximately $22 billion in 2009 revenues. Think about that. American businesses and households were spending $22 billion a year to store stuff they could not cram into their houses and offices! And make no mistake about it, households account for a big chunk of that business: Nearly one in ten U.S. households rent a self-storage unit. To grasp the magnitude of the self-storage business, consider this: Total self-storage space in the U.S. amounts to 2.3 billion square feet — about 80 square miles, an area three times the size of Manhattan — just to accommodate the overflow of stuff too precious to bury in the landfill.[187]

Now, think how the accumulation of stuff gets leveraged into mass over-spending and under-saving. First, there's the cost of buying the stuff. Second, there's the cost of housing and storing the stuff. You pay interest, taxes and insurance on the space, at an average cost of $80 per square feet in basic construction costs. And, don't forget, you also pay to heat and air-condition space for the care and comfort of your stuff. Finally, to help pay that inflated mortgage, both spouses work, typically full-time. Their combined incomes boost the family into a higher tax bracket, with the result that they pay higher taxes. Finally, because they're working longer hours, they experience a time famine and outsource domestic chores at considerable extra cost. Talk about a treadmill — give me a hamster wheel any day!

Simplify, Simplify, Simplify

Life isn't about accumulating more stuff. He who dies with the most toys does not win. "Family and relationships — not money and power — are at the heart of what Americans most value," writes Ken Dychtwald, CEO of the Age Wave consulting firm in "Retirement at the Tipping Point." "We are almost twice as likely to define success as 'having loving family and friends,' than by having wealth. And having strong relationships has become twenty times more important than wielding 'power and influence.'"[188]

In the "Retirement at the Tipping Point" survey, 56 percent of the respondents said the best thing about money was "feeling secure." Next came "being able to help my family and loved ones" (42 percent), "having freedom/choices" (37 percent) and "being independent" (33 percent).

"Accumulating huge piles of stuff that spill out of my closets when I open the door" did not make the list.

In other words, having money is a good thing, but not for the material possessions it buys. Bucks in the bank provide security, independence, and the ability to help others, all benefits that far outlast the brief rush that comes from buying more stuff. Most important of all from my perspective, emancipating yourself from mammon — reducing your living expenses and building up savings — will position you to survive Boomergeddon.

Cutting spending is not easy, but it can be done. Millions of American families have done so in response to the recession. The key is to systematically review where you spend money.

Housing. The fastest, easiest way to curtail spending is to move to a smaller abode. According to the Bureau of Labor Statistics' household expenditure survey in 2008, 34 percent of all consumer dollars were spent on home mortgage or rent.[189] That's where the big bucks are. Size is not the only factor determining the value of a residence, of course. There is also "location, location, location," as we shall discuss below in the context of transportation. But all other things being equal, a smaller dwelling is a less expensive dwelling.

For most people, an obstacle to moving to a smaller residence is the perception that there would be no place to put all their stuff. That's why the process of restructuring your lifestyle and domestic finances must begin with the ruthless purging of possessions. When thinking of how much of those old clothes, knick-knacks and yard tools you really need, consider the price of storage. The average cost of basic construction is roughly $80 per square foot.

The second step is to analyze how much of your square footage is wasted. Do you really need a living room? Most people do most of their "living" in the kitchen and family room. Living rooms are architectural relics of the days when people admitted guests and visitors to a room for formal entertainment. No one but royalty and the rich do that anymore. When you invite your friends over, everyone hangs out near the food and the big-screen TV.

Do you really need a guest room? Sure, it's nice to have a place for out-of-town guests and family to lay their heads. But how often do they visit? Do not forget the alternate opportunity cost. On the assumption that a bedroom adds $10,000 to the cost of your house, you could have bought a similar house without the room for a smaller mortgage. Between interest, insurance and property taxes, you could be saving $500 a year! If relatives come to town, you could put them up in the nearest Holiday Inn for a couple of nights and still come out ahead.

Can the kids share a room? Sure, every child will lobby relentlessly for his or her own room. But do they really need their privacy? Sharing a room worked out for Wally and the Beaver back in the 1950s. Continue through every room in the house. Would you really suffer a diminishment in your standard of living if you didn't have it? Are there portions of a room that go unused, filled perhaps with chairs and couches that nobody sits on, or sideboards whose drawers are filled with useless stuff? Can you live with smaller rooms?

Finally, don't forget the lot your house sits on. How important is that big, ½-acre yard to you? Do you really enjoy mowing the lawn, raking the leaves and pulling the weeds it takes to maintain that acreage – – or do you pay someone else to do so? Some people truly do love their gardens. If you're one of them, ask yourself: Could you be almost as happy tending a postage-stamp garden on a much smaller lot?

Transportation. The second largest category of household expenditures is transportation. For all practical purposes, that means automobiles. When you total up the purchase price, the financing costs, the insurance, the maintenance, repairs and gasoline, cars account for 17 percent of the household budget. There are many ways to economize. Next time you purchase a car, buy a less expensive model. Never lease a car — always buy. And don't trade in after two or three years, the period during which the car depreciates most rapidly. Holding on to a car for longer can save significant dollars. Keeping a car long enough to pay off the loan is even better: Bank what you had been spending on the car payment to build a kitty towards the next car purchase. Ideally, pay for the vehicle in cash.

Another way to save money on cars is to own fewer of them. If you have a three-car household, try living with two. If you have a two-car household, try living with one. Admittedly, that may be impractical in some locations. Most neighborhoods developed within the past 50 years — the "burbs" — have been designed around the automobile. If you live in a cul de sac subdivision, commute 20 miles to work, and find all the conveniences of civilization segregated in strip shopping centers, then walking, biking and mass transit are not serious alternatives. But some communities do offer transportation options.

Manhattan is famous as a location where residents don't need to own a car — indeed, where owning a car is a hindrance because there's no point in driving and the cost of parking is astronomical. You can get along fine just walking, riding the subway or hailing a cab. If you need to transport something heavy, just call a delivery service. Saving the expense of owning a car is a major bonus to living in Manhattan. Too bad everything else is so hideously expensive.

A more livable community where it is possible to live a car-free lifestyle is Arlington, Va., the county across the Potomac River from Washington, D.C. Over the course of the past 40 years, Arlington has transformed itself from a typical, auto-centric, bedroom community into one of the most livable places in the United States. While preserving its traditional neighborhoods of single-family houses, Arlington has encouraged dense development around its METRO heavy rail stations that link it to Washington, D.C., and neighboring jurisdictions. Arrayed around a quarter-mile radius of the subway stations is a mix of residential apartments, commercial offices, retail space and public amenities that make it possible for many residents to meet many of their daily needs on foot. To reach neighborhoods not served by the subway, Arlington maintains a dense network of bus routes. Between the heavy rail and the buses, the county has the highest rate of mass transit usage in the U.S. outside of New York City. But the options don't end there. Arlington has laced the county with a network of biking trails. And for residents who simply cannot do without a car on an episodic basis, the county has arranged with Zipcar to position its rental-by-the-hour cars at convenient locations around the county.

While Arlington may set the U.S. gold standard for the car-free lifestyle, there are many other communities with pedestrian-friendly communities served by mass transit. If you live in one, consider buying or renting in a location where the options of walking, biking, car sharing or mass transit will allow you to dispense with a car.

Of course, such locations go for a premium price precisely because they provide that lifestyle alternative and they tend to be in short supply. In a word, you pay more for a location that allows you to live without a car. And that brings us to a critical insight in your quest to drive down your living expenses: The cost of housing and transportation are inextricably intertwined. In every metro area in the U.S., you can find less expensive real estate located on the metropolitan periphery. But there is a trade-off for the lower mortgage: a longer commute and higher transportation costs. Longer commutes add to your time famine, and the higher transportation costs may render your mortgage savings illusory. Housing and transport combined account for half your living expenses. You must consider the two in tandem.

Food and health care. Like housing and transportation, food and health care are inseparably bound. Food accounts for 12.7 percent of the family budget and out-of-pocket health care expenditures 5.9 percent — totaling nearly one consumer dollar out of five.

As Americans are acutely aware, what we eat and drink has a direct bearing on our health. We eat way too much, and most of what we consume is unhealthy. Poor nutrition contributes directly to obesity, and obesity is a scourge that contributes to any number of expensive and debilitating medical conditions such as heart disease, diabetes and arthritis. Those chronic diseases increase out-of-pocket payments for doctors' visits, medical tests and medication, not to mention co-payments for surgery should things go radically wrong. Obesity also leads to disabilities that require in-home assistance, yet another cost. Good health is its own reward, and that reward comes with one heck of a fringe benefit — lower household expenses.

You can get a pretty good idea of what kind of food America eats and in what quantities by visiting a grocery store. The shelf space in a Kroger or a Food Lion is a small Darwinian universe in which only the fit survive. If a category's sales grow, the shelf space devoted to it expands. If a product's sales slows, its share of shelf space declines. Observe how the shelf space in your favorite store is allocated. Invariably, a full aisle is devoted to the trashiest of junk food — salt- and fat-laden snacks like Fritos, Cheetohs and potato chips on one side, and carbonated drinks in their infinite varieties of sugared and sugar-free, caffeinated, non-caffeinated, colas and lemon-limes on the other. Compare the space devoted to garden greens... and ice cream. Compare the space dedicated to healthy multi-grain bread... and to white bread, pastries, bagels, rolls, buns, muffins, cupcakes, Ho Hos and Ding Dongs. Compare the square footage allotted to blueberries, strawberries and other fresh fruits... and to cookies, candy and sugar-drenched breakfast cereals. It is no accident that Americans are the fattest people on the face of the planet. We are what we eat.

Fortunately, we have one thing going for us in our struggle for better nutrition. Eating less saves money! For every 12-pack of Coca-Colas you refrain from buying, you save money. For every bag of Fritos you put back on the shelf, you save money. For every carton of Edie's gourmet death-by-chocolate, super creamy ice cream you leave in the refrigerator case, you save money.

Here's another remarkable finding based upon extensive personal research: Eating smaller portions cuts calories and saves money, too. As the nutritionists advise, eat until you're full... and then stop! Grilling hamburgers? Make smaller patties. Serving those giant Perdue chicken breasts? Cut them in half. Whipping up a packet of delicious Zatarain's black beans and rice? Save half a pot for tomorrow night's dinner.

It is often said that eating healthier food is more expensive. That is true no doubt for fresh fruits and vegetables, which are indispensable for any balanced diet. But fruits and vegetables constitute a relatively small share of the typical family's grocery bill — about 11.5 percent. If you cut out enough cookies, cake, ice cream, French fries, soft drinks, chips, dip, pretzels, cheese whiz and other garbage, you can double your consumption of fruits and vegetables and still save money.

Food is only one half the health equation; exercise is the other. Membership in a local health club may be a good investment, but it doesn't take a gymnasium or a wall of treadmills and stair climber machines to stay in decent physical condition. A few square feet on an empty patch of rug provides enough space to do pushups, squats, crunches, stretches and lower-back exercises. A metal rod in the garage gives you a chin-up bar. The intersection of your kitchen counters provides a place to do dips. Jogging outdoors costs nothing more than gym shorts, a t-shirt and a pair of athletic shoes. Power walking doesn't even require running apparel.

The biggest barrier to exercise is motivation. If feeling better and looking better doesn't give you motivation, then try this: Better health equals fewer trips to the doctors, fewer medications, fewer encounters with the health care system and, consequently, lower outlays for medical services. Staying healthy also keeps you out of the hospital, where medical errors and disease transmission are rampant.

The last thing you expect when you check into a hospital is to wind up sicker than when you started. But a 2005 study found that 20 percent of the 391 patients tracked over several days in intensive-care and coronary-care units in an unnamed academic hospital experienced "adverse events" that had nothing to do with their original illness. Nearly half were preventable. Administration of medications was the single-most frequent problem.[190]

Hospitals hire epidemiologists, whose job is to prevent the spread of disease, for a reason: With the possible exception of heroin dens and leper colonies, hospitals are among the most disease-prone dwellings on the planet. A recent study concluded that sepsis (a bloodstream infection) and pneumonia acquired in U.S. hospitals affected nearly 250,000 people in 2006, killing 48,000, and ran up medical bills by $8.1 billion. Said co-author Anup Malani: "In some cases, relatively healthy people check into the hospital for routine surgery. They develop sepsis because of a lapse in infection control — and they can die."[191]

There are so many reasons to take control of your health: Feel better, look better, save money. To borrow a phrase from Nike, just do it. Stop smoking, eat better, exercise more. Those are the top three health commandments, but there are others. If you are sentient, you know them. Unless you're aching for a case of melanoma, don't roast yourself in the sun like a pig on a rotisserie. Don't drink until you puke and pass out. For that matter, don't drink and drive — and, by the way, do wear your seat belts. Don't eat lead paint. Don't play with asbestos. Don't play in toxic waste. You may feel entitled to health care, but society cannot afford to fix what you spent 65 years running down in the expectation that somebody else would take care of your problem.

The one issue I'm sympathetic to is the difficulty of finding the time to exercise, especially when you're working long hours, commuting long distances, ferrying the kids around town, volunteering, running errands and doing chores around the house. Being a responsible member of society is really time consuming. If time is an issue, think of ways to shave your commitments. Can you spend fewer hours at work? Can you buy a house that offers a shorter commute? Can you turn the commute into exercise, either biking or walking? Can you raise "free range" children who spend more time playing in the neighborhood and less time in structured activities like soccer league and music lessons that require parents to chauffeur them?

If all else fails — I know this would be a real sacrifice, but life is all about making hard choices — could you spend less time watching television? The average American watches 153 hours of television per month. One hundred and fifth-three hours! Get off your lard butt, America, and put down the remote! If you can't bestir yourself to cut your TV time by one tenth and get 15 hours of exercise a month, don't come whining to the rest of us about your poor health and expect us to pick up the tab!

Utilities and public services. This category gobbles up 7.3 percent of discretionary consumer spending. On average, electricity and natural gas cost $1,900 per year, although the sum approaches $3,000 a year for higher-income families. Investing in energy conservation and solar power represents a tremendous opportunity to go "off the grid." Insulation, smart meters, solar hot-water heaters and solar electric-generating panels are among the options available to consumers.

Think of investments in conservation and energy generation the same way you would with any other investment. What financial payback can you realistically expect? What are the risks that the payback might not materialize? And how do the risk-adjusted rewards compare to alternate investments that you might make?

Thanks to energy credits and the prospect of increasing electric rates, the payback for residential users is competitive in some states. Depending upon the cost of electricity, the prevalence of sunshine and the ubiquity of tax credits, you can recoup your investment within eight years. Factor in the convenience of still having electricity when ice storms, snow storms, thunder storms, tornadoes and hurricanes knock out your neighbors' power. Consider also the likelihood that utility-provided power rates will increase as the price of fossil fuels increase and as greener but more expensive alternative fuel sources are folded into the electric rate base. Finally, calculate the tax consequences. Let's assume, for purposes of argument, that after paying the cost of installing and financing the solar units you save $500 a year in electric and/or natural gas bills. By converting taxable financial assets into a non-taxable reduction in expenses, you insulate a nice chunk of your household budget from inflation, deflation, higher taxes, currency fluctuations, spiking interest rates or whatever else Boomergeddon has to throw at you.

Stuff. The BLS expenditure survey indicates that households spend 15 percent on categories that I refer to generically as "stuff." These include home furnishings, entertainment, apparel, housekeeping supplies, personal care and entertainment. A few general notes:

If you move to a smaller house, you need less furniture to fill it. Get rid of the hand-me-downs from your parents' attic and keep the best pieces. Taking a long-term perspective, you're better off buying fewer quality pieces that preserve their value over a long period of time — perhaps even become heirlooms — rather than buying cheap and barely serviceable furniture, and then trading up.

The same rule applies to clothing. If you have smaller closets, invest in superior quality garments that hold up longer to wear and tear and are less likely to go out of style. It may be worthwhile engaging a clothing consultant to build a wardrobe of pieces that can be mixed and matched for a wide variety of looks.

Above all, distinguish between fleeting desires and legitimate needs. Break the habit of "retail therapy" — shopping as a form of entertainment. Go for quality over quantity. Simplify your life. Avoid clutter. Embrace the ethic that less is more — except when it comes to your bank account.

Paying down debt. Paying down debt is such an essential and widely recognized part of preparing for retirement that I hesitate to insult your intelligence by mentioning it. But there are a few points worth emphasizing. The global capital glut made borrowing easier by driving down U.S. interest rates and reducing the cost of carrying debt.

If your debt consists mainly of a fixed, long-term mortgage around 5 percent, you're in good shape. But if you owe large balances on your credit cards and require financing to purchase your automobiles, you are vulnerable to the rising rates that are sure to come. Remember, the world will gradually shift to a global capital shortage over the next 10 to 20 years. If you are stuck on the debt treadmill, you will pay dearly.

Now, you might be thinking, what if Boomergeddon leads to a revival of inflation? That would be good for all debtors, not just the federal government. Why should I pay off my debt? Why not just roll it over until Boomergeddon hits and let inflation do the heavy lifting for me? There is an undeniable logic to such a notion, but it is fraught with risk. Inflation will indeed diminish the size of your debt in inflation-adjusted terms. But consider what also occurs after Boomergeddon. Foreign creditors won't satisfy themselves with yanking their money out of U.S. Treasuries, they will unload other U.S.-denominated assets, leaving the U.S. starving for capital. Given the chaos and uncertainty set loose by Boomergeddon, interest rates will shoot higher — in all probability at a rate faster than inflation.

Let us say that you owe $50,000 in debt over and above your mortgage. Let us also stipulate that in the year following Boomergeddon inflation leaps to 10 percent and the prime interest rate jumps from 6.5 percent (about double the rate prevailing in April 2010) to 18.5 percent. And, to be generous, let us further assert that your credit record is so estimable that banks will lend to you at the prime rate. In such circumstances, the value of your non-mortgage debt would shrink by $5,000 but your interest payments would increase by $6,000. In sum, you would fall $1,000 behind. Congratulations!

But, you retort, inflation would shrink the value of your mortgage as well, so you still would come out ahead. Yes, that could be true, but you would be playing a dangerous game. Boomergeddon will spark more than the default of the federal government. It will push the country into severe economic downturn: a routine business recession magnified by the loss of the federal government's deficit-spending stabilizers, the flight of foreign capital and sky-high interest rates. With the economy in the tank, you cannot count on your house preserving its value, even with inflation pushing general prices higher. Moreover, there is no guarantee, as banks tighten lending standards, that you would be able to tap the equity in your house. With your non-mortgage debt piling up, you could be forced into selling your house to remain solvent. Entering the world of Boomergeddon deeply in debt is not a risk you want to take.

Unless you're inclined to gamble with your retirement, you need to set a goal of paying down all your non-mortgage debt. Your debt repayment strategy should follow a straightforward logic: Pay off debt with the highest interest charges first. Start with your credit cards, and then move on to your auto loans. Build up your bank account balance so you can pay for your next car in cash. Then think seriously about paying down your mortgage.

If you're a bit of a gambler and your mortgage is fixed at a low rate of interest, you might consider keeping it. A 30-year loan at 5 percent interest will look pretty sweet a decade from now when interest rates are higher, and it will look even sweeter when Boomergeddon kicks in and a surge of inflation whittles down the "real" inflation-adjusted size of your principle. But such a happy scenario is contingent upon you having paid down the rest of your debt and having enough cash flow or liquid assets to meet the mortgage payments in perilous times. If you can swing it, eliminating that monthly payment will dramatically lower your monthly expenses and provide the most insulation from the vicissitudes of Boomergeddon. Most importantly, paying off your mortgage will provide a lot more peace of mind.

Working Longer

Once you have done everything you can to reduce your overhead, the next step is to determine when you can retire. As confirmed by market research surveys too numerous to bother citing, Boomers have resolved to delay retirement in order to preserve their retirement living standards. But "retirement" doesn't mean the same thing to Boomers that it did to older generations.

For the G.I. Generation and much of the Silent Generation, re-tirement represented the day you stopped work for your employer, pocketed your gold watch, signed up for Social Security and started hanging around home and driving your wife batty. There was a clear de-marcation between work and non-work. Boomers, by contrast, in-creasingly regard retirement as a process that comes in phases. The process begins when they stop full-time work for an employer and be-come eligible to start receiving a pension, tap their 401(k) plan or draw Medicare. Instead of embarking upon a life of leisure, however, many Boomers anticipate doing one of three things: (1) down-shifting from full-time to part-time work, often as a consultant or independent con-tractor, (2) launching a small business, typically a home-based business; or (3) taking a lower-paying job, often for a non-profit organization, that offers more personal fulfillment. Phased-in retirement represents a compromise between bolting from the workaday grind and generating the income needed to support a retirement that could well last longer than 20 years.

If you work for an employer who provides medical insurance as a fringe benefit, that's a big reason to continue working at least until you reach 65 and qualify for Medicare. You want to avoid paying for health care insurance in the open market as a 63- or 64-year-old. Even under Obamacare, which limits how much insurance companies can charge older people, the differential is still significant.

There are other advantages to delaying retirement. Working one more year allows you more time to build up your retirement nest egg. It also means one year less of retirement you have to fund out of your sav-ings. That logic applies not only to your personal savings but your Social Security: Social Security benefits typically increase 8 percent for each year you defer signing up. Ordinarily, a guaranteed 8 percent return would be an attractive proposition. However, you cannot ignore the impact that Boomergeddon will have on Social Security outlays some 16 to 17 years from now. It is hard to counter the logic behind the idea that you should "take what's yours" while the government still can afford to give it to you.

Deferring retirement may not sound like an attractive option to Boomers who patterned their lifestyle expectations on the experience of their own parents. Given the century-long trend toward earlier retirements, you might have assumed that you can start a life of leisure earlier than your parents did. Well, it's time for a major attitude adjustment. Unless you expect to inherit a large sum or managed to become independently wealthy, that scenario is not in the cards. Waaah. Get over it. Life isn't fair. Besides, you're privileged enough as a Boomer as it is. You probably earned a lot more money over your lifetime than your mom and dad did. And if you failed to save enough, whose fault is that? What's more, thanks to the miracle of modern medicine, you're likely to live a lot longer than they did — and you didn't hear them bellyaching about how they got shortchanged in the life-expectancy department, did you? Take the bitter with the sweet and do the responsible thing: Work longer.

Picking Where to Live

Boomers who extend their working careers tend to stay put, especially if they are expected to show up at the office every day. However, some have the flexibility as consultants or free-lancers to live anywhere they can access the Internet. As for those who quit work altogether upon retirement, there are no job-related constraints at all.

According to a survey conducted earlier this year by Del Webb Corp., a developer of communities for "active seniors," one third of all 64-year-old Boomers say they would like to move to a new home — and three-quarters of that group would move out of town.[192] That leaves roughly three out of four Boomers who prefer to "age in place," living in the same community and staying connected to friends, family and neighbors. Given the fact that Boomers tend to cite "family and friends" as the thing they value most out of life, the desire to age in place makes total sense. Far be it for me to suggest that anyone think otherwise. I live in Virginia, along with my parents and all of my siblings (well, one sister lives across the Potomac River in Washington, D.C., but that's close enough), and everyone in my wife's family lives within relatively easy driving distance in North Carolina. So, I understand the stay-at-home impulse. When Boomergeddon comes, it will be a great comfort to have your family and friends nearby. You can cling to each other for mutual support while the U.S.S. Welfare State slinks into the inky abyss.

However, if your foremost goal is surviving Boomergeddon, aging in place may not be the optimum strategy. The key to preserving your living standards, as I have argued, is to keep your living expenses as low as you can. One way to do that is to pick a place with a lower cost of living than where you live now. As much as you might wish to live out your retirement in Manhattan, San Francisco or a dozen other metropolitan regions that are so desirable that the wealthy have priced them beyond the means of the middle class, you probably cannot afford to. Fortunately, the United States is a big country. There are thousands of places to choose from. In fact, North America is a big continent. You have even more options if you are willing to live in Mexico, Panama, Costa Rica or other developing countries where the U.S. dollar goes a long way.

If you are inclined to consider moving to a less expensive location within the confines of the U.S., there are several handy tools to help you in your search. The Council for Community and Economic Research publishes the ACCRA Cost of Living Index, which you can access for free via CNNMoney.com[193] and other websites. The ACCRA methodology tracks prices for 60 different items in several broad categories across most U.S. metropolitan areas.

By comparing the cost of living for different metro areas, you can find ways to significantly lower your monthly expenditures. For example, it takes a $100,000 salary in Bergen-Passaic, N.J., neighboring New York

City, to get what $76,756 will buy you in Harrisonburg, Virginia, a livable college town in the heart of the beautiful Shenandoah Valley. Specifically:

Groceries will cost	16 %	less
Housing will cost	40 %	less
Utilities will cost	17 %	less
Transportation will cost	10 %	less
Health care will cost	8 %	less

Another example: it takes a $106,866 salary in Cleveland, Ohio, to buy you what $100,000 will get you in Myrtle Beach, S.C.

There is one important limitation to the CNNMoney and related COL tools. They compare "salaries," not income, which implies that the cost of living categories are weighted to compare the buying power of people of working age. Retirees, of course, tend to have much higher medical expenses. Therefore, someone researching a prospective retirement home should give greater weight to the medical component of the cost of living. Ideally, there would be a means to compare average Medicare costs, as opposed to the cost of private health care plans for working-age people.

As it turns out, such an online tool exists. The Dartmouth Atlas website displays a map that compares annual Medicare expenditures of different "hospital referral regions" across the U.S.[194] Returning to our comparison of Bergen-Passaic and Harrisonburg, we find that the discrepancy in Medicare costs is significantly higher than the 8 percent differential noted by the CNNMoney tool. Average Medicare reimbursements per enrollee in the Hackensack, N.J., hospital referral region were 35 percent higher in 2006 than in the Charlottesville, Va., region. Presumably, a similar differential also exists in the out-of-pocket expenses incurred by Medicare enrollees.

Cost of living is not the only geographic factor to take into account when planning for Boomergeddon. When the federal government defaults on its debt, it won't be in a position to send much aid to state and local governments, as it has during the recent downturn. Consequently, you'll prefer living in a state that can maintain basic services on its own — services like a police force... and a functioning court system... and prisons. Retirement won't be any fun if you spend it cowering in dread of marauding post-apocalyptic motorcycle gangs out of a Mad Max movie.

It doesn't take much imagination to suggest that a state like California, which literally resorted to issuing I.O.U.s in place of tax refunds last year, will find itself bearing a more uncomfortable resemblance to the near-bankrupt nation of Greece than just its Mediterranean climate. Currently, Moody's still rates California's general obligation debt as investment grade, Baa, a level that historically has shown a minimal number of defaults — 0.13 percent, to be precise.[195] Thus, the official party line from the Governator on down is that California has a wonderful future ahead of it. But give the Golden State another 10 to 15 years to run up its unfunded public pension liabilities and erode its tax base by chasing more middle-class citizens and small businesses out of the state, and the situation will look considerably bleaker. Indeed, California and its profligate peers such as Illinois, Massachusetts and New Jersey — let's see how the new deficit-hawk governor, Chris Christie, fares before removing the Garden State from the list — may well precede the United States into Boomergeddon.

The best bet is to make your home in a state with AAA-rated finances. That leaves you with a choice of Delaware, Georgia, Maryland, Missouri, North Carolina, Utah and Virginia. The three main rating agencies, Standard & Poor's, Moody's and Fitch, take into account the strength of the state's economy, its debt structure, its financial condition, demographic factors, and the management practices of the state government. States with growing populations and economies are deemed a better credit risk than states whose citizens and businesses are fleeing. States with chronic deficits and mounting debts are thought to be riskier. States with stronger financial controls — such as not is-suing I.O.U.s in place of tax refunds — are better bets.

While you're checking the stats for the states, Google the credit rating for any municipality you might consider living in. You'll find, for example, that S&P downgraded its rating for Los Angeles' $1.9 billion in general obligation bonds from AA to AA- in February. S&P opined that the city still needs to slash thousands of positions and $400 mil-lion in expenses.[196] Just think if you were living in L.A. when Boomergeddon shattered the market for sovereign debt. You could get a three-fer: a nation, a state and a city all in default!

Boomers are old enough to remember the Los Angeles riots of 1992 that followed the televised police beating of Rodney King. More than 50 people were killed, more than 4,000 were injured, 12,000 people were arrested and more than $1 billion in property was damaged.[197] Now, imagine how big a riot might get if stoked by a deep recession and mas-sive cuts to poverty programs. Then, contemplate how a riot might spread if budgets of the L.A. police and the California national guard were cut by a third, and the unionized police force was on strike.

Call me crazy, but I'd rather not be caught in L.A. under those cir-cumstances. I'd much rather be hunkered down in the AAA-rated com-monwealth of Virginia and the AAA-rated county of Henrico (outside of the capital city of Richmond) when Uncle Sam goes broke. Virginia's constitution prohibits state and local governments from borrowing money to balance their budgets, so I figure there's only so much trou-ble our politicians can get into. Our General Assembly did skirt the re-striction against borrowing by dipping into the Virginia Retirement System till by $650 million this year, but our pension liabilities still aren't as bad as those of many other states. Maybe Virginia's bond rat-ing will slip to an A or A- rating by the time Boomergeddon rolls around, but even that is creditworthy enough to keep paying the police, the judges and the prison guards.

Here in the Old Dominion, we understand that life in the state of nature can be nasty, brutish and short. We still hew to the old-fashioned idea that the primary role of government is to protect life and property from the anarchic "state of nature." The cost of living is no bargain basement here — the Richmond region is a little higher than the national average — but I'll take the trade-off. If nothing else, come Boomergeddon, I figure I'll save a lot of money that other people are investing in shotgun shells and concertina wire.

The Passive Resistance of the Productive Classes

In 1957 Ayn Rand published her greatest work, *Atlas Shrugged,* a novel set in a dystopian United States enervated by an all-intrusive government. In the book, the great minds who create wealth and drive the economy forward decide they have had enough and, led by the mysterious John Galt, drop out of sight. In effect, they go on strike, depriving society of the contributions of its most productive and innovative members. As the economy falls apart, Americans come to understand the true source of prosperity.

Atlas Shrugged is a classic among those who yearn for a smaller government. In the half century since Rand wrote, the federal government has grown bigger than ever, commanding a greater share of society's resources than in any peace-time era of its history. But there is no sign in the United States of a John Galt or anyone like him. Steve Jobs, who is America's most widely hailed living innovator and perhaps its greatest, is ... it pains me to say this ... a hard-core Democrat. Having donated over the years $228,000 to Democrats and $1,000 to Republicans,[198] Jobs would not appear at first blush to be a good candidate to lead a Galt-like strike against the leviathan state. Bill Gates, the nation's richest man, spreads his political bets between both parties. Warren Buffett, the nation's second wealthiest, is a confirmed Democrat. Neither one has the making of a John Galt. Other American billionaires are divided fairly evenly in their sympathies between the Donkey Clan and the Elephant Clan. A few may contribute to small-government political candidates and free-market think tanks, but none seem disposed to launch a revolution.

As for those of us in the yeoman class of hard-working, self-supporting, tax-paying men and women, we don't have the luxury of going on strike. We make a living by selling our skills in the marketplace. We must work to eat. Acting as individuals, we would hurt only ourselves by going on strike and we would change nothing. Unlike Rand's protagonists, we lack the power to bring the economy to a halt.

But we can do the next best thing: We can step off the treadmill. Call it the passive resistance of the productive classes. By adopting the strategy I outline in this chapter — spurning the lifestyle of buying more stuff, working harder and paying more taxes — we can not only insulate ourselves from Boomergeddon, we can slough off our servitude as tax-paying drones. Think of the impact if 20 million producers — roughly one American out of ten in the workforce — revolted against the redistributors by jumping off the spend-work-tax treadmill. What a political statement! We would shrink the tax base by hundreds of billions of dollars and reduce the tax take by tens of billions.

Passive resistance on such a scale would send a shudder of fear through the political class. The progressive elites would denounce our recalcitrance as a threat to all that is holy and just: By working less and spending less, we would be sabotaging the economy, causing job layoffs, crimping tax revenues and plunging the country even deeper into deficits and debt. Americans should keep on spending, they would say. It's our patriotic duty to keep the economy growing and tax collections flush. Translation: We should sacrifice our well-being so they can continue looting the country.

And what sacrifices would the partisans of the political class make for the common good? What privileges would they relinquish? What tribute would they return? What liberties would they restore? To that question the worm tongues of the media either would fall silent or mutter their usual prevarications.

Through our passive resistance, the productive classes can accelerate the onset of Boomergeddon and precipitate the inevitable crisis to come. The sooner the corrupt and tyrannical institutions of the leviathan state crash, the sooner we can begin to build anew.

Chapter 9
Salvaging the Future

$1 Trillion or Bust

I have argued that Boomergeddon, the day of reckoning, is all but inevitable. The special interest constituencies are too entrenched, the partisan politics too gridlocked, the public's sense of entitlement too pervasive and the law of compounding interest too remorseless for the political system to right itself. Only a full-blown crisis — a true catastrophe, not a sharp rap on the knuckles like the recession just past — will bring an end to Politics As Usual. Only when there is near-universal agreement that the New Deal/Great Society paradigm of activist, expansionist government has failed, not just in the United States but across Europe and even in Japan, will Americans insist upon a more financially sustainable contract between government and the people.

That is not a message that many want to hear, certainly not lovers of the leviathan state, nor even those who share my conviction that overbearing government is suffocating the country. It is not in the American temperament to back off from a brawl. I can imagine readers thinking, "Bacon may be right about that Boomergeddon thing, but if I'm going down, I'm going down fighting."

Well, bully for you! In deference to your ornery nature, I will lay out in this final chapter what I think it will take to avert national calamity. I'm not betting my personal finances on it, but I do believe that if the national mood shifts decisively enough, and if it shifts soon enough, it is theoretically possible to head off Boomergeddon. But make no mistake: We have passed the point where half measures will save us. There is no "muddling through" the mess we have created. While there may be tens of billions of dollars of "waste, fraud and abuse" worth rooting out, we need to cut *hundreds* of billions of dollars.

266

We must enact deep-rooted change to the size, scope and efficiency of government at all levels — state and local included (the topic for another book) — and we must move with urgency. We are in a race against time: We must restore credibility to United States finances before the Electronic Herd loses confidence in government's will to honor its debt.

How much time do we have? That is difficult to say. Market psychology is volatile and unpredictable. I have suggested that the political status quo can continue stumbling forward until 2027, based on the premises that (1) our economic decision makers still have enough flexibility to weather an economic downturn later this decade, but (2) financial and demographic trends will turn so decisively against the U.S. in the 2020s that there will be no surviving the next recession. If by some miracle the government avoids default in 2027, the combined weight of the Age Wave, entitlements, rising global interest rates, a runaway national debt and bond-holder skittishness induced by the fiscal collapse of other economically advanced nations will push us over the precipice. A more likely scenario is that Boomergeddon will explode sooner than expected, ignited by unanticipated events — a nuclear bomb exploding in the Middle East, perhaps, sovereign default by Japan or the United Kingdom, or a breakdown of civil order in China. Thus, any package of tax and spending reforms must be enacted well before 2020, otherwise it will be a matter of too little, too late.

How much do we have to cut? Well, let's see. According Obama's own 10-year forecast, deficits will bottom out at $706 billion in 2014, stay fairly level for four more years, then head up to more than $1 trillion a year by 2020. Of course, that assumes no recessions. The reality is that a recession is inevitable. To cut enough spending to ensure that surpluses and deficits balance over the course of a business cycle, we need to carve at least $1 trillion out of a budget that is $3.5 trillion and growing.

One can argue that we don't have to cut the budget by a full $1 trillion. All we have to do is shrink deficits to the point where they inflate the national debt at a rate slower than the economy is growing. So, for instance, if we reduced the deficit to 3.0 percent of the economy (about $350 billion) but the GDP was growing by 3.5 percent, we would be making progress. Slow progress, to be sure, but heading in the right direction. After a couple of decades, the national debt would move out of the danger zone — and we'd spare ourselves a lot of cost-cutting agony.

Wrong! The metric we need to watch is not the national debt but the interest we pay on that debt. The gentle-glide-to-solvency idea might work if interest rates stayed pinned down to their current low levels. But they will not. As rates rise over the next decade, payments on the debt will outpace economic growth by a wide margin. Therefore, Boomergeddon is not a fate we can ease ourselves out of. We must freeze the national debt in its tracks or by 2020 higher interest rates will consume us.

Absent fundamental change, trillion-dollar deficits will be routine by the end of the decade, even under the best of economic conditions. The interest rate on 10-year Treasury bonds will be 5 percent, by Obama's calculation, and twice as high in the estimation of others. The interest payments on *a single year's* worth of deficits will amount to between $50 billion and $100 billion — larger than the entire 2011 budget for the Department of Education, bigger than that of the Department of Energy two times over. The interest on the total $20 trillion debt will be between $912 billion (Obama's scenario) and $1.8 trillion (mine). At that point, the similarities to Greece's predicament today will be impossible to ignore.

Assuming that we embrace the goal of cutting a trillion drachmae, er, dollars, per year, what balance of spending cuts and higher taxes do we aim for? Here, my philosophical prejudices come into play. All other things being equal, I believe it is preferable to balance the budget by cutting spending than by raising taxes. Curtailing the size of government is a moral imperative: It expands the sphere of liberty. Smaller government is also a practical necessity: It diminishes the scope of rent-seeking activity that misallocates resources on a massive scale. Over the long run, economic growth will be stronger, tax revenues higher and deficits lower with a smaller, more efficient government.

Any platform must be leavened, however, by a recognition that reform must pass a divided Congress and a gauntlet of special interests. It will be impossible to bring the budget into balance without the cooperation of some Democrats who share their clan's strong predilection for raising taxes. Thus, while I deem tax increases to be anathema, I also acknowledge that they are unavoidable. The trick is to select a revenue-raising mechanism that induces as little job-killing and tax-avoidance behavior as possible.

One last note before we jump into the briar patch: Social Security should be one of the easier problems to fix. We took note in Chapter 2 of the wide range of options available for adjusting Social Security taxes and benefits. I would reject any proposal that would raise the payroll tax on the grounds that such a measure would fall disproportionately upon younger generations that are already buckling under the weight of high college debts, income taxes, payroll taxes and the redistribution of wealth from young to old under Obamacare. Also, I would exclude any proposal to extend Social Security benefits to any new categories of recipients. We simply are not in a position to expand entitlements to anyone right now. Patching gaps in the system will have to wait until the future, when we are out of the fiscal woods.

One Social Security reform should garner widespread political buy-in: increasing the retirement age for younger generations. When Social Security was enacted in 1935, the life expectancy was 60 for men and 64 for women. Today, average life expectancy has increased by 15 years for men and 16 for women, yet the retirement age has increased only two years for Americans born after 1959. Life expectancy continues to advance by roughly one year per decade. Increasing the retirement age by one year for younger workers — those born after 1969, for instance — should pose no great hardship. I am confident that, if polled, most would say they would greatly prefer to delay retirement than to pay higher payroll taxes. The principle of raising the retirement age, I believe, is sound. The details of how fast to phase in the new retirement age, I leave to the actuaries.

A second easy-to-swallow reform is the introduction of a new indexing formula for future benefits. Under the current arrangement, an individual's Social Security benefits are based upon his or her average career earnings. To determine average career earnings, income from previous years is adjusted upward by the increase in the average wage level, an approach called "wage indexing." Because wages usually exceed inflation, wage indexing provides higher benefits than increasing benefits based on the Consumer Price Index, an approach referred to as "price indexing." Shifting to a hybrid wage index/CPI index would gradually reduce Social Security payouts to future beneficiaries, yet keep them ahead of inflation. It's not an ideal solution but it would rack up big savings over the decades.

One idea advanced by Rep. Paul Ryan in his "Roadmap for America's Future" is to create individual accounts for Americans under 55.[199] The idea didn't fly when President Bush advanced it, however, and it won't fly in any Congress in which the Democrats hold enough seats to sustain a filibuster. The Dems are viscerally opposed to anything that smacks of Social Security privatization, and they will not endorse any legislation that contains it. Personally, I like the idea of allowing wage earners to opt into individual accounts, but restoring long-term integrity to the nation's finances is the top priority. Bipartisan agreement is required, and any bells and whistles that might jeopardize the restoration of Social Security's fiscal balance should be stripped from any reform legislation. The idea of phasing in individual accounts can be revisited one day when the nation's fiscal condition is on the mend. Remember, fixing Social Security is the "easy" reform, a mere warm-up for the slugfest to come. The country cannot afford to get bogged down in an emotional debate that derails the reform.

One more point to bear in mind about Social Security: As important as it is to fix the program, it is almost incidental to the larger job of putting federal finances back on a sound footing. The Social Security trust fund will last 27 years before it is exhausted. Boomergeddon will arrive long before then. Patching up Social Security will do nothing to stave off Boomergeddon, and it will only create the illusion that Social Security benefits are safe. The fact is, if the federal government defaults on its general obligation debt, the nation will have no means with which to honor its Social Security trust fund debt. There is no side-stepping the need to cut that $1 trillion per year.

Paul C. Light, a professor at New York University, argues that streamlining government could save $1 trillion over the next 10 years. He recommends cutting the number of presidential appointees, eliminating needless management layers in the bureaucracy, cutting the contracting workforce, increasing federal productivity, merging duplicate programs and deep-sixing programs that simply do not produce results.[200] That averages out to $100 billion a year — good money if you can actually get it. Let us assume, for purposes of argument, that streamlining federal government can deliver all those savings, yielding a 10 percent down payment on our ultimate objective. How do we cut the other $900 billion?

I have identified five broad initiatives for which it may be possible to cobble together a coalition of enough members of the Donkey Clan and Elephant Clan to pass into legislation and, if a Tea Party-like revolution could put a sympathetic occupant in the White House, get enacted into law. Combine the fiscal impact of all these reforms, and we'll get close to achieving that $1 trillion goal. The measures include:

- Ending corporate welfare: Save $100 billion.
- Adopting the Fair Tax: Increase revenue by $350 billion.
- Cutting discretionary domestic spending: Save $117 billion.
- Cutting national security spending: Save $100 billion.
- Improving health care productivity and quality: Save $60 billion a year (with caveats).

I shall discuss each one in turn.

End corporate welfare

The private sector has extended the field of competition from the marketplace to the political arena. There are more trade associations in Washington, D.C., more lobbyists, more PACs and more money than ever before. The special interests are continually seeking to gain some advantage — subsidies, tax breaks, cheap credit, tariffs, trade restrictions, regulatory changes, and the list goes on. Given the willingness of Congress to insert itself into any and all corners of the economy, almost every business sector is affected.

Direct federal expenditures on behalf of individual corporations — a practice widely known as "corporate welfare" — is the easiest to identify. In fiscal 2016, the feds spent $92 billion in direct and indirect subsidies, mainly for agriculture, exports and technology, concluded a Cato Institute study.[200] The Department of Agriculture, appropriately enough, maintains the biggest hog trough: By Cato's reckoning, that one department accounted for $43.2 billion in corporate welfare, largely for crop and farm support, most of which went to corporate farms. Back in 2007, when the study was written, no other department came close. The Department of Defense was a poor runner up, spending $11.8 billion on applied R&D funding, with an assortment of other departments and independent agencies divvying up the balance.

Of course, the Cato study was written before TARP became a household acronym and opened the sluice gates for corporate welfare under the guise of combating the recession. In 2008 the Bush administration and Congress agreed to spend $29 billion to support the merger of Bear Stearns and JPMorgan Chase, and another $85 billion to bail out insurance giant American International Group. Then followed $700 billion to salvage the banking system under the Troubled Asset Relief Program, which morphed into an all-purpose bailout fund to relieve favored constituencies such as the unionized automobile industry. Under Obama, some $49 billion in TARP money went to keep General Motors alive, while billions more went to Chrysler. The stimulus piñata showered billions more upon favor seekers with any remote connection to conservation and renewable energy: wind turbines, solar cells, clean coal technologies, carbon dioxide sequestration, smart grids and high-speed rail. Apply for a grant, pitch a good story, and win some money.

TARP and ARRA were sold to the American public as one-time expenditures. But once the funds are distributed, the programs create new constituencies that hire lobbyists and donate to political campaigns with the goal of perpetuating the largesse. Predictably, a number of these "temporary" handouts, conceived for the purpose of countering the recession, will make the leap into full-time wards of the state. If Cato updated its corporate-welfare report today, it undoubtedly would find annual corporate-welfare expenditures totaling well over $100 billion.

In theory, it should be possible to assemble a coalition of Democrats and Republicans to scale back corporate welfare. Democrats are inclined to look unfavorably upon giveaways to corporations. Republicans often cast themselves as defenders of business, but they don't believe that government is very good at picking winners and losers. Neither party defends corporate welfare in the abstract.

Yet the privileges proliferate.

The survival of agricultural subsidies is testimony to the staying power of corporate welfare. In 1996, a Republican-controlled Congress voted to phase out farm subsidies by 2002. The rollback was easily agreed to because agricultural commodity prices were high and farming was profitable. The phase-out stayed on track for two years — until farm prices dropped. Congress promptly passed an "emergency" bill to help the farmers, then did so again. Instead of eliminating the subsidies in 2002, President Bush caved into the farming interests. He signed a new six-year appropriation that was estimated at the time to cost taxpayers $99 billion in direct subsidies over six years. There is no evidence to suggest that Congress has grown a spine since then. Indeed, as this book was going to press, our august legislative body was on the brink of creating a $50 billion "orderly liquidation fund" to bail out creditors of bankrupt financial institutions.

Threatened by the loss of billions of dollars in subsidies, protected industries will lobby for their lives. The political class will predict the complete ruin of corn farming, aircraft exports and solar panel manufacturing. The opposition will be relentless. Taking on the welfare CEOs won't be easy. Still, if voters decide to throw the bums out, as they are clearly in the mood to do, a new Congress populated by enthusiastic, pitchfork-waving rubes from the provinces might find itself energized enough to send the lobbyists scurrying back to their paymasters.

When corporate welfare measures are considered in isolation, the benefits are concentrated among a few recipients but the costs are diffused among millions of taxpayers. Under normal circumstances, it pays businesses to hire lobbyists to angle for subsidies worth millions of dollars; it does not pay individual taxpayers to hire lobbyists to oppose subsidies that cost them only pennies. But if all the cuts are packaged together and sold as an assault on corporate welfare, the prospect of lopping $100 billion off the annual deficit just might prove enticing enough to motivate voters — at least the half of the electorate that pays income taxes — to cheer legislators on.

Reform the Tax Code

Hollowed out by credits and deductions too numerous to list, the U.S. tax code is rotten to the core — a tree trunk infested by beetle-like pleaders who bore deeper and deeper, chewing through the heartwood. Tax breaks for businesses amount to more than $105 billion. Tax breaks for individuals total more than $760 billion. The black market, where people avoid paying taxes of any kind, is estimated to be roughly $1 trillion. If taxed on the same basis as the rest of the economy, the underground economy would yield tens of billions of dollars in revenue.

To capture more revenue lost to all those exemptions, Congress raises general tax rates. Higher rates punish the middle-class schmucks too gainfully employed to take refuge in the underground economy and too poor to avail themselves of elaborate tax schemes. A broader, flatter tax code would apply the same rules to everyone, and it would increase tax revenues without inducing the kind of unproductive tax avoidance that undermines economic growth.

Perhaps the best known flat-tax proposal has been tirelessly popularized by Steve Forbes, publisher of *Forbes* magazine. His proposal would scrap the entire personal income tax code and replace it with a formula so simple that he claims it would fit on a single post card. The Forbes flat tax would exempt the first $36,000 in income for a family of four, then tax all income above that amount at a flat rate of 17 percent. In theory, the plan would yield roughly the same revenue as the current tax code while saving taxpayers the expense, and frequently the agony, of tax preparation. The top rate would be so low that high-income taxpayers would have little incentive to dodge taxes, thus steering financial capital into more productive endeavors and stimulating economic growth.[202]

The Forbes plan has been criticized for being insufficiently "progressive" — it doesn't squeeze as much out of the rich as the current tax code does. Perhaps so. That's a trade-off I'm personally happy to make if the simplified plan would encourage the rich to invest more of their money in new wealth- and job-creating ventures than in tax shelters. However, if the class warriors in Congress insist upon penalizing the super-rich for the sin of being super-rich, it is easy enough to make the flat tax more progressive. For instance, create a second bracket of 25 percent for income over, say, $500,000. (Just be sure to index it for inflation.) The fact that we don't hear such counter-proposals indicates to me that progressives want to retain a system that is so complex and opaque that taxpayers don't know how badly they are getting hosed.

In his "Roadmap for America's Future," Congressman Paul Ryan deals with the lack of progressivity in the Forbes plan. Like Forbes, he would eliminate all deductions (except for a tax credit for health care), and he would provide a generous standard deduction of $39,000 for a family of four. Then he would apply a 10 percent tax rate for joint incomes of up to $100,000. In a move that should please progressives, he would tax income at a 25 percent rate for any amount over that. Additionally, he would replace the corporate income tax, currently the second highest among the advanced economies of the world, with a border-adjustable business consumption tax of 8.5 percent. Ryan's plan would limit the total federal tax take to 19 percent of the GDP.[203]

In my humble opinion, both plans would be vastly preferable to the travesty of a code that we tolerate today. I do have one concern. By leaving the personal and corporate income taxes in place, both plans invite the special interests to begin boring back into the code when nobody else is looking. One of President Ronald Reagan's great achievements was the Tax Reform Act of 1986, which reduced the number of tax brackets from 11 to three and expunged innumerable tax breaks. But after two-and-a-half decades, the pleaders have riddled the tax code with more holes and tunnels than an ant colony. It's the nature of the system.

An alternative tax reform proposal has been introduced in Congress under the name of the Fair Tax Act. In a nutshell, the Fair Tax would replace all federal taxes with a single national sales tax. As a consumption-based tax, the Fair Tax is superficially similar to the Value Added Tax (VAT) idea floated by the Obama administration. But it is different in very important ways. The Fair Tax would be the sole tax; it would not be imposed in addition to existing taxes. Unlike the VAT, which would be paid by businesses at each step in the added-value chain and thus invisible to taxpayers, the Fair Tax would be collected at the retail level. Citizens would know exactly how much they were paying — 23 percent, to be exact, under the current Fair Tax proposal.[204] If they were unhappy, they would know exactly whom to hold accountable.

A Fair Tax would offer at least three game-changing advantages:

- A 23% tax rate would collect $358 billion more than the taxes it replaces, according to the Americans for Fair Taxation, making a meaningful contribution toward balancing the budget. Yet it would not diminish incentives for working harder and producing more taxable income.

- Not only would the Fair Tax save taxpayers the cost and headaches of tax preparation, like the Forbes and Ryan flat tax plans would do, it would drive a stake through the heart of the Infernal Revenue Service, abolishing it entirely, which the flat-tax plans would not.

- Shifting from an income-based tax to a consumption-based tax would reward thrift and punish prodigality. It would help Americans accumulate savings in preparation for their retirement, and it would reduce the excesses of a consumer-driven economy such as indebtedness and the accumulation of stuff.

To address complaints that the tax was unfair to the poor and middle class, the Fair Tax plan calls for mailing every American family a "prebate" at the beginning of each month to offset taxes on expenditures equal to the federal poverty level. In effect, anyone under the poverty line would pay no tax, and those above it would pay only on the portion that exceeded the poverty line.

Admittedly, upon passage of Fair Tax legislation, the special interests would immediately set to work, begging to exempt all manner of products and services from the national sales tax. But the payback for lobbying and PAC contributions is weaker. If you finagle an income tax break for your widget-manufacturing company, that's money in your pocket. If you wheedle an exemption for widgets from the sales tax, you don't benefit directly — the break goes to the people buying the widgets. It puts money in their pockets, not yours. You may benefit indirectly if people purchase more widgets than they would have otherwise, but that's more problematic. Given enough time, the political class would corrupt the Fair Tax, just as it corrupted Reagan's tax simplification, and voters eventually would have to insist upon another round of house cleaning. But the incentives would be duller, so it should take longer for the corruption to set in.

No reasoning or evidence will persuade the political class, however. The beneficiaries of Politics as Usual will mobilize to defeat the Fair Tax idea, not because their minions and apologists are worried that it will fail to accomplish its stated objectives, but because they are worried that it will succeed. And with good reason: The Fair Tax threatens the transfer of billions of dollars of booty from taxpayers to Washington's special interests. But Reagan overcame heavy opposition to his tax simplification plan by appealing directly to the people. The Fair Tax, like proposals to end corporate welfare, offers a big enough benefit that the politically inert middle class could be aroused to action. If the Tea Party movement elects enough of its partisans into Congress and elects a sympathetic president as well, the Fair Tax could become reality — and it could get the country some $350 billion closer to a balanced budget.

Cut Discretionary Spending

President Obama proposes to freeze discretionary spending — not immediately, when tough decisions are called for, but next year, 2011, when the rhetoric will be forgotten. Even then, there is less than meets the eye to the supposed belt tightening. This year (2010), according to Obama's own budget numbers, discretionary spending shoots up by $157 billion, or 14.6 percent. To give you an idea of what a vast expansion of federal spending we're talking about, consider this: That's more than this year's funding for the entire Department of Housing and Urban Development ($58 billion), Department of Education ($56 billion), Department of Energy ($29 billion) and Department of the Interior ($12.4 billion) combined. In sum, the "freeze" locks spending into place at such a bloated level that it makes Jabba the Hut look like an anorexic worm.

How's this for a bone-crushing, fiscal nihilist proposal? Let's roll back Obama's spending freeze to 2009 levels. That would mean reverting to spending levels that prevailed before the president and Congress approved a 7.9 percent increase in security spending and the 26.5 percent (not a typo) in discretionary, non-security spending. In theory, hacking $117 billion from non-security funding shouldn't be so hard. (I'll talk about security spending later.) After all, the government managed to function very well at 2009 levels, even if the economy didn't. Making the job easier, outlays for food stamps and other social safety net programs should recede as the economy enters a new phase of economic expansion and unemployment drifts lower.

Given the fiscal peril the nation faces, reverting to 2009 spending levels may strike you, the taxpayer, as eminently reasonable. But rest assured, any effort to restrain spending would set off a firestorm. Discretionary spending is the preserve of the political class. The legions of lawyers, lobbyists, trade association executives, policy wonks, Astroturf organizers, pleaders, fixers, plumbers and all their fellow travelers don't live off of the $2.2 trillion allocated each year to entitlements and interest payments on the national debt, they live off that $1.4 trillion in discretionary spending. What's more, they are media savvy, politically canny and connected. Their media spinners will go all out warning of a parade of horribles: of gaping wounds to government programs, of devastation wrought upon American industries, of jobs lost in the heartland, of widows dispossessed, orphans made homeless and the poor ground under foot.

Gutting discretionary spending is not for the faint of heart. The political pros will pull out the big knives to defend their booty. Even if reformers prune programs one year, the lobbyists will creep back into the Congressional committee chambers when the cameras are gone to get their money reinstated. Government programs are like weeds. Unless you pull them out by the roots the spending programs always grow back.

That's why an incremental spread-the-misery approach will not work. Budget cutters need to shock and awe the opposition. They need to take out entire federal departments. Instead of trimming the Department of Education by 10 percent, go for the whole caboodle. Preserve one or two legitimate functions, such as measuring and tracking student performance across the 50 states, and get rid of all the rest.

There is little in the Departmental budget that doesn't duplicate — and hobble with strings and mandates — what state/local governments are already doing.

The same goes for the Department of Energy. Preserve one or two core functions, such as collecting statistics and funding basic research, and abolish the rest, along with all the subsidies, loans, tax breaks, and loan guarantees. You want energy efficiency? Put all forms of energy — oil, gas, coal, nuclear, solar, wind, biofuels — on a level playing field and let the private sector allocate capital to projects that offer the greatest return on investment. Chasing the rent-seekers from the temple and sending clear price signals to the marketplace is the single-greatest thing we can do to optimize the mix of energy sources and promote conservation. If you think fossil fuels enjoy an unfair advantage in the marketplace because the costs associated with pollution are "externalized," as the economists might say, meaning that the costs are borne by the public, then slap on a carbon tax — and apply the revenues to deficit reduction! Let the corporations and venture capitalists, not the politicians and bureaucrats, decide which risks to bear and which projects to fund.

Targeting the entire Department of Energy may come across as the ultimate example of political tilting at windmills. One might as well mount old Don Quixote upon his steed and point him toward a General Electric 2.5-megawatt wind turbine. But in the arena of discretionary spending, as in corporate welfare and tax reform, the opposition of the special interests and their servants in Congress can be overcome by mobilizing the electorate. The secret is to set an objective — helping to avert Boomergeddon by shrinking the deficit by another $117 billion — that is big enough and ambitious enough to get voters excited.

Conduct an Orderly Withdrawal

Forget about the $127 washers and $544 spark plugs.[205] There is a huge amount of money to be saved in procurement reform but any campaign to wring inefficiency out of the Pentagon supply chain is likely to meet the same fate as past efforts. Some 14 waves of iterative reforms since 1971 have subjected purchases to ever-closer scrutiny and added ever lengthier review processes. The result? Weapons systems have become more complex and more unaffordable at an exponential rate.[206] (If you spotted a direct parallel between "controlling costs" in the health care and defense sectors, bingo, you win the prize.) Among other reasons for the Pentagon's behemoth budget, expense controls are hampered by an unauditable accounting system — actually 4,150 different systems, according to a 2006 count[206] — and a cumbersome Base Realignment and Closing (BRAC) process that slows the rationalization of the base structure to a crawl.

The Pentagon bureaucracy is bigger, badder and more dug in than the 101st Airborne at Bastogne. The infamous iron triangle of the military-industrial complex, in which defense contractors, congressmen and senior military brass advance the interlocking interests of their corporations, districts and services, has defied all but the most marginal and incremental of reforms. Although the enormity of the task should not dissuade President Obama or anyone else from trying to wring efficiencies from the system, it would be foolhardy to pin hopes of balancing the U.S. budget and averting Boomergeddon upon the remote prospect that someone, somehow, finally will succeed in doing so. No, the only sure-fire way to squeeze $100 billion a year or more out of the $527 billion defense budget within a few years' time is to realign the strategic priorities of the U.S. to match the size of its pocketbook. Inevitably, that will require decommissioning entire army divisions, mothballing entire aircraft carrier flotillas and scrapping epic-cost weapons systems.

This is not an easy argument for me to make — I am driven to it by necessity. My dad was a submarine skipper in the Navy, and one of the biggest thrills of my youth was riding with him in the conning tower of the U.S.S. Tench as it cruised up the York River from Norfolk to Yorktown. To this day, I love military hardware. No, I *luuuurve* military hardware. When I'm channel surfing, I flip over to Cable TV's Military

Channel to learn what I can about the latest warships and fighter planes on the drawing boards. Stealth bombers and anti-missile lasers are way cooler than even the iPhone. Military equipment is the most awesome stuff ever invented. But the U.S. is rapidly reaching the point where it cannot afford everything the admirals and generals would like to have. Their awesome machines are breaking the bank.

The top brass is as unwilling as every other special interest to make the sacrifices required to restore fiscal sustainability. But trust me, they will regret their foot dragging when Boomergeddon arrives and their war-making apparatus grinds to a halt. We can only hope that the U.S. is not engaged in active combat when that day comes.

We must ask ourselves: Can we afford to continue paying the staggering expense of patrolling the world's mean streets as policeman? We all know the answer: Not for long. That leads to the next question: If our projection of power abroad is fiscally unsustainable, which of the following two alternatives is preferable: Hang tough, expending blood and treasure, until Boomergeddon strikes like a lightning bolt, choking the flow of fuel and supplies to our forces overseas and putting our men at risk? Or adapt now to fiscal realities and create a strategic vision that we can afford?

It makes far more sense, I maintain, to manage an orderly withdrawal now than to retreat helter skelter 15 years from now at times and under conditions not of our choosing. Change comes slowly in the military — talk about turning around a battleship! — so we need to begin thinking immediately about what our international priorities should be and what military force structure we will require to support them. What follows are some preliminary thoughts to get the process moving in the right direction.

War on Terror/Middle East. Al Qaeda has been strategically stalemated, if not defeated. The bombing of the World Trade Center was Osama bin Laden's greatest victory, and the likes of it are not likely to be repeated. We may have to contend with an endless parade of shoe bombers, underwear bombers, even car bombers from abroad, as well as occasional homegrown killers like Nidal Hasan, the Fort Hood shooter. We will stop some of them, others will get lucky and, yes, Americans will die. But let us be realistic. Forty thousand Americans are killed violently in automobile accidents every year. Roughly 15,000 are murdered. For that matter, more than 1,000 Americans drown in pools and bathtubs yearly, but we have not declared a Global War on Drowning. As spectacular as they are, terrorist attacks killing people by the dozens or even hundreds will not unravel a society of 310 million. We need to make every reasonable measure to prevent such assaults, but the threat does not justify prosecuting wars in such a way as to drive our country into fiscal insolvency.

If there is one thing we should have learned from eight years spent "draining the swamps" of terrorism in Iraq, Afghanistan and other countries, it is that the job will be long, protracted and thankless. Nation building is the mission of a generation, not of a few years. At some point we must ask, is it a job we need, or can afford, to undertake ourselves?

Some analysts believe that support for terrorist movements is on the decline. Much of the Muslim world feels increasing revulsion for the indiscriminant slaughter of civilians, nearly all of them fellow Muslims. Scholars and jurists are increasingly outspoken in their rejection of terrorism on theological grounds. A straw in the wind: Prominent Muslim scholars attending a worldwide conference convened by the Global Centre of Renewal and Guidance earlier this year issued a religious declaration condemning terrorism by Islamists in Somalia.[208] A few days later, Tahir-ul-Qadri, a Pakistani, issued a 600-page fatwa in a comprehensive rebuttal of the theological arguments advanced by al Qaeda and its sympathizers.[209]

While Islam in the popular American imagination is associated with the fundamentalist Wahhabi sect practiced by the Saudi sheikhs, preached in Saudi-financed madrassas and embraced by al Qaeda, the religion is diverse. Mirroring similar debates that have taken place in

Christianity and Judaism, Muslims are wrestling with theological questions of how to practice their religion and live a righteous life in an increasingly interconnected world amidst accelerating technological, economic and social change. As Thomas P.M. Barnett argues in "Great Powers," the religion is undergoing a transformation on its periphery that could counter the reactionary, Medieval Wahhabism of the Middle Eastern heartland. Barnett sees challenges emerging from America where Muslim women are seeking a more prominent role for their gender; from Europe, where it is only a matter of time before Islamic parties begin participating in a pluralistic political process; and from East Asian countries like Malaysia and Indonesia, predominantly Muslim nations that are developing market-friendly and democracy-tolerant societies. To that list of challengers I would add Turkey, heir to the Ottoman Empire, whose Islamist rulers oversee one of the world's fastest economic growth rates, and Iraq, whose citizens have suffered more from al Qaeda-inspired terrorism than anyone else. The Grand Ayatollah Sistani, one of the leading clerics in the Shia Muslim world, has blessed the nascent democratic institutions of that country, limiting the role for clerics such as himself to judicial matters. The Iraqi democratic experiment in the heart of the Middle East will stimulate the debate over the relationship between religion and the state throughout the Muslim Arab world, if not beyond.

The possibility that al Qaeda is losing the war of ideas within Islam does not preclude jihadists from prevailing through force and intimidation. Public beheadings have a way of trumping the spirit of free inquiry. The Taliban, which is closely allied with al Qaeda, could yet prevail in Afghanistan, and if it takes power there, its brethren across the Hindu Kush could ramp up efforts to destabilize Pakistan. An American withdrawal from the region would be trumpeted throughout the Islamic world as a great triumph. Militant Islamists then could boast that they had defeated two superpowers, first the Soviet Union and then the United States. Humbling the crusaders would restore the movement's tarnished credibility and reignite recruiting and fund raising.

Let us consider the worst-case scenario. Let's say a U.S. withdrawal rekindles militant Islam. Would such a resurgence harm our newly re-defined interests? Insofar as jihadists would enjoy a safe haven in Afghanistan or in the tribal territories of Pakistan to dispatch more minions like the Times Square bomber to the U.S., the potential exists for an uptick in terrorist attacks. But it is easy to exaggerate the danger. Once the U.S. withdrew from the Middle East, the priorities of the Islamists would change. They would despise us no less; they would become no less vehement in their detestation of what they consider to be our depraved and decadent culture. We need entertain no illusions that their hearts would soften in the least. But the jihadists would have other preoccupations. Once U.S. forces withdrew from the region to the confines of the coral flyspeck in the Indian Ocean known as Diego Garcia, out of sight and out of mind, the victorious militants would shift their attention from the "far" enemy, the U.S., to the "near" enemy, the impious regimes presiding over the Islamic countries they wish to convert into a new caliphate.

If the militants fail to assume power anywhere, the U.S. loses nothing. Indeed, we could rightfully say that we won our strategic gamble. If they do take control of the apparatus of state, an interesting thing will happen: It will become apparent to all that radical Islam is not a unified force. The extremists have cooperated tactically in order to expel the U.S. from the region, but the rules of tribal society still apply. In the words of a Somali saying:

> *Me and my clan against the world;*
> *Me and my family against my clan;*
> *Me and my brother against my family;*
> *Me against my brother.*[210]

Ancient ethnic divides — Pashtuns, Uzbeks, Kurds, Arabs and Persians — will persist in the Middle East. The Sunni-Shia schism, which dates back to the 7th-century death of Ali, cousin of the prophet Mohammed, will burn undiminished. In the absence of a dominating U.S. presence against which to unify, the Arab states of the Persian Gulf will continue to fear domination by the Shiites of Iran, and the Sunnis will continue to regard the Shiites as apostates. Even if a militant group hell bent on jihad seizes control of a state, what are the chances that it will accept the primacy of a militant group that came to power somewhere else? About zero. If you think you have a direct pipeline to Allah, you're not going to accept the interpretation of the Koran proffered by some other imam or mullah just because he thinks he has a pipeline to Allah too. No, you fight to establish your authority as the one true voice of Islam. Even if your long-term aim is to one day plunge the Great Satan into the boiling tar pits of hell, you're a lot more worried about the threat to your legitimacy posed by the other guy than you are about the United States sitting on the other side of the world.

There are only three reasons why Americans should care what happens in the Middle East after we depart. One is humanitarian. We don't like to see people butchering each other. But let us be brutally honest. People slaughter one another in other parts of the world — some 25 million people have died in the Congo's endless warfare — without anyone losing any sleep. If a village is massacred in the rain forest and Westerners are not around to see it, does the gunfire still make a sound? Unless there is a CNN crew to file video by 7 p.m., routine acts of barbarism will not greatly trouble the American mind.

The second reason is more practical: We don't want to see anyone dominate the Persian Gulf oilfields. If someone cuts off the spigot, 99 percent of the globe will be in a world of hurt. Of course, others will be hurting even more than the U.S. The Chinese, Japanese and Indians are far more dependent upon Persian Gulf oil than we are, which suggests that they have an even greater stake in the stability of the region than we do. Instead of acting as a spoiler, as the Chinese have done in our diplomatic effort to block the Iranians from developing nuclear weapons, why not invite them to share the responsibility of keeping the sea lanes open? Beijing's mandarins have been getting a free ride for years. Let them contemplate a world in which Iran controls the Straits of Hormuz. Let them assume some of the burden of keeping the oil flowing.

The third reason we need to worry about the Middle East is the proliferation of nuclear weapons. The Pakistanis have the bomb. The Israelis have the bomb. The Iranians soon will have the bomb. If the Iranians get the bomb, the Saudis, the Egyptians and maybe the Turks might want one too. That sounds like a volatile situation. Fortunately for us, what none of them have is inter-continental ballistic missiles, which means none of them have the means to deliver one of those bombs to the United States. In other words, nuclear proliferation is very much more the problem for the regional powers located within the estimated 5,000-mile range of Iran's Shahab-6 than it is a concern of ours. Admittedly, the radioactive fallout from dozens of exploding nuclear bombs would disperse throughout the world, making it indirectly our problem too. But that should not distract us from the essential point: Once the U.S. announces its unwillingness to share the burden of policing the Middle East, regional powers will perceive their interests in the region very differently.

China, Russia, India and Turkey, all located on the edge of the Middle East, have far more to lose than the United States from the spread of anarchy and instability on their borders. They will be the recipients of unwanted refugees, destabilizing insurgencies and weapons of mass destruction. They have no choice but to get involved — in effect, replacing the United States as the cops on the regional beat. Admittedly, they may be no more successful than we have been in maintaining order. Indeed, if we bungle the hand-off, the competition of regional powers for influence and control could become destabilizing itself. But even that would be the problem of the regional powers, not us. If we chose to maintain a minimalist connection to the region, it would be to ensure that no single power dominated the oilfields or closed the sea-lanes. With cruise missiles, Stealth bombers, a couple of aircraft carrier flotillas and an Indian Ocean base at Diego Garcia, we would be in a position to tilt the balance of sea power if need be.

As fraught with risk as a strategic withdrawal may seem, we must contemplate the world in the aftermath of Boomergeddon, in which we withdraw precipitously, leaving a power vacuum that invites disorder, adventurism, and the intervention of regional powers. If we show foresight and begin the process of disengagement now, we can avoid the worst effects of retreat. Our foreign policy should aim to construct a diplomatic framework for engaging China, Russia, India and Turkey as partners in the new order. The challenge would be to persuade them that it is in everyone's best interest to maintain political stability and open trade rather to carve up the region into spheres of influence. In the long run, a collaborative approach would best preserve the open-trade system that has benefited all the world's major economies and would pose fewer risks than an unbridled competition for influence.

There is no guarantee that we will be able to construct such a framework. But if we wait for Boomergeddon, it will be too late to even try. In the great unraveling that follows, we will have no leverage over anyone.

Europe. Why do we maintain a major military presence in Europe? What are we defending against? A wave of Russian tanks surging across the plains of Northern Europe? That scenario has been a fantasy ever since the disintegration of the Soviet Union. The Russians don't have that capability, and they don't seek it.

The political survival of Vladimir Putin, Dmitry Medvedev and the industrial oligarchs depends primarily upon Russia's ability to generate revenue through the sale of oil and gas. Accordingly, the primary focus of Russian foreign policy has been to control the movement of energy supplies via pipelines and ports from Russia and from the former Soviet republics to the outside world. Secondarily, the regime's survival hinges upon its ability to suppress the separatist movements in Russia's Islamic territories. While the Russkies may entertain ambitions to extend their influence over the Ukraine, Belarus and the Baltic republics, they are content to do so by manipulating energy supplies and appealing to ethnic Russian minorities — not through military conquest. Militarily, the Russians have their hands full in the Caucasus.

Even if Russia did adopt a belligerent attitude toward Europe, whose responsibility is it to deal with the threat? Ours — or the Europeans'? The European Union has a population of 495 million people, Russia 145 million. The EU has an economy of $16.4 trillion, Russia roughly $1.3 trillion. The EU is at peace within its borders. Russia has restive minority populations to control. By what stretch of the imagination are the Europeans incapable of defending themselves? If the Europeans cannot muster the will to protect their own interests, why should the U.S. make sacrifices to do so for them?

The U.S. presence in Europe is a Cold War relic. Americans can no longer afford to subsidize Europe's defense. The time for free riding is over. We should shut down the bases, send the boys home and demobilize any military formations that don't contribute to our scaled-down strategic interests. Once we have made the decision to depart, we should use the pace and timing of our withdrawal as diplomatic leverage to extract from Russia whatever concessions we can regarding its military posture on the European frontier.

Korea. If there is one thing that everyone in the international community can agree upon, it is that North Korea is big trouble. Not only does the renegade state possess nuclear weapons and the means to deliver them, it maintains the world's largest artillery force, some 11,000 pieces, that could bring down a rain of fire upon South Korea's capital city of Seoul, located only 50 miles from the border. Moreover, the North Koreans defy the most basic norms of international behavior. The regime starves its people while the ruling elite lives in luxury. The country is the world's greatest proliferator of nuclear and long-range missile technology. It abducts Japanese civilians for nefarious intelligence purposes, it runs the world's largest counterfeiting operation, and, in the most recent outrage, it torpedoes South Korean naval vessels during peacetime. The only thing worse than the Pyongyang regime clinging to power would be the Pyongyang regime losing its grip on power. None of the country's neighbors wants to deal with millions of refugees fleeing the world's largest prison camp.

Granted, the Norks are a big problem. But why are they our problem? Why aren't they the problem of their immediate neighbors: South Korea, China, Russia and Japan? Were it not for the vestigial Cold War mentality in which the U.S. takes upon itself the obligation of trying to settle every crisis the world over, we would be perfectly happy to let those nations hash out their differences with North Korea all by themselves.

Nukes aside, South Korea should be able to handle its northern neighbor all by itself. The South matches up against the North like Arnold Schwarzenegger against Woody Allen... Well, OK, like Arnold versus a very paranoid Woody armed with a Glock 37. Look at the stats. Population: 50 million versus 24 million. Gross Domestic Product: $832 billion versus $28 billion. The Norks are the most militarized society on the face of the planet. But guess what, the South Koreans are the second most militarized society. Their army is smaller but more modernized. Here's my question: Other than to act as a trip-wire to ensure our involvement should the North ever invade the South again, why do we need to maintain 29,000 of our armed forces in South Korea?

If the South needs a nuclear umbrella, we can provide it. But we cannot afford to maintain a small army on the Korean Peninsula or supporting forces in Japan. We need to slowly divest ourselves of the situation, turning responsibility over to those countries most intimately affected by North Korea's erratic behavior, shutting down our bases and decommissioning our troops. If we had unlimited resources, sure, we would be happy to take on the burden. But we don't.

Taiwan. Taiwan is the only other potential flashpoint where the

U.S. might confront a large, well-armed conventional military force, in this case China's. Unlike Europe and South Korea, Taiwan may not be able to stand on its own. The match-up is hopelessly lopsided. China, 1.3 billion population; Taiwan 23 million. China, $5 trillion economy; Taiwan, $400 billion. China, $80 billion in military expenditures, Taiwan, $10 billion. Taiwan's main defense is the 80-mile-wide Formosa Strait, a formidable obstacle. While China would be hard-pressed to launch and supply an invasion force across that body of water today, it could develop that capability in the future.

The U.S. must choose between conflicting considerations. On the one hand, we feel an obligation to protect Taiwan, a free-market democracy that respects human rights and poses no threat to anyone. While we may shrink from the task of imposing democracies on others, Taiwan has made the evolution from dictatorship to democracy on its own. We share core values. On the other hand, the Taiwan issue is incredibly touchy for the mainland Chinese, who show no signs of budging from their "one China" policy. We want to coax Beijing into sharing the burden of what Barnett calls "closing the Gap," or bringing political stability to failed states, opening up their economies to investment, nurturing the growth of a middle class, and laying the foundation for an evolution to democracy. We cannot do that by ourselves, especially if we are shrinking our military footprint across the globe. We need China's cooperation, and aligning ourselves with Taiwan could be a major obstacle to getting it done.

That said, Taiwan's greatest protection is not the Formosa Strait or even its military. It is China's integration with the global economy. China is not the autarkic state it was under Mao Tse-Tung. Outsiders, Taiwanese businesses the foremost among them, invest billions of dollars in China every year. Foreign markets are critical to China's economic health. Foreign companies manage a large share of China's exports. Invading Taiwan for whatever reason would be construed around the world as an act of colossal recklessness, disrupting Foreign

Direct Investment, crimping exports, and potentially leading to the lay-off of millions of jobs. And it would invite a devastating response for which China would have no counter: the blockade of oil imports by al-most anyone — like India — wishing to thwart the rise of Chinese hege-mony. Above all else, China's leaders are pragmatic. They know they have everything to lose and very little to gain from a war with Taiwan.

Surely, the U.S. can thread the needle between the divergent prior-ities of protecting Taiwan and coaxing China into assuming a more re-sponsible role as a rising world power. If we can pull it off, we create the strategic conditions that allow us to close our bases in Okinawa, which support 20,000 Marines, Navy and Air Force personnel, and bring the boys (and girls) home. As the linchpin of our military power in East Asia, including the defense of Korea and Japan, Okinawa is not a base we would relinquish lightly. But should we ever feel compelled to proj-ect force into the East China Sea, we could always do so from Guam, which is 1,600 miles away.

Our military strategists undoubtedly would treat such a prospect as heresy. As always, my retort is this: Consider your options in 2027 when your funding suddenly gets chopped by 30 percent. What hor-rendous choices will you face then? It is better to make the hard choices ourselves than to have others thrust the decisions upon us.

Enact Real Health Care Reform

As president Obama rightly observed, there is no budgetary reform without health care reform. Unfortunately, the bill he signed takes the U.S. in the wrong direction. While the bill may accomplish the goal of provid-ing health care coverage to an estimated 22 million Americans, it does so at a frightful cost to the deficit. Among other budgetary tricks, the Oba-manants claim deficit neutrality by paying for six years of programs with 10 years of revenue. My personal nomination for the Enron Accounting of the Year Award goes to the shyster who decided to count revenues from the CLASS long-term insurance intitiative while neglecting to include the long-term liability of actually providing the long-term care. If a private insurance company kept its books that way, its senior executives could rightfully be convicted of fraud. Moreover, additional costs keep on surfacing. In the immortal words of House Speaker Nancy Pelosi, "We have to pass the bill so that you can find out what is in it, away from the fog of controversy."[211]

The Congressional Budget Office is one of the organizations tasked with finding out what is in the bill. On May 11, CBO Director Douglas W. Elmendorf wrote a letter identifying an estimated $115 billion in expenditures over 10 years that it had not previously enumerated. Some of that sum reflects spending on existing programs affected by the legislation, but much of it is new, such as $5 billion to $10 billion for the IRS to enforce tax elements of the bill, and a like amount for Medicare and Medicaid Services to implement the programmatic changes. Even those numbers, Elmendorf added, do not cover all the potential budgetary implications.[212]

Another embarrassing gaff was the insertion of a measure deleting the tax break for companies offering drug coverage in their corporate retirement plans. When ATT, Caterpillar and others announced billions of dollars in write-offs to reflect their new liability, outraged Congressmen called a hearing to investigate the flagrant political timing of the announcements — then sheepishly canceled it when they realized that the corporations were following Generally Accepted Accounting Procedures. At this point it remains unknown how many companies will curtail their drug benefits, forcing Medicare to pick up the cost, but the liability could be large.

Bottom line: Health care spending is heading for a budgetary train wreck. Democrats in Congress are shoveling more coal into the furnace, and Republicans are too busy yelling at them to bother looking for the hand brake. The GOP grasps that running against the deficit spending inherent in the health care bill is good politics, but the party proposes no clear alternative. Some pundits dream of rolling back the expansion of entitlements, but the Dems will not give up their dream of universal (or near-universal) coverage. Put bluntly, there is zero chance of repealing the Patient Protection and Affordable Care Act while Obama is in office, or even if he is voted out of office and there are still 40 Democrats in the Senate to sustain a filibuster. As for the Republicans' ideas of permitting inter-state competition of insurance companies and tightening up on tort law, such modest reforms fall far short of the transformative change needed to make a dent in Medicare and Medicaid spending.

What follows is a description of how to restrain runaway health care spending without triggering a no-win war with Democrats or invoking everyone's worst fear, the rationing of access to health care. The transformation of the health care industry along these lines will take years to take effect, meaning that the fiscal benefit will take years to materialize. Even so, the payoff could be significant. By one estimate, described below, modernization of U.S. health care delivery could save $600 billion between now and 2020, and even more in the out years.

Get employers out of health care. There is no logical reason that Americans' access to health care insurance should be tied to their employment status. The practice of offering medical insurance as a "fringe benefit" is an unanticipated outcome of World War II wage-and-price controls. Major employers offered the insurance as a way to skirt the caps on pay increases. Unlike wages and salary, the benefit was not deemed taxable, so it spread throughout the economy after the war.

Making employers central players in the health care system precipitates a cascade of undesirable consequences. When employers provide health care coverage, they negotiate with insurance companies to offer plans that optimize the interests of the employer, not the employee. Businesses want plans that are easy to administer, so, typically, insurers offer three variations on the same theme: an HMO (managed care) product, a more expensive PPO product that limits employees to a pre-selected network of hospitals and doctors, and an expensive, unrestricted plan. If employees want a plan attuned to their family budget, tolerance for risk or desire for preventive medicine, they have to look elsewhere. Trouble is, no one wants to pay with after-tax dollars.

Take away the tax differential, and people would compare the products offered by their employers to other insurance plans on the open market. One way that insurers could distinguish themselves would be to offer plans that truly practiced preventive medicine and "managed" care like the early HMOs idealistically proposed to do. With a few rare exceptions, employers are unwilling to pay for insurers to invest upfront resources to improve employee health over a period of years. Why is that? The reason is workforce turnover. It makes little sense for employers to sign a multi-year contract with an insurer to invest money in preventive and managed care for the long-term benefit of employee health if 20 percent of the workforce leaves the company every year. Given the reality of churn, employers select the insurer who can deliver insurance for the lowest cost in the year ahead.

Consequently, insurers look for one main thing when cutting deals with hospitals and physicians: not a proven track record of positive outcomes, just the steepest possible discount on procedures. Because hospitals and doctors are rewarded for performing procedures — more stent inserts and more gall bladder surgeries mean more money, regardless of results — they have little incentive to organize their practices to achieve the medically meritorious but financially fatal effect of improving outcomes and reducing the demand for their services. In sum, don't blame the docs, don't blame the insurers, don't even blame the employers for the relentlessly short-term focus of medical practice. Blame the tax break.

Promote the right kind of insurance competition. After eliminating the employer's role as middleman, the next step is to tear down the legal and regulatory apparatus that hinders competition between insurance companies. Think about it: There is plenty of competition for auto insurance, life insurance and homeowners insurance. Why isn't there more competition for health care insurance? Is it because executives who run health care insurance companies are greedier or more predatory than their counterparts in life and auto? Or is it that health care insurance is more heavily regulated? Unless someone discovers a mean-person gene in medical insurance executives that cannot be found in auto-insurance executives, I'm inclined to believe that the difference in behavior can be attributed to the different rules that govern each insurance line.

Republicans propose allowing insurers to compete across state lines. In theory, consumers would be able to select from policies originating in any state, effectively bypassing local insurance mandates. These mandates, inserted by special interest groups lobbying state legislatures, compel insurance policies to cover items as varied as mammography screenings, contraceptives and mental illness, or to include services by particular medical practitioners like chiropractors, optometrists and acupuncturists. While any one mandate may seem reasonable, the cumulative result is that insurers lose the flexibility to design their own health care plans. In effect, the minimum standards are established by government fiat, regardless of what the buyer can afford.

Imagine if legislators mandated the features in every automobile sold, whether new or used. The car must have side-door air bags, leather seats, an iPod dock, antilock braking systems, electronic stability systems, impact-absorbing interiors, back-up sensing systems, GPS navigation and a hybrid engine that gets at least 35 miles per gallon. Lawmakers could praise themselves for their worthy intentions. Everyone should drive a safe, comfortable, ecologically sensitive car, shouldn't they? Just one little problem: Such cars can't be manufactured for less than $35,000 (to pick a number out of thin air in order to make a point) and half the population can't afford them. No problem. Declare a car supply crisis, lambaste greedy auto executives in public hearings for failing the public, and create government subsidies for those who can't buy the government-designed cars!

Anything that sidesteps state insurance mandates would be an improvement over the status quo. If North Dakota has fewer mandates and an insurance company there offers a better deal, then the GOP bill would allow you do business with the company in North Dakota. Unfortunately, the bill would not address the problem of federally mandated insurance requirements, and it is entirely predictable that the special interests would switch their lobbying efforts from state legislators to Congress. The legislation might bring temporary relief, but before long the national insurance market would get gooed up with mandates emanating from Washington.

Another reason why the GOP brand of insurance competition falls short is that it does nothing to change the dynamic in which insurers compete solely on the basis of price. If Big Insura offered insurance products with the same short-sighted price-discounting focus as the products on the market today, then the market will not advance very far. Insurers need to compete on the basis of providing health care value, the best combination of price and quality.

To drive transformational change, insurers (including Medicare and Medicaid) need to re-think their relationship to the patient/customer. Instead of negotiating deals with hospitals and physician groups for the lowest prices on specific billable items, leaving the patient out of the equation, they need to empower patients to seek the best deals (price and quality) for the treatment of their medical condition.

Regina Herzlinger draws a picture of how such consumer-driven health care might work, using the example of a fictional patient, Jack Morgan, who has been diagnosed with kidney failure. The insurer gives him $40,000 a year over five years, the amount typically spent (in 2007) on male end-stage renal disease. Jack has $200,000 of buying power — enough money to attract anyone's attention. In Herzlinger's example, he contracts with an integrated team of specialists for a bundled service; the $40,000 a year covers all costs. With a five-year time horizon, Jack's team is incentivized to provide treatments, such as a kidney transplant, that might cost more up-front but would reduce annual treatment costs on the back end. The healthier they keep him, the less money they spend in the end and the more profit they make.[213]

Such a scenario would require three key changes from common practice. The first is the willingness of an insurer to pay a team of doctors, nurses and other professionals focused on treating kidney disease as a bundled service. No more billing for each X-ray, blood test and tablet of aspirin. Everything is covered. The second is the ability to contract to provide care over a five-year period of time. What's to stop unscrupulous physicians from taking the money and short-changing Jack on care? That's where the third key change comes in. Insurance companies would compete for patients on their ability to keep them alive and well. In an efficiently functioning health care system, cost and quality data would be readily available to all consumers.

Create market transparency. One of the biggest obstacles to market-driven health care is the fact that there is, er, no market. You don't know the price of a particular procedure until you get billed. In the rare instance that you ask beforehand, the doctor probably doesn't know. Except for routine procedures, there's not much point in calling around — you'll never get an answer. As for comparing the quality of different hospitals and doctors, forget it. Even for procedures as basic as, say, coronary bypass operations, very few institutions keep the information in a format that would allow you to contrast the record of Hospital A with Hospital B.

One reason providers don't like tracking outcomes is that the data can be used carelessly. Just because Hospital A experiences more mortalities on the operating table than Hospital B doesn't mean that its quality is deficient. The difference could stem from the fact that Hospital A takes the riskier patients. If its results were properly adjusted for sickness, or morbidity, Hospital A actually might prove to be better.

While prickly, such issues can be addressed. Groups around the country have been wrestling with them for years. Furthermore, one of the best things to come out of Obamacare is a requirement that health care providers begin reporting quality data. Health and Human Services will work with industry groups to select the most pertinent measures and decide how to organize and present it. Then the data will be made public to anyone who can make good use of it — either hospitals and doctors who want to benchmark themselves for the purposes of quality improvement, or third parties who package the data in a way that is accessible to patient/consumers.

Within a few years, it should be possible to shop for the best hospitals on the basis of criteria more meaningful than how much they spend on advertising, and for doctors on criteria more relevant than how much other doctors like them. If insurers can canoodle providers into posting public prices for bundled services, like the $40,000 price tag for a year's worth of renal-disease treatment mentioned above, then consumers will have much of the information they need to make informed choices and drive change in the marketplace. Also, as genuine markets emerge, insurers may find a new value proposition: applying their intimate knowledge of local health care markets to help patient/consumers make the often-difficult tradeoffs between price and quality. Wouldn't that be a turn-around? Instead of acting as a gatekeeper denying care to patients, insurers could evolve into their guides and advocates to ensure that they received the very best care.

Eliminate barriers to business innovation. Once providers become focused on delivering health care value, the industry will be primed for a business revolution. The future will belong to multidisciplinary teams that specialize in treating chronic diseases and complex medical conditions with great efficiency. Abundant research has shown that the providers with the best medical outcomes are those who perform the most procedures. In a word, practice makes perfect. As manufacturers of products from cell phones to microchips have proven over and over, quality is synonymous with productivity. Learning how to perfect the diagnosis, deliver the correct course of treatment, eliminate errors, and provide follow-up care leads to better medical outcomes at lower cost.

In a market-driven health care system, the industry will evolve away from jack-of-all-trades-and-master-of-none medical facilities toward what Regina Herzlinger calls "focused factories," where the owner/entrepreneurs are fanatically devoted to the pursuit of excellence. Scrutinizing cost and outcomes data to see how they compare with competitors, these medical entrepreneurs are driven to relentless improvement. As learning organizations, they scour the literature for state-of-the-art technologies, procedures and delivery systems. They lay out their facilities, equip them and staff them in order to maximize productivity and quality. When medical outcomes are widely publicized, the practice of poor medicine will be punished ruthlessly; superior quality will be rewarded by more patients and higher profits.

We will see focused factories emerge in fits and starts here in the U.S. — and at light speed overseas. Dr. Devi Shetty, a Bangalore, India, heart surgeon, has built one of the most efficient heart hospitals in the world. While the typical American hospital charges between $20,000 and $100,000 to perform open-heart surgery, the 1,000-bed Narayana Hrudayalaya Hospital charges $2,000 on average — and, arguably, provides better quality outcomes. Remarkably, one-third of the hospital's patients are poor farmers. They are covered by an insurance plan, crafted in partnership with the state of Karnataka, costing $3 per person per year and reimbursing the hospital $1,200 for a surgery, slightly less than its $1,500 break even.

How does Shetty do it? By paying Third World wages to his hospital staff? No, cardiac surgeons earn between $110,000 and $240,000 annually — less than in America, perhaps, but not exactly coolie wages. By cutting corners on quality? Well, no. Quality comparisons are difficult to make but they tend to favor Narayana Hrudayalaya. The hospital reports a 1.4 percent mortality rate within 30 days of coronary bypass graft surgery, one of the most common procedures, compared with an average of 1.9 percent in the United States in 2008. If the data were adjusted for the morbidity of the patients treated — many Indians lack access to basic health care and suffer from more advanced cardiac disease when they are admitted — the quality comparisons would favor Narayana Hrudayalaya even more.

Shetty delivers superior quality and outcomes by adopting a manufacturing model of process efficiency and quality control. "Japanese companies reinvented the process of making cars. That's what we're doing in health care," Shetty says. "What health care needs is process innovation, not product innovation."

There is a revolution in medical care occurring in the world, and India is at the epicenter. But it is not the only player. The phenomenon of medical tourism is growing by leaps and bounds. To Americans retiring in Latin American, inexpensive housing in beautiful locations is not the only lure. They frequently find high-quality — and lower cost — health care in developing nations as well. Indeed, last year, Shetty was planning to expand his business to the Western Hemisphere. When the *Wall Street Journal* reported on his activities last November, he had just inked a deal, subject to approval by local authorities, to build a hospital in the Cayman Islands to deliver lower-cost care to Americans willing to make an hour-and-a-half flight from Miami.[214]

Why not build the hospital in the United States? The *Journal* did not address that question, but the answer is obvious. Too many regulations, too many barriers to doing business. The Stark law restricts doctors from owning an interest in facilities to which they refer patients. Certificate of Public Need law allows established hospitals to block interlopers from building surgery centers or other facilities for which there is no demonstrated "need" — in other words, which competes with an existing hospital. These barriers to innovation must be swept away. Innovators like Shetty should be encouraged to enter the U.S. market and shake up the established way of doing business.

How does reform of the private market for health care help reduce spending on Medicare and Medicaid? The revolution in productivity and quality will improve outcomes and lower prices for everyone, including Medicare and Medicaid patients. While Obamacare plans to trot out a half dozen or so pilot programs for Medicare, an unshackled private sector would conduct thousands of pilot projects, otherwise known as new business ventures. The results of the private-sector tests will be digested and lessons learned far more quickly than they possibly could percolate through the Department of Health and Human Services, no matter how many Ph.D.s of the John F. Kennedy School of Government are employed on staff or as consultants. It will take endless experimentation, success and failures and many iterations of new delivery models to reap the productivity and quality gains that analysts think are achievable. Rapid innovation will come from the private sector. Whatever innovation emerges from the public sector will be glacially slow — and will depend upon insights generated from the private sector in the first place. Letting Washington dictate the rate of medical-delivery innovation would be disastrous.

Health, education and social services actually lost ground in terms of productivity between 1995 and 2005, compared to average economy-wide growth of 2.4 percent annually, notes David Cutler a Harvard economist. If health care productivity simply kept pace with national norms, the economy would save unimaginable sums. Cutler estimates that health care modernization, which he defines as "investing in infrastructure; measuring what is done and how well it is performed; rewarding high-value care, not just high-volume care; and realigning consumer incentives to encourage better health behavior" — could save $600 billion in public health spending over the next decade and $9 trillion over the next 25 years.[215]

Think of that: Health care modernization properly executed could trim federal government spending by billions and provide better quality of care for all. Only elite policy makers in government and academe believe, however, that top-down reform directed by government (and guided by elite policy makers) will lead to the transformation that Cutler is looking for. Politicians and bureaucrats in Washington, D.C., will never spur the innovation needed to salvage health care in America. Only a tidal wave of creative destruction powered by entrepreneurs operating in free markets can create the disruptive, transformative change required to avert Boomergeddon.

Coming Up Short

I've sketched out a broad approach that could cut $100 billion in corporate welfare, shrink discretionary spending by $117 billion, unwind $100 billion in military spending, and save as much as $60 billion a year on average this decade through health care reform. To those sums add $350 billion in addition revenue generated by the Fair Tax and the $100 billion Paul Light thinks can be saved by streamlining government. Total it all up and you get about $817 billion.

That's a large sum, but it is still short of the $1 trillion we're aiming for. And remember, achieving those reforms would take years of brutal political warfare to legislate and years more to implement. The savings will not materialize all at once. From one perspective, that's a good thing. Slashing $800 in federal spending overnight in a $12 trillion to $13 trillion economy could push the nation back into a deep recession. We need to ease our way back to fiscal solvency. But would closing the budget gap by $800 billion over several years get us out of the swamp? The national debt would grow by multiple trillions of dollars while the reforms took effect. Eventually, there would be another recession, and deficits would balloon again — just not as badly as if the changes had not been made. All the while, the size of the national debt would continue to grow. If interest rates rose as well, interest payments on the swelling debt would take on a life of their own. The question with the unknowable answer is this: Would the Electronic Herd be impressed enough with our deficit-taming efforts to keep on lending?

I don't know. But I have given it the best shot I've got. If you want to save the good ol' USA from a fiscal meltdown, push these proposals.

Better yet, refine and improve upon them. Elect like-minded Congressmen to enact them. Commit yourself to saving the country from Boomergeddon.

But don't bet your financial future on the naive hope that our dysfunctional and myopic political culture would permit the changes I have described. Too many vested interests have too much to lose. While you work for change, cover your bases. Slenderize your lifestyle, live with less, pay down debt and save what you can. In sum, do everything on a personal level that you are urging the federal government to do, because if Boomergeddon does detonate, Uncle Sam will not be there to take care of you. You will be on your own.

Chapter 10
The End of an Era

The Global Financial Crisis of 2007-2008 is now history, but national and world events have yet to settle into a pattern that could be called normal. In the six months since I began writing this book, the Greek debt crisis has exposed the fragile economic and fiscal health of Europe, the United States' major trading partner and geopolitical ally. The Euro sprinted past the dollar in the race to the bottom as financial markets grew increasingly skeptical of the ability of the democratic welfare states — including the United States — to meet their long-term debt obligations. With riots erupting in Athens to protest the terms of the European Central Bank-engineered bailout, voters in Germany punished their ruling party in mid-May for squandering their tax dollars on a people who showed little sign of appreciating their sacrifice. Oblivious to the dangerous shift in global investor sentiment, the Obama administration rammed through health care legislation, which in exchange for a fleeting expansion of the welfare state will accelerate the rush to Boomergeddon and its calamitous dismantling of that very same welfare state. In reaction to the voracious appetite of government, the Tea Party has gathered strength, morphing in a few short months from scattered protests in town hall meetings into a formidable grassroots organization capable of mounting serious challenges to the Republican Party establishment.

I am heartened by the fact that the American people have channeled their anxieties about deficits, the national debt and the endless encroachment of the central government into a national movement. Yet I remain realistic. The emergence of the Tea Party as a political force does not yet change the underlying political or fiscal fundamentals that lead inexorably to Boomergeddon.

The political class remains immensely powerful, and it senses the first real threat to its power since the 1994 Gingrich insurrection. Initially, commentators for elite media outlets dismissed Tea Party activists as a rent-a-mob orchestrated by conservative special interest groups. When that interpretation proved too divergent from reality to maintain with a straight face, the Politics As Usual apologists sought to marginalize Tea Partiers by referring to them as "tea baggers," a contemptuous term with a sexual connotation. In this updated portrayal, the Tea Party consisted of an ignorant rabble of rustics, cranks, gun lovers, spittoon users and *Deliverance* creatures. Then, when a *New York Times* poll found that Tea Partiers were better educated and had higher incomes than the national norm, the media re-cast the movement as the "populism of the privileged," to use the words of *Washington Post* columnist and tool of the political class E.J. Dionne, Jr.[216] In the latest line of thinking, Tea Partiers are affluent, white and conservative, driven not by rational thought but deep anxieties about a complex world and racial prejudice against the nation's first African-American president! What the elite opinion makers will never do is credit the movement for what it really is: a populist revolt against the parasitical political class and its bankrupt philosophy of governance.

Democrats have endorsed the negative depiction, understanding quite accurately that, from whatever wellsprings of resentment it draws upon, the Tea Party threatens the spend-and-elect status quo. Insofar as the Dems view themselves as the party of big government dedicated to the redistribution of wealth, they perceive clearly that they have the most to lose from this middle-class uprising. Republicans are more ambivalent. On the one hand, their philosophy, if not their practice, preaches the virtues of small government and fiscal responsibility. On the other, establishment candidates find themselves under fire by deficit hawks and Tea Party sympathizers for their manifest failure to live up to their ideals. Will the K-Street Republicans try to co-opt the movement, or will they ultimately reject it as an alien entity? It may take years before the struggle for the soul of the Republican Party is finally resolved.

While the Tea Party does represent, to my mind, the greatest hope for pulling the country back from the brink of Boomergeddon, as of this writing the movement has yet to cohere as a political force with a cohesive agenda. It is one thing to inveigh against deficits, taxes and the national debt, it is quite another to agree what needs to be done about them. Tea Partiers may propel the Rs to electoral gains in November, but it's not clear that the Elephant Clan has the will to defy the organized special interests in Washington, D.C., much less to make transformative reforms that can return the country to a sustainable fiscal trajectory. As long as Obama is president, until January 2013 at the very least, even the eviction of the Donkey Clan as the majority party in Congress will result in little change for two more years. By then, the nation will be $3 trillion deeper in hock, the economy will be as hooked as ever upon Keynesian spending stimulus to keep growing, society's "unmet needs" will be as acute as always, the evaporation of the Medicare Part B trust fund will be looming on the horizon, and foreign investors will be even more antsy about the ability of the U.S. to repay its debt.

Taxpayers may vehemently oppose deficit spending and the mounting national debt, but those who pay no federal income taxes — about 43 percent of the population, according to the center-left Tax Policy Center[217] — will oppose with equal vehemence any move to cut entitlements, and both parties will demagogue anyone who proposes to touch Social Security and Medicare. Just look what the Democrats did to George Bush's proposal to reform Social Security, and observe how Republicans accused Obamacare of undermining Medicare. Any change, if it comes, will likely be incremental and insufficient to divert the federal government from its downward slide.

With each passing day, the United States seems to be following the script written by William Strauss and Neil Howe in their eerily prescient 1997 book, "The Fourth Turning," which predicted that the country would enter a lengthy crisis between 2005 and 2025.[218] Crises come every four generations, or roughly every 80 years: first the American Revolution, then the Civil War and then the Great Depression/World War II. And now, after the passage of another four generations, we are due for another cataclysm.

The premise of these latter-day Nostradami was that human societies follow cycles of history as generations succeed one another in predictable patterns. Each generation fits an archetype — Prophets, Nomads, Heroes and Artists — molded by the generations that precede them and in turn molding those that follow. Each cycle of the four generations coincides with four phases. First comes the epochal "high" marked by a strong sense of national unity, faith in institutions, settled values and communal sense of purpose. Then follows an awakening, in which new ideals are articulated and institutions attacked, though not overturned. Just as fall supplants summer, there follows an unraveling, in which politics become increasingly divisive, faith in institutions erode, and traditional ideals are more deeply called into question. Finally, society enters a turning point — a crisis — in which the old order is swept away, a new contract is forged between government and the people, new values are celebrated and new institutions arise.

As a student of history, I am not entirely comfortable with this typology. It would seem all too easy to impose a generational framework on American history and select examples of prophets, nomads, heroes and artists from the multitude of historical figures available to choose from, forcing some into the typology and ignoring those that don't fit. But I'm a great believer in prediction. If someone can look 10 to 15 years ahead and foresee outcomes that elude everyone else, then I perk up and pay attention. Maybe the prognosticator is lucky... but maybe he knows something that the rest of us do not. In the case of Strauss and Howe, they divined developments that no one else foresaw at the time.

Remember, the United States was fairly upbeat in 1997. The Soviet Union had collapsed, China had not emerged as an economic rival and the name Osama bin Laden was known to only a few. The Internet boom offered a world of limitless possibilities. Alan Greenspan was hailed as a genius for vanquishing the business cycle. The U.S. was running a budget surplus, and the public debate was what to do with all the money. Other than the acrimonious partisanship in Washington, it seemed the best of times. But Straus and Howe saw the nation unraveling, soon to enter a deep crisis. One of the signs, they wrote, would be a financial crisis in 2005 or soon thereafter.

"As the crisis mood congeals," they wrote, "people will come to the jarring realization that they have grown helplessly dependent on a teetering edifice of anonymous transactions and paper guarantees." (Can anyone say "credit default swaps"?) "The era will have left the financial world arbitraged and tentacled. Debtors won't know who holds their notes, homeowners who owns their mortgages, and shareholders who run their companies."

The Boomers' old age will loom, said Strauss and Howe, "exposing the thinness in private savings and the unsustainability of public promises." Millennials (young adults, also known as Generation Y, around 28 years old or younger) will face debts, tax burdens and two-tier wage structures. There will be a Great Devaluation, "a severe drop in the market price of most financial and real assets.... a free-falling price in a market with no buyers."

Does any of this sound familiar?

Looking beyond the financial crisis, Strauss and Howe describe how elders, their savings decimated, will become more dependent than ever upon government even as government becomes more overextended and less able to meet its obligations. Mid-lifers (commonly known as Generation X) will get stuck with higher taxes during their peak earning years.

According to "The Fourth Turning," the old order will seem ruined beyond repair. "Like a magnet passed over society's disk drive," the authors write, the crisis will erase the social contract and clear the books of vast unpayable promises to which people had come to feel entitled.

The nation could well enter a depression or get dragged into traumatic foreign wars. But eventually, after the 20-year crisis, the nation will emerge transformed. The Fourth Turning will be a time of glory or ruin. "The emergent society may be something better, a nation that sustains its Framers' visions with a robust new pride. Or it may be something unspeakably worse."

We are still in the early phases of the crisis. To my mind, the worst has yet to come. The Global Financial Crisis of was a dress rehearsal for the fast approaching Sovereign Debt Crisis. That trauma will afflict most of the European countries, even France and Germany eventually, as well as Japan, North America and the less fiscally disciplined of the developing countries. The Sovereign Debt Crisis will pull even fiscally responsible nations like China into its maw. As the world's biggest creditor, China will have the most to lose from the U.S. default: trillions of dollars of wealth tied up in U.S. Treasuries. Additionally, its export-driven economy will get slammed by the collapse in buying power from what once had been the richest countries in the world. Hysteria will sweep through financial markets globally. As credit shuts down, the economies of the richest nations will be unable to stimulate their economies by means of Keynesian deficit spending. Economic misery will ensue on the scale of the Great Depression.

Although it may be theoretically possible to extricate ourselves along the lines I described in Chapter 9, the prospects that the political class, either of the two party/clans or even a majority of the American people will be willing to make the necessary sacrifices are remote. Although Americans should strive to bring deficits under control in the hope of dampening the disaster to come, we also must maintain a steely eyed realism about the odds of success.

The critical struggle, the outcome of which is not foreordained, is this: What follows Boomergeddon? How will Americans diagnose what went wrong? Whom will they hold accountable? Will Americans depose the political class, or will they bow down to it? What new institutions will arise from the ashes? Will we move to a social contract based upon personal responsibility, free markets, stronger civic institutions and a smaller, more accountable government that focuses on doing a few things very well? Or will we, as we did in the 1930s, move toward a corporatist state with the interests of business cartels, labor unions and other constituencies mediated by a powerful government?

In the great American tradition of assigning blame and punishing the innocent, the political class will attribute the catastrophic failure on the last vestiges of a free marketplace. The Krugmans and Reichs of the 2020s will argue that the surest path to recovery will be to entrust political elites with more power over a broader swath of American life. But in the minds of many, the leviathan state will be thoroughly discredited. The lovers of liberty will demand a new contract between citizen and government: from the New Deal to a No Deal. They will seek to shrink the scope of government power, invent mechanisms for individuals to weave their personal safety nets, and to stop rewarding the reckless, the profligate and the indolent. Because the calamity of Boomergeddon will far surpass the suffering engendered by the Global Financial Crisis, the mother of all meltdowns may inspire a rebellion so powerful that insurgents actually will manage to dismantle the political class and burn (figuratively, of course) the Imperial City to the ground before being seduced by its temptations. But no outcome is preordained. If those who foresee the calamity succeed in framing the debate that follows Boomergeddon, and if they press their case with conviction, their vision of the post-apocalyptic world may prevail.

Appendix A
The "Head for the Hills" Scenario

Chmura Economics & Analytics ran a number of scenarios to see what would happen when we plugged different growth and interest-rate assumptions into the 10-year forecast contained in the Obama administration's proposed 2011 budget. The head-for-the-hills scenario assumes that (1) the economic expansion is one percentage point slower than forecast, (2) interest rates will stay subdued for three years as turmoil in European financial markets creates a flight to safety that keeps interest rates low on U.S. Treasuries, (3) interest rates then surge for any number of possible reasons, such as sovereign defaults in Europe sparking a global financial panic, and drive the weighted average of U.S. Treasuries up to 10 percent by 2020, and (4) the spike in interest rates slams the brakes on the aging business expansion, pushing the U.S. into a recession in 2018 and 2019.

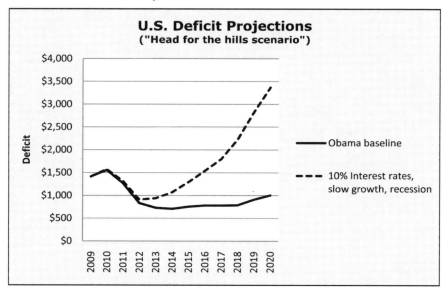

Under this scenario, the annual deficit would reach $3.4 trillion in 2020, more than three times the level projected by the O Team. The national debt would escalate to $35 trillion — equivalent to 170 percent of the GDP, far higher than the 115 percent debt/GDP ratio in a near-insolvent Greece. Of course, conditions would be so extreme and volatile that the wheels would come off the economy and the budget long before 2020. Boomergeddon would come early.

If you find the growth and interest-rate assumptions in this scenario to be plausible, we would suggest that you waste no time — purchase yourself a cabin in the mountains of Montana and stock up on canned foods.

Appendix B

Appendix B
Obama Budget Forecasts

10-Year Forecast, FY 2011 Budget (In $billions, published Feb. 1, 2010)						
Outlays:	**2010**	**2011**	**2012**	**2013**	**2014**	**2015**
Appropriated ("discretionary") programs:						
Security	855	895	827	811	825	845
Non-security	553	520	475	456	457	465
Subtotal, appropriated programs	1,408	1,415	1,301	1,267	1,283	1,310
Mandatory programs:						
Social Security	715	730	762	801	845	893
Medicare	451	491	501	556	623	652
Medicaid	275	297	274	292	313	336
Troubled Asset Relief Program (TARP)	−73	11	10	7	6	3
Allowance for jobs initiatives	12	25	8	3	2	
Allowance for health reform	6	−7	−17	2	30	72
Other mandatory programs	737	619	570	547	546	544
Subtotal, mandatory programs	2,123	2,165	2,107	2,208	2,364	2,500
Net interest	188	251	343	436	510	571
Disaster costs	1	3	4	4	4	5
Total outlays	3,721	3,834	3,755	3,915	4,161	4,386
Receipts:						
Individual income taxes	936	1,121	1,326	1,468	1,604	1,733
Corporation income taxes	157	297	366	393	445	411
Social Security payroll taxes	635	674	720	766	809	856
Medicare payroll taxes	180	192	208	223	237	251
Unemployment insurance	51	60	67	73	77	79
Other retirement	9	8	9	9	9	9
Excise taxes	73	74	81	85	87	88
Estate and gift taxes	17	25	23	24	26	28
Customs duties	24	27	32	35	37	39
Deposits of earnings, Federal Reserve	77	79	67	59	52	48
Allowance for jobs initiatives	−12	−25	−8	−3	−2	
Allowance for health reform		16	18	39	58	74
Other miscellaneous receipts	18	17	17	17	18	18
Total receipts :	2,165	2,567	2,926	3,188	3,455	3,634
Deficit	1,556	1,267	828	727	706	752

10-Year Forecast, Proposed FY 2011 Budget
(In $billions, published Feb. 1, 2010)

Outlays:	2016	2017	2018	2019	2020	Total
Appropriated ("discretionary") programs:						
Security	862	885	907	931	955	8,743
Non-security	475	486	497	511	529	4,871
Subtotal, appropriated programs	1,337	1,371	1,405	1,442	1,484	13,614
Mandatory programs:						
Social Security	945	1,002	1,064	1,130	1,201	9,373
Medicare	724	757	791	881	953	6,927
Medicaid	362	389	419	451	487	3,619
Troubled Asset Relief Program (TARP)	1					39
Allowance for jobs initiatives						38
Allowance for health reform	101	100	100	104	106	590
Other mandatory programs	563	567	568	616	637	5,775
Subtotal, mandatory programs	2,696	2,815	2,942	3,182	3,384	26,363
Net interest	627	681	733	786	840	5,777
Disaster costs	5	5	5	5	5	46
Total outlays	4,665	4,872	5,084	5,415	5,713	45,800
Receipts:						
Individual income taxes	1,856	1,980	2,102	2,223	2,338	17,752
Corporation income taxes	449	463	473	486	502	4,285
Social insurance and retirement receipts:						
Social Security payroll taxes	911	954	1,000	1,044	1,084	8,819
Medicare payroll taxes	267	280	293	307	318	2,578
Unemployment insurance	79	78	77	76	77	743
Other retirement	9	9	9	9	10	89
Excise taxes	89	90	90	91	92	867
Estate and gift taxes	30	32	35	37	40	298
Customs duties	42	44	47	49	52	404
Deposits of earnings, Federal Reserve	50	52	55	57	59	578
Allowance for jobs initiatives						−38
Allowance for health reform	86	93	101	110	119	712
Other miscellaneous receipts	18	18	19	19	19	180
Total receipts :	3,887	4,094	4,299	4,507	4,710	37,268
Deficit	778	778	785	908	1,003	8,532

Proposed FY 2011 Budget
(In $billions, submitted February 1, 2010)

Outlays:	2016	2017	2018	2019	2020	Total
Appropriated ("discretionary") programs:						
Security	862	885	907	931	955	8,743
Non-security	475	486	497	511	529	4,871
Subtotal, appropriated programs	1,337	1,371	1,405	1,442	1,484	13,614
Mandatory programs:						
Social Security	945	1,002	1,064	1,130	1,201	9,373
Medicare	724	757	791	881	953	6,927
Medicaid	362	389	419	451	487	3,619
Troubled Asset Relief Program (TARP)	1					39
Allowance for jobs initiatives						38
Allowance for health reform	101	100	100	104	106	590
Other mandatory programs	563	567	568	616	637	5,775
Subtotal, mandatory programs	2,696	2,815	2,942	3,182	3,384	26,363
Net interest	627	681	733	786	840	5,777
Disaster costs	5	5	5	5	5	46
Total outlays	4,665	4,872	5,084	5,415	5,713	45,800
Receipts:						
Individual income taxes	1,856	1,980	2,102	2,223	2,338	17,752
Corporation income taxes	449	463	473	486	502	4,285
Social insurance and retirement receipts:						
Social Security payroll taxes	911	954	1,000	1,044	1,084	8,819
Medicare payroll taxes	267	280	293	307	318	2,578
Unemployment insurance	79	78	77	76	77	743
Other retirement	9	9	9	9	10	89
Excise taxes	89	90	90	91	92	867
Estate and gift taxes	30	32	35	37	40	298
Customs duties	42	44	47	49	52	404
Deposits of earnings, Federal Reserve	50	52	55	57	59	578
Allowance for jobs initiatives						−38
Allowance for health reform	86	93	101	110	119	712
Other miscellaneous receipts	18	18	19	19	19	180
Total receipts :	3,887	4,094	4,299	4,507	4,710	37,268
Deficit	778	778	785	908	1,003	8,532

10-Year Forecast - Economic Assumptions
(In $billions, submitted February 1, 2010)

	2013	2014	2015	2016
Gross Domestic Product (GDP):				
Levels, dollar amounts in billions:				
Current dollars	17,433	18,446	19,433	20,408
Real, chained (2005) dollars	15,027	15,633	16,194	16,714
Chained price index (2005 = 100), annual avg.	116	117.9	120	122
Percent change, 4th quarter over 4th quarter				
Current dollars	6.0	5.7	5.2	5.0
Real, chained (2005) dollars	4.2	3.9	3.4	3.1
Chained price index (2005 = 100)	1.7	1.7	1.7	1.8
Percent change, year over year:				
Current dollars	6.0	5.8	5.3	5.0
Real, chained (2005) dollars	4.2	4.0	3.6	3.2
Chained price index (2005 = 100)	1.7	1.7	1.7	1.8
Incomes, billions of current dollars:				
Corporate profits before tax	1,915	1,924	1,998	2,031
Employee Compensation	9,626	10,247	10,855	11,447
Wages and salaries	7,776	8,288	8,783	9,263
Other taxable income	3,830	4,049	4,218	4,434
Consumer Price Index (all urban)				
Level (1982–84 = 100), annual average	230.8	235.5	240.2	245.1
Percent change, 4th quarter over 4th quarter	2.0	2.0	2.0	2.1
Percent change, year over year	2.0	2.0	2.0	2.0
Unemployment rate, civilian, percent:				
Fourth quarter level	7.0	6.2	5.7	5.4
Annual average	7.3	6.5	5.9	5.5
Federal pay raises, January, percent:	NA	NA	NA	NA
Military				
Civilian	NA	NA	NA	NA
Interest rates, percent:				
91-day Treasury bills	4.0	4.1	4.1	4.1
10-year Treasury notes	5.2	5.3	5.3	5.3

10-Year Forecast - Economic Assumptions
(In $billions, submitted February 1, 2010)

	2017	2018	2019	2020
Gross Domestic Product (GDP):				
Levels, dollar amounts in billions:				
Current dollars	21,373	22,329	23,312	24,323
Real, chained (2005) dollars	17,190	17,643	18,091	18,543
Chained price index (2005 = 100), annual avg.	124.3	126.5	128.8	131.1
Percent change, 4th quarter over 4th quarter				
Current dollars	4.5	4.5	4.4	4.3
Real, chained (2005) dollars	2.7	2.6	2.5	2.5
Chained price index (2005 = 100)	1.8	1.8	1.8	1.8
Percent change, year over year:				
Current dollars	4.7	4.5	4.4	4.3
Real, chained (2005) dollars	2.8	2.6	2.5	2.5
Chained price index (2005 = 100)	1.8	1.8	1.8	1.8
Incomes, billions of current dollars:				
Corporate profits before tax	2,058	2,076	2,087	2,150
Employee Compensation	12,024	12,612	13,197	13,792
Wages and salaries	9,733	10,198	10,667	11,134
Other taxable income	4,662	4,857	5,073	5,305
Consumer Price Index (all urban)				
Level (1982–84 = 100), annual average	250.3	255.5	260.9	266.4
Percent change, 4th quarter over 4th quarter	2.1	2.1	2.1	2.1
Percent change, year over year	2.1	2.1	2.1	2.1
Unemployment rate, civilian, percent:				
Fourth quarter level	5.3	5.2	5.2	5.2
Annual average	5.3	5.2	5.2	5.2
Federal pay raises, January, percent:	NA	NA	NA	NA
Military				
Civilian	NA	NA	NA	NA
Interest rates, percent:				
91-day Treasury bills	4.1	4.1	4.1	4.1
10-year Treasury notes	5.3	5.3	5.3	5.3

10-Year Forecast - Economic Assumptions
(In $billions, submitted February 1, 2010)

	2017	2018	2019	2020
Gross Domestic Product (GDP):				
Levels, dollar amounts in billions:				
Current dollars	21,373	22,329	23,312	24,323
Real, chained (2005) dollars	17,190	17,643	18,091	18,543
Chained price index (2005 = 100), annual avg.	124.3	126.5	128.8	131.1
Percent change, 4th quarter over 4th quarter				
Current dollars	4.5	4.5	4.4	4.3
Real, chained (2005) dollars	2.7	2.6	2.5	2.5
Chained price index (2005 = 100)	1.8	1.8	1.8	1.8
Percent change, year over year:				
Current dollars	4.7	4.5	4.4	4.3
Real, chained (2005) dollars	2.8	2.6	2.5	2.5
Chained price index (2005 = 100)	1.8	1.8	1.8	1.8
Incomes, billions of current dollars:				
Corporate profits before tax	2,058	2,076	2,087	2,150
Employee Compensation	12,024	12,612	13,197	13,792
Wages and salaries	9,733	10,198	10,667	11,134
Other taxable income	4,662	4,857	5,073	5,305
Consumer Price Index (all urban)				
Level (1982–84 = 100), annual average	250.3	255.5	260.9	266.4
Percent change, 4th quarter over 4th quarter	2.1	2.1	2.1	2.1
Percent change, year over year	2.1	2.1	2.1	2.1
Unemployment rate, civilian, percent:				
Fourth quarter level	5.3	5.2	5.2	5.2
Annual average	5.3	5.2	5.2	5.2
Federal pay raises, January, percent:	NA	NA	NA	NA
Military				
Civilian	NA	NA	NA	NA
Interest rates, percent:				
91-day Treasury bills	4.1	4.1	4.1	4.1
10-year Treasury notes	5.3	5.3	5.3	5.3

Acknowledgements

A work such as this is not the product of a single mind, no matter how creative (or in my case, no matter how demented). I owe so much to the contributions and encouragement of others.

First and foremost, I must thank Matt Thornhill and John Martin with the Boomer Project who introduced me to the field of Baby Boomers and generational analysis. Matt and John are two of the most creative guys I know, and it has been a pleasure working with them — and learning from them — over the past two years. As much as I owe them, they bear no responsibility for the conclusions reached in this book, which are entirely my own.

A close second on my thank you list is Steve Martin (no relation to John), the publisher of Oaklea Press. When the idea for Boomergeddon was nothing more than a rough outline, Steve saw its potential. He is the one who encouraged me to throw caution to the winds. Without his guidance and support, "Boomergeddon" never would have made it to print.

Thirdly, I want to express my gratitude to Chris Chmura and Xiaobing Shuai with Chmura Economics & Analytics who applied their expertise in economic modeling to the Obama administration's 10-year budget forecast. By testing the sensitivity of the O Team's deficit projections to alternate growth-rate and interest-rate assumptions, they helped me draw much stronger conclusions than I could have based on my own innumerate hunches.

To Sidney Gunst and Annie Tobey, I owe many of the insights contained in Chapter 8, "Surviving Boomergeddon." It was during a series of brainstorming sessions for one of Sidney's business ventures that Sidney, Annie and I developed the schematic approach by which Americans can lower their household expenditures, pay down debt and become more self reliant. I can hardly wait for Sidney to launch the enterprise. It's one thing to articulate an idea. But if you really want it to spread, figure out how to make money from it.

I also must credit my parents for the content of this book, for better or worse. I formulated many of the insights contained here, too numerous to mention, during marathon conversations with my mother. To my father, I owe my advocacy of the Fair Tax as well as many useful comments on a rough draft. To both, I owe the love of liberty and self-reliance that permeate my writing.

I thank Ed Risse, Peter Galuszka, "Groveton" and the regulars on the Bacon's Rebellion blog (http://baconsrebellion.blogspot.com) for sustaining one of the most thoughtful and civil public policy blogs anywhere. I posted long sections of "Boomergeddon" on the blog for critique. The feedback was invaluable. Ed and I have been collaborating so long that it is hard to know where his ideas leave off and mine begin. To Peter, I am especially grateful for his close reading of the manuscript.

I am obliged to Steve Nash for his unflagging encouragement of my writing, even though my ideas don't always mesh with his own; his wife Linda, one of the serial entrepreneurs who are reinventing the delivery of health care; Conaway Haskins, my guide into the Alice-and-the-Looking-Glass world of the nation's capital; Billy Mock, for acting as sounding board for my crackpot economic theories; and Tanner Powell for his insights into the financial menace posed by public employee unions.

To Sandra Baker, my eagle-eyed proof reader, goes the credit of making the manuscript presentable to the public.

No list of debts and obligations would be complete without acknowledging the stimulating discourse of the West End Gentlemen's Eating, Drinking and Bloviating Club, where I have been privileged to engage in the most stimulating conversation around a Virginia dinner table since Thomas Jefferson and James Monroe last supped together.

Last but not least, I thank Laura for her endless patience with my endless writing. Being my wife is not an easy avocation.

End Notes

Most of the sources that I drew upon to write "Boomergeddon" can be found on the Internet. In most cases you can find them by typing the title (in quotation marks) into a search engine. If that doesn't work, you can find all the notes with links directly to the sources on the "Boomergeddon" website at *www.boomergeddon.us.*

That's *.us,* folks, not *.com.*

A Different Kind of Retirement Book

1 "The Wealth of the Baby Boom Cohorts after the Collapse of the Housing Bubble"; David Rosnick and Dean Baker; Center for Economic and Polity Research; February 2009.
2 "Family Caregivers: What they Spend, What They Sacrifice"; Donna L. Wagner, Ph.D.; November 2007.
3 "America's Changing Workforce: Recession Turns a Graying Office Grayer"; Paul Taylor, Research Director; Pew Research Center; September 2009.
4 "Students Borrow More than Ever for College"; Anne Marie Chaker; *Wall Street Journal;* September 4, 2009.
5 "Boomers Digging into Retirement Savings, Opening their Homes to Support Adult Kids Suring Recession"; press release; VibrantNation.com; June 15, 2009.
6 "Retirement at the Tipping Point: The Year That Changed Everything"; Ken Dychtwald, Ph.D.; Age Wave and Harris Interactive; May 2009.
7 "Long-Term Care Costs and the National Retirement Risk Index"; Center for Retirement Research at Boston College; Alicia H. Munnell, Anthony Webb, Francesca Golub-Sass and Dan Muldoon; March 2009.

Chapter 1: The Imperial City

8 "Farewell Address by the President to the Nation"; President William Jefferson Clinton.
9 "The Budget and Economic Outlook: Fiscal Years 2002-2011"; Congressional Budget Office; January 2001.
10 "Budget of the United States Government, Fiscal Year 2011: Summary Tables"; March 2010.
11 "Preliminary Analysis of the President's 2011 Budget"; Congressional Budget Office; March 5, 2010.
12 "State of the Union Address"; President William Jefferson Clinton; January 23, 1996.
13 "I.O.U.S.A."; Addison Wiggin and Kate Incontrera; John Wiley & Sons; 2008.
14 "Obama Blames Financial Woes on Bush"; Josh Gerstein; *Politico.com;* February 24, 2009.

15 "Obama Gets Highest Approval on Iraq, Lowest on Deficit"; Frank Newport; The Gallup Organization; September 17, 2009.

16 "71 percent Angry at Federal Government, Up Five Points Since September"; Rasumussen Reports; November 30, 2009.

17 "How Big Are Total Individual Income Tax Expenditures, and Who Benefits from Them?"; Leonard Burman, Eric Toder and Christopher Geissler; paper presented at the American Social Sciences Association annual meeting; January 5, 2008.

18 "Estimates of Federal Tax Expenditures for Fiscal Years 2008-2012"; report prepared by the staff of the Joint Committee on Taxation for the House Committee on Ways and Means and the Senate Committee on Finance; October 31, 2008.

19 "Build America Pays off on Wall Street"; Ianthe Jeanne Dugan; *Wall Street Journal;* March 10, 2010.

20 "Near-Zero Rates Are Hurting the Economy"; David Malpass; *Wall Street Journal;* December 4, 2009.

21 "Lobbyists Terminating Their Federal Registrations at Accelerated Rate"; Dave Levinthal; OpenSecrets.org; November 2, 2009.

22 "Cosmetic Surgeons Get Reid to Tax Tanning Salons Instead"; Barnara Martinez; *Wall Street Journal;* December 22, 2009.

23 "Revolving Door: Top Agencies"; OpenSecret.org website.

24 "Daschle Pays $100K in Back Taxes Over Car Travel"; Ceci Connolly; *The Washington Post;* January 30, 2009.

25 "Obamanomics: How Barack Obama is Bankrupting You and Enriching His Wall Street Friends, Corporate Lobbyists, and Union Bosses"; Timothy P. Carney; Regnery Publishing, Inc.; 2009.

26 "Supercapitalism: The Transformation of Business, Democracy and Everyday Life"; Robert B. Reich; Alfred A. Knopf; New York; 2007.

27 Career Guide to Industies, 2010-2011 Edition, Table 1; Bureau of Labor Statistics.

28 "Personal Income by Selected Large Metropolitan Areas: 2005 to 2007"; U.S. Census Bureau.

29 "The Envy List"; Barbara Vaida; *National Journal;* April 2, 2010.

30 "Federal Pay Ahead of Private Industry"; Dennis Cauchon; *USA Today;* March 5, 2010.

Chapter 2: The Ten-Year Outlook

31 "Remarks by the President in the State of the Union Address"; President Barack Obama; January 27, 2010.

32 "Budget of the Government of the United States, Fiscal Year 2011".

33 "An Analysis of the President's Budgetary Proposals for Fiscal Year 2011"; Congressional Budget Office; March 24, 2010.

34 "2010 Retirement Confidence Survey"; Employee Benefit Research Institute; March 2010.

35 "Sun Life Unretirement Index Reports Almost Half of Americans Would Not Contribute

to Social Security"; SunLife Financial; March 16, 2009.

36 "Status of the Social Security and Medicare Programs: A Summary of the 2009 Annual Reports"; Social Security and Medicare Boards of Trustees; May 2009.

37 "Social Security Trust Funds"; Douglas Elmendorf; Director's Blog; Congressional Budget Office; March 31, 2010.

38 "Fixing Social Security: Adequate Benefits, Adequate Financing"; Virginia P. Reno and Joni Lavery; National Academy of Social Insurance; October 2009.

39 "Is There a Right to Social Security?"; Michael Tanner; The Cato Institute; November 25, 1998.

40 The Boomer Project, a market research company, specializes in generational marketing. I worked with Matt as Senior Vice President-Publishing.

41 "Estimated Life Expectancy at Birth in Years, by Race and Sex: Death-registration States, 1900-28, and United States, 1929-2001"; National Vital Statistics Reports, Vol. 52, No. 14, February 18, 2004

42 World Population Prospects: The 2008 Revision Population Database; the United Nations.

43 "U.S. Diabetes Cases to Double, Costs Triple by 2034"; Julie Steenhuysen; Reuters; November 27, 2009.

44 "Chronic Care: A Call to Action for Health Reform"; AARP Public Policy Institute; March 2009. Data reproduced from Johns Hopkins Bloomberg School of Public Health analysis of Medicare claims data, 2006, and Medical Expenditure Panel Survey, 2005.

45 "2009 Alzheimer's Disease Facts and Figures"; Alzheimer's Association.

46 "Forecasting the Cost of U.S. Healthcare"; Robert Fogel; *The American;* September 3, 2009.

47 "Are Baby Boomers Doomed to Disability?"; Daniel J. DeNoon; *WebMD Health News.*

48 "Baby Boomers Will Create a Joint Replacement Boom"; Virginia Rohan; *NewJersey.com;* January 18, 2010.

49 "Middle-Aged Americans Reporting More Mobility-Related Disabilities"; press release; Rand Corporation; April 6, 2010.

50 "The Hepatitis C Generation"; Sarah Kliff; *Newsweek;* January 11, 2010.

51 "Illicit Drug Use among Older Adults"; National Survey on Drug Use and Health; December 29, 2009.

52 "Increasing Substance Abuse among Older Adults Likely to Create Sharp Rise in Need for Treatment Services in Next Decade"; press release, Substance Abuse and Mental Health Services Administration; January 8, 2010.

53 "HIV/AIDS Surveillance Report: Cases of HIV Infection and AIDS in the United States and Dependent Areas, 2007"; Centers for Disease Control and Prevention.

54 "Study finds drop in age-related hearing problems"; Malcolm Ritter; Associated Press; January 26, 2010.

55 "'Baseline Projection of Current Policy by Category"; The Budget for Fiscal Year 2011; Office of Management and Budget; March 2010.

56 "Love Is (Not) All You Need"; Mary A. Fischer; *AARP: The Magazine;* March 2010.

57 "Never Enough: America's Limitless Welfare State"; William J. Voegeli; Encounter Books; 2010.

58 "An Analysis of the President's Budgetary Proposals for Fiscal Year 2011"; Congressional Budget Office; March 2010.

59 "Business Cycle Expansions and Contracts"; National Bureau of Economic Research website.

60 "Treasury Issues Update on Status of Support for Housing Programs"; U.S. Department of the Treasury press release; December 24, 2009.

61 "Barclays: Treasury Should Boost Fannie Lifeline to $300 Billion"; Nick Timiraos; *Wall Street Journal;* December 11, 2009.

62 "CBO's Budgetary Treatment of Fannie Mae and Freddie Mac"; Congressional Budget Office; January 2010.

63 "Housing Agency Reserves Fall Far Below Minimum"; Nick Timiraos; *Wall Street Journal;* November 13, 2009.

64 "Pension Benefit Guaranty Corporation Annual Management Report: Fiscal Year 2009"; November 13, 2009.

65 "CBO's Estimate of the President's Budget"; An Analysis of the President's Budgetary Proposals for Fiscal Year 2011; March 2010.

Chapter 3: Health Care Deform

66 "Dissecting the Real Cost of ObamaCare"; Paul D. Ryan; *Wall Street Journal;* March 4, 2010.

67 "Health Reform That Won't Break the Bank"; Peter Orszag and Nancy-Ann DeParle; *The Washington Post;* March 5, 2010.

68 "The Prognosis for National Health Insurance: A Virginia Perspective"; Donna Arduin; Arduin, Laffer & Moore Econometrics; Virginia Institute for Public Policy; September 2009.

69 Redefining Health Care: Creating Value-Based Competition on Results; Michael Porter and Elizabeth Olmsted Teisberg; Harvard Business Press; 2006.

70 "Who Killed Health Care?"; Regina Herzlinger; McGraw-Hili; 2007.

71 The Patient Protection and Affordable Care Act; Title III-Improving the Quality and Efficiency of Health Care, Part II-National Strategy to Improve Health Care Quality.

72 The Patient Protection and Affordable Care Act; Section 3023-National Pilot Program on Payment Bundling.

73 The Patient Protection and Affordable Care Act; Section 3001-Hospital Value-Based Purchasing Program.

74 The Patient Protection and Affordable Care Act; Section 3991I-Collection and Analysis of Data for Quality and Resource Measures.

75 The Patient Protection and Affordable Care Act; Section 3021-Establishment of Center

for Medicare and Medicaid Innovation Within CMS.

76 The Patient Protection and Affordable Care Act; Section 3022-Medicare Shared Savings Program.

77 The Patient Protection and Affordable Care Act; Section 933-Health Care Delivery System Research.

78The Patient Protection and Affordable Care Act; Section 3403-Independent Medicare Advisory Board.

79 The Patient Protection and Affordable Care Act; Section 6003-Disclosure Requirements for in-Office Ancillary Services Exception to the Prohibition on Physician Self-Referral For Certain Imaging Services.

80 "Obamacare Has a Poison Pill for Doctor-Owned Hospitals"; Rob Bluey; *The Examiner;* May 4, 2010.

81 "The Case for Public Plan Choice in National Health Reform"; Jacob S. Hacker; Institute for America's Future.

82 "We're Governed by Callous Children"; Peggy Noonan; *Wall Street Journal;* November 5, 2009.

83 "Obama's Health Care Town Hall in Portsmouth"; transcript; *New York Times;* August 11, 2009.

84 "Medicare Is No Model for Health Reform"; Grace-Marie Turner and Joseph R. Antos; *Wall Street Journal;* Sept. 11, 2009.

85 "Medicare Fraud Costs Billions of Dollars Each Year, CMS Officials Testify"; *Medical News Today;* April 23, 2007.

86 "2009 National Health Insurer Report Card"; American Medical Association; 2009.

87 "Drug Makers Raise Prices in Face of Health Care Reform"; Duff Wilson; *New York Times;* November 15, 2009.

88 "Rx Watchdog Report: Drug Prices Continue to Climb Despite Lack of Growth in General Inflation Rate"; AARP Public Policy Institute; Insight on the Issues; November 2009.

89 "Top Industries: Most Profitable"; *Fortune Magazine.*

90 "Drug Industry"; Value Line Investment Survey; January 15, 2009.

91 "Research and Development in the Pharmaceutical Industry"; Congressional Budget Office; October 2006.

92 "Pharmaceutical Pricing Policies in a Global Market"; Elizabeth Docteur and Valerie Paris; Organization for Economic Cooperation and Development; 2008.

93 "Obama's Preventive Care Pitch"; Jonathan LaPook; CBS News; September 10, 2009.

94 Letter to the Subcommittee on Health, Committee on Energy and Commerce; Douglas W. Elmendorf; August 7, 2009.

95 "Study Raises Questions About Cost Savings from Preventive Care"; Lori Montgomery; *The Washington Post;* September 1, 2009.

96 "Screening for Breast Cancer: U.S. Preventive Services Task Force Recommendation Statement"; *Annals of Internal Medicine;* November 17, 2009.

97 "Do Doctors Practice Defensive Medicine?"; Daniel P. Kessler and Mark B. McClellan;

The Quarterly Review of Economics and Finance; May 1996.

98 "2008 Update on U.S. Tort Cost Trends"; Towers Perrin; 2008.

99 "Medical Malpractice Tort Limits and Health Care Spending"; Congressional Budget Office; April 2006.

100 "Evidence on the Costs and Benefits of Health Information Technology"; Congressional Budget Office; May 2008.

101 "Medicare Reimbursements per Enrollee: 2006 Medicare Reimbursements by Hospital Referral Region"; the Dartmouth Atlas of Health Care; www.dartmouthatlas.org.

102 "Mayo Clinic in Arizona to Stop Treating Some Medicare Patients"; David Olmos; Bloomberg; December 31, 2009.

103 "The Physicians' Perspective: Medical Practice in 2008"; The Physicians' Foundation; 2008.

104 "Texas Doctors Opting out of Medicare at Alarming Rate"; Todd Ackerman; *Houston Chronicle;* May 17, 2010.

105 "The Complexities of Physician Supply and Demand: Projections Through 2025"; Association of American Medical Colleges; November 2008.

Chapter 4: Debt Shock

106 "The Graying of the Great Powers: Demography and Geopolitics in the 21st Century"; by Richard Jackson and Neil Howe, with Rebecca Strauss and Keisuke Nakashima; Center for Strategic & International Studies; 2008.

107 "Global Imbalances: Recent Developments and Prospects"; Ben S. Bernanke; September 11, 2007.

108 "Equity Gilt Study 2010: Chapter 1 - From Feast to Famine"; Tim Bond; Barclays Capital; February 2010.

109 "Genworth 2009 Cost of Care Survey"; Genworth Financial; April 2009. The figure cited covers the cost of providing skilled nursing care 24 hours a day in a private room.

110 "Fast Facts"; National Center for Education Statistics. The most recent year listed, 2006-07, was $9,683. My $10,000 figure assumes that the cost has increased in the past four years.

111 "2009 Annual report of the Boards of Trustees of the Federal Hospital Insurance and Federal Supplementary Medical Insurance Trust Funds"; May 12, 2009.

112 "Monthly Statistical Snapshot, December 2009"; U.S. Social Security Administration, Office of Retirement and Disability Policy; December 2009.

113 "Federal Spending on the Elderly and Children"; Congressional Budget Office; July 2000.

114 "Global Aging and Financial Markets"; Richard Jackson; presentation at the Macroeconomic Advisers, LLC, 16th annual Washington Policy Seminar; September 7, 2006.

115 "OECD Factbook 2009: Economic, Environmental and Social Statistics."

116 "Personal Saving Rate"; Bureau of Economic Analysis, National Economic Accounts; December 22, 2009.

117 "Principal Funds Addresses Need for Diversified Income in Retirement"; Principal Financial Group; press release; January 27, 2010.

118 "China's Long March to Retirement Reform: The Graying of the Middle Kingdom Revisited"; by Richard Jackson, Keisuke Nakashime and Neil Howe; Center for Strategic & International Studies; April 22, 2009.

119 "India's savings rate to drop to 34 percent"; Rediff India Abroad; October 16, 2008.

120 "Mainland China Budget for 2009"; Thomas Shik and Joanne Yim; Hang Seng Bank Limited; May 13, 2009.

121 "Comparison of Personal Saving in the National Income and Product Accounts (NIPAs) with Personal Saving in the Flow of Funds Accounts (FFAs)"; Bureau of Economic Analysis, National Economic Accounts; January 29, 2010.

122 "Bernanke delivers Blunt Warning on U.S. Debt"; Patrice Hill; *The Washington Times;* February 25, 2010.

123 The Lexus and the Olive Tree; Thomas Friedman; Farrar, Steaus & Giroux; 1999.

124 "Japan's Ratings Outlook Cut on Lack of Hatoyama Plan"; Bloomberg; January 26, 2010.

125 "U.K. May Lose AAA Rating at S&P as Finances Weaken"; Lukanyo Mnyanda; Bloomberg; May 21, 2009.

126 Table "Risk Premiums by Rating Class" in "Country Risk Premiums"; webpage; San Jose State University Department of Economics; April 16, 2010.

127 "Moody's Warns U.S. Could Lose Triple-A Rating"; Ken Sweet; FOXBusiness; December 8, 2009.

127 "Global Financial Stability Report: Meeting New Challenges to Stability and Building a Safer System"; International Monetary Fund; April 2010.

129 "Operations of the Combined OASI and DI Trust Funds, in Current Dollars, Calendar Years 2009-85"; 2009 OASDI Trustees Report; May 12, 2009.

130 "On the Brink: Inside the Race to Stop the Collapse of the Global Financial System"; Henry M. Paulson Jr.; Hachette Book Group, Inc.; 2010.

131 "The Forgotten Man: A New History of the Great Depression"; Amity Shlaes; Harper Perennial; 2008.

Chapter 5: No Way Out

132 "Fiscal Scare Tactics"; Paul Krugman; *New York Times;* February 4, 2010.

133 "Deficits and the Future"; Paul Krugman; *The New York Times;* December 1, 2008.

134 "Deficit Hysteria"; Paul Krugman; The Conscience of a Liberal blog, *The New York Times;* November 23, 2009

135 "Don't Succumb to Deficit Hysteria"; Robert Reich; Robert Reich's Blog; August 25, 2009.

136 "Time to Throw Some Water on the Deficit Hysteria Fire"; L. Randall Wray and Yeva Nersisyan; Wall Street Pit; February 18, 2010.

137 "U.S. Chamber Urges Obama, Congress to Rethink Climate Push"; Michael Burnham; January 12, 2010.

138 "Debt and Deleveraging: The Global Credit Bubble and Its Economic Consequences."; McKinsey Global Institute.; January 2010.

139 "February Oversight Report: Commercial Real Estate Losses and the Risk to Financial Stability"; Congressional Oversight Panel; February 10, 2010.

140 "An Overview of the Housing/Credit Crisis and Why There Is More Pain to Come"; T2 Partners LLC; April 3, 2009.

141 "Foreclosure Activity Decreases 9 Percent in April"; press release; RealtyTrac; May 13, 2010.

142 "Factors Affecting Implementation of the Home Affordable Modification Program"; Neil M. Barofsky; Office of the Special Inspector General for the Troubled Asset Relief Program; March 25, 2010.

143 "Housing in America: The Next Decade"; John K. McIlwain; Urban Land Institute; March 2010.

144 "Recession Continues to Batter State Budgets; State Responses Could Slow Recovery"; Elizabeth McNichol and Nicholas Johnson; Center of Budget and Policy Priorities; February 25, 2010.

145 "Public Pension Promises: How Big Are They and What Are They Worth?"; Robert Novy-Marx; Joshua D. Rauh; Social Science Research Network; December 18, 2009.

146 "Citizen's Report on the Troubled Asset Relief Program (TARP)"; Fiscal year 2009; United States Department of the Treasury, Office of Financial Stability; March 2, 2010.

147 "Overview of Funding"; Recovery.gov; March 15, 2010.

148 "Feds to End Mortgage Purchase Program"; Jon Hilsenrath and Luca Di Leo; *Wall Street Journal;* March 16, 2010.

149 "The Graying of the Great Powers"; Richard Jackson and Neil Howe; Center for Strategic & International Studies; 2008.

150 "The Coming Entrepreneurship Boom"; Dane Stangler; Ewing Marion Kauffman Foundation; June 2009.

151 China Nutritional Profile; World Health Organization; 2005.

152 That estimate is based on U.S. petroleum imports of roughly 10 million barrels per day. Source: U.S. Energy Information Administration website; "Oil: Crude and Petroleum Products Explained."

153 "Global Trends 2025: A Transformed World"; National Intelligence Council; November 2008.

154 "Growth in a Time of Debt"; Carmen M. Reinhart and Kenneth S. Rogoff; NBER Working Paper No. 15639; January 2010.

155 "Mapping the Global Muslim Population: A Report on the Size and Distribution of the World's Muslim Population"; The Pew Forum on Religion and Public Life; October 2009.

156 "Europe's Muslim Street"; Omer Taspinar; The Brookings Institution; March/April 2003.

157 "Terrorists Promise More Attacks Like 9/11"; Steven Stalinsky; *The New York Sun;* Sep-

tember 6, 2006.

158 "America Alone"; Marc Steyn; Regnery Publishing; 2006.

159 "More Americans Sever U.S. Ties as IRS Gets Rougher"; Martin Vaughan; *Wall Street Journal;* April, 2010.

160 "Individual Income Tax Returns with Positive Adjusted Gross Income (AGI): 1986-2006"; Internal Revenue Service; March 2010.

161 "Using Inflation to Erode the U.S. Public Debt"; Joshua Aizenman and Nancy Marion; National Bureau of Economic Research; December 2009.

162 "Paul Ryan: The GOP's Answer to the 'Party of No'"; Alex Altman; *Time;* February 17, 2010.

Chapter 6: Bye, Bye, American Empire

163 "The Next 100 Years"; George Friedman; Doubleday; 2009.

164 "Freedom in the World 2010"; Freedom House; 2010.

165 "Budget of the United States Government, Fiscal Year 2011"; Office of Management and Budget; 2010.

166 "Quadrennial Defense Review Report"; Department of Defense; February 2010.

167 "Base Structure Report: Fiscal Year 2008 Baseline"; Department of Defense; 2008.

168 "Fact Book FY08"; Defense Energy Support Center; 2008. See also "Department of Defense Fuel Spending, Supply, Acquisition, and Policy"; Anthony Andrews; Congressional Research Service; September 22, 2009.

169 "The Failed States Index 2009"; *Foreign Policy* and The Fund for Peace; 2009. Countries are scored on the following criteria: demographic pressures, refugees, group grievances, human flight, economic decline, de-legitimization of the state, public services, human rights, security apparatus, factionalized elites and external intervention.

170 "Great Powers: America and the World After Bush"; Thomas P.M. Barnett; G.P. Putnam's Sons; 2009.

171 "Why AirSea Battle?"; Andrew J. Krepinevich; Center for Strategic and Budgetary Assessments; 2010.

172 "Country Analysis Briefs: China"; U.S. Energy Information Administration website.

Chapter 7: Safety Net Unraveled

173 "The Madoff Scam: Meet the Liquidator"; Morley Safer; 60 Minutes; September 27, 2009.

174 "What They Said about Fan and Fred"; *Wall Street Journal;* September 25, 2003.

175 "Operations of the Combined OASI and DI Trust Funds, in Constant 2009 Dollars"; 2009 Trustees Report.

176 "Social Security to Start Cashing Uncle Sam's IOUs"; Stephen Ohlemacher; Associated Press; March 14, 2010.

177 "2010 Del Webb Baby Boomer Survey"; Del Webb Corp.; April 13, 2010.

178 "German Pensioners Kidnap and Torture Their Investment Advisor"; Roger Boyes; *The Times;* June 24, 2009.

179 "Computing a Retired-Worker Benefit"; Social Security Online.

180 A Deeper Look at the Fed's Inflation Debate"; Jon Hilsenrath; *Wall Street Journal;* April 5, 2010.

181 "Argentina's Sovereign Debt Restructuring"; J.F. Hornbeck; Congressional Research Service; October 19, 2004.

182 "Argentine Pensioners Turn to Prostitution"; BBC; July 19, 2002.

Chapter 8: Surviving Boomergeddon

183 "Will Health Care Costs Bankrupt Aging Boomers?"; Richard W. Johnson and Regina Mommaerts; Urban Institute Retirement Program; February 2010.

184 "The Alternative Minimum Tax and Effective Marginal Tax Rates"; NBER Working Papers 7662; National Bureau of Economic Research; 2003.

185 "Median and Average Square Feet of Floor Area in New One-Family Houses Sold by Location"; National Association of Home Builders; October 13, 2009.

186 "Housing Facts, Figures and Trends"; National Home Builders Association; March 2006.

187 "2010 Self-Storage Association Fact Sheet"; Self Storage Association website; current as of April 1, 2010.

188 "Retirement at the Tipping Point: The Year That Changed Everything"; Ken Dychtwald; Age Wave and Harris Interactive; May 2009.

189 "Consumer Expenditure Survey: Current Expenditure Tables (2008)"; Bureau of Labor Statistics.

190 "The Critical Care Safety Study: The Incidence and Nature of Adverse Events and Serious Medical Errors in Intensive Care"; Jeffrey M. Rothschild, et al; Critical Care Medicine; August 2005.

191 "New Study Shows Sepsis and Pneumonia Caused by Hospital-Acquired Infections Kill 48,000 Patients; cost $8.1 Billion to Treat"; press release; Extending the Cure; February 2010.

192 "2010 Del Webb Baby Boomer Survey"; Del Webb Corp.; April 13, 2010.

193 "How Far Will My Money Go in Another City?"; CNNMoney.com; http://cgLmoney.cnn.com/tools/costofliving/costofliving.html.

194 "Medicare Reimbursements per Enrollee"; The Dartmouth Atlas of Health Care.

195 "Cumulative Historic Default Rates"; Municipal Bond Fairness Act; September 9, 2008.

196 "Los Angeles Debt Rating Cut by S&P; Mayor 'Confident'"; Ryan Flinn; Bloomberg; February 23, 2010.

197 "The Los Angeles Riots, 1992"; USC Libraries website.

198 NewsMeat Campaign Contribution Search.

Chapter 9: Salvaging the Future

199 "A Roadmap for America's Future"; U.S. Rep. Paul Ryan.

200 "Washington's $1 Trillion Opportunity"; Paul C. Light; *Wall Street Journal;* May 25, 2010.

201 "The Corporate Welfare State: How the Federal Government Subsidizes U.S. Businesses"; Stephen Slivinski; Cato Institute; May 14, 2007.

202 "Flat Tax Revolution: Using a Postcard to Abolish the IRS"; Steve Forbes; Regnery Publishing; July 2005.

203 "Federal Tax Reform; A Roadmap for America's Future"; Paul Ryan; U.S. House of Representatives website.

204 "More Fair Tax Basics"; Americans for Fair Taxation; FairTax.org website; May 4, 2010.

205 "Spare Parts Horror Stories, Part II: $127 Washer Shows Military Procurement Not Yet Fixed"; Project on Government Oversight; January 21, 1997.

206 "US Defense Procurement Reform: An Animated Presentation"; *Defense Industry Daily;* March 10, 2009.

207 "The Pentagon's Broken Bookkeeping"; *Defense Industry Daily;* February 26, 2006.

208 "Anti-terrorism declaration for Somalia by Leading Global Islamic scholars"; press release Global Centre for Renewal and Guidance; March 15, 2010.

209 "Islamic scholar Tahir ul-Qadri Issues Terrorism Fatwa"; Dominic Casciani; BBC News; March 2, 2010.

210 "Insurgents, Terrorists and Militias: The Warriors of Contemporary Combat"; Richard H. Schultz Jr. and Andrea J. Drew; Columbia University Press; 2006.

211 "Video of the Week"; The Heritage Institute; March 10, 2010.

212 Letter to the Hon. Jerry Lewis, ranking member, Committee on Appropriations, U.S. House of Representatives"; Douglas W. Elmendorf; Congressional Budget Office; May 11, 2010.

213 "Who Killed Health Care?"; Regina Herzlinger; McGraw-Hill; 2007.

214 "The Henry Ford of Heart Surgery"; Geeta Anand; *Wall Street Journal;* November 25, 2009.

215 "Health System Modernization Will Reduce the Deficit"; David M. Cutler; Center for American Progress Action Fund; May 8, 2009.

216 "The Tea Party: The Populism of the Privileged"; E.J. Dionne, Jr.; *The Washington Post;* April 19, 2010.

217 "Tax Units with Zero or Negative Tax Liability, 2009-2019"; Tax Policy Center; April 14, 2009.

Chapter 10: End of an Era

218 "The Fourth Turning: What the Cycles of History Tell Us About America's Next Rendezvous with Destiny"; William Strauss and Neil Howe; Broadway Books; 1997.

Index

Index

Index

Index

Index

Index

Index

344

Index

Index

Index

Index

Index

Index

Index

Help Make a Difference

Are you bummed about Boomergeddon? Do you want to help spread the alarm?

Here are some easy ways to help that won't cost you a dime:

1. Visit the Boomergeddon blog at *www.boomergeddon.us* to read regular updates, fulminations and excoriations.

2. Link to the blog from your own website or blog. Links improve search engine results, drive more traffic to the Boomergeddon blog and spread the message to unsuspecting Web surfers. Mwa ha ha!

3. Tell all your Facebook friends that they must buy the book or you will mercilessly de-friend them.

4. Post a book review on the "Boomergeddon" page at Amazon.com. Be sure to say good things, though. If we don't like your review we will mercilessly de-friend you! Mwa ha ha!

Here are some ways to help that will cost you -- but will be well worth the expense:

1. Mail a copy of "Boomergeddon" to your congressperson with a hand-written note: "Dude, Wake up and smell the coffee!" The more copies our representatives receive from constituents, the more they'll get the message. If people send enough copies, your congressperson might even feel compelled to read the book–or at least tell an aide to read it for him!

2. Order bulk copies and give them to people you know. Your conservative friends will thank you. Your liberal friends will be annoyed -- which is almost as gratifying. (We offer discounts. Contact Oaklea Press at oakleapress.com for details.)

3. Ask Jim Bacon to speak to your group or organization in person. Imagine, you can see him in *vibrant 3-D* without wearing those funny red and green glasses! (For details, check his profile at his speaker's bureau, arnettandassociates.com.)

If you really, *really* want to help Jim carry on his valuable work, send money directly. No traveler's checks, please!